LATIN AMERICA PROFILED

LATIN AMERICA PROFILED

Essential facts on society, business and politics in Latin America

Edited by Barry Turner

ST. MARTIN'S PRESS
NEW YORK

LATIN AMERICA PROFILED

St Martin's Press, Scholarly and Reference Division,
175 Fifth Avenue, New York, N.Y. 10010

First published in the United States of America in 2000

Printed in the United Kingdom

ISBN: 0–312–22995–X

Library of Congress Cataloging-in-Publication Data
Latin America profiled: essential facts on society, business, and politics in Latin America/edited by Barry Turner.
   p. cm. — (SYB factbook series)
   Includes bibliographical references and index.
   ISBN 0-312-22995-X (pbk.)
    1. Latin America I. Turner, Barry. II. Series
   F1408 .L37 2000
   918—dc21

                            99-053353

Contents

ARGENTINA 1

Territory and Population 2
Time Zones 3
Key Historical Events 3
  Pre-Columbian 3
  Spanish Rule 4
  Independence 5
  Peron 5
  Galtieri, the Falklands and Modern
    Argentina 6
  Menem 7
Political Chronology for the Century
    9
Cultural Chronology for the Century
    12
Leading Cultural Figures 15
  Jorge Luis Borges 15
  Carlos Gardel 15
City Profile 16
  Buenos Aires 16
    Tourist Information 17
    Taxis 17
    Postal Services 18
    Internet Access 18
    Landmarks 18
    Catedral Metropolitana
      (Metropolitan Cathedral) 18
    Plaza de Mayo (May Square) 19
    Casa Rosada (Presidential
      Palace) 19
  Museums and Galleries 19
    Museo Nacional de Bellas Artes
      (National Museum of Fine
      Arts) 19
    Museo Nacional de Arte
      Decorativo (National

    Museum of Decorative
      Arts) 19
    Museo de Arte
      Hispanoamericano Isaac
      Fernandez Blanco (Museum
      of Hispano-American Art) 20
    Museo Histórico Nacional
      (National Historical Museum)
      20
    Museo de Arte Moderno
      (Museum of Modern Art) 20
  Theatre and Opera 21
    Teatro Colón (Colón Theatre) 21
Social Statistics 21
  Statistics Offices 21
  Climate 22
Constitution and Government 22
  National Anthem 23
  Recent Elections 23
  Current Administration 24
  Political Profiles 24
    Dr Fernando de la Rúa 24
    Carlos Alberto Alvarez 25
    José Luis Machinea 26
    Adalberto Rodríguez Giavarini 27
    Ricardo López Murphy 27
    Carlos Menem 28
    Carlos Ruckauf 29
  Local Government 29
Defence 30
  Army 30
  Navy 30
  Air Force 30
International Relations 31
Economy 31
  Policy 32
  Performance 33
  Budget 33
  Currency 33

Banking and Finance 33
  Major Banks 34
  Stock Exchanges 35
  Chambers of Commerce 35
  Weights and Measures 36
Energy and Natural Resources 36
  Electricity 36
  Oil and Gas 36
  Minerals 36
  Agriculture 37
  Forestry 37
  Fisheries 37
Industry 38
  Top Ten Companies 38
  Labour 38
  Trade Unions 38
International Trade 39
  Imports and Exports 39
Communications 40
  Roads 40
  Rail 40
  Civil Aviation 40
  Shipping 41
  Telecommunications 41
  Postal Services 42
Social Institutions 42
  Justice 42
  Religion 42
  Education 43
  Health 43
    Health Requirements 43
  Welfare 44
Culture 44
  Broadcasting 44
  Cinema 44
  Press 45
Tourism 45
  Tourist Organization 45
  Visas 45

Festivals 45
Public Holidays 46
Social Etiquette 46
Diplomatic Representatives
  47
Further Reading 47

BRAZIL 49
Territory and Population 50
Time Zones 52
Key Historical Events 53
  Pre-Colombian 53
  Portuguese Exploration 53
  Brazilian Independence 54
  Pedro II and the Creation of the
    Republic 55
  Vargas 55
  Economic Crisis and Military Rule
    56
  Recent History 57
Political and Social Chronology for
    the Century 58
Leading Cultural Figures 63
  Emiliano Di Cavalcanti 63
  Lúcio Costa 63
  Oscar Niemeyer 64
  Heitor Villa-Lobos 65
Major Cities 66
  São Paulo 66
    Introduction 66
    Tourist Information 67
    Financial and Currency 67
    Post Services 68
    Internet Services 68
    Rail 68
    Landmarks 69
      Cathedral of the Sé 69
      *São Bento Monastery and
        Basilica 69*

Praça da República and Edificio
  Italia 69
Memorial da América Latina
  70
Museums and Galleries 70
MASP 70
MAC (Museu de Arte
  Contemporânea) 70
Museu de Arte Moderna 71
Paulista Museu 71
Museu de Arte Sacra de São
  Paulo (Museum of Sacred Art)
  72
MIS (The Museum of Image and
  Sound) 72
Theatre and Opera 73
Teatro Municipal 73
Teatro Alfa-Real 73
Aliania Francesca 73
Italia 73
Cacilda Becker 73
Paiol 73
Ruth Escobar 73
Rio de Janeiro 74
Introduction 74
Tourist Information 75
Financial and Currency 75
Taxis 76
Postal Services 76
Internet Access 76
Landmarks 78
Catedral Metropolitana
  (Metropolitan Cathedral)
  78
Pão de Açúcar (Sugar Loaf)
  78
Monumento Cristo Redentor
  (Christ the Redeemer)
  78

Museums and Galleries
  78
Museu Historico Nacional (Praça
  Marechal Âncora) 78
Museu de Arte Moderna
  (Museum of Modern Art)
  79
Museu da Chácara do Céu
  79
Museu Nacional de Belas Artes
  (National Fine Arts Museum)
  80
Espaço Cultural dos
  Correios (Cultural Corridor)
  80
Theatre and Opera 80
Teatro Municipal 80
Metropolitan 80
Brasília 81
Introduction 81
Tourist Information 82
Financial and Currency 83
Internet Access 83
Landmarks 83
Catedral Metropolitana 83
Television Tower 84
Juscelino Kubitschek Memorial
  84
Praça dos Tres Poderes 84
Museums and Galleries 84
Museum of Art of Brasília
  (Museu de Arte de Brasília)
  84
Museum of North-eastern Art and
  Tradition (Museu de Arte e
  Tradição) 85
Historical Museum of Brasília
  (Museu Histórico de Brasília)
  85

Catetinho Museum (Museu do
Catetinho) 85
Currency Museum of the Central
Bank (Museu de Valores do
Banco) 85
Theatre and Opera 86
Claudio Santoro National Theatre
(Teatro Nacional Claudio
Santoro) 86
Brasília Arena Theatre
(Concha Acustica de Brasília)
86
Dulcina Theatre (Teatro Dulcina)
86
Further Information 86
Social Statistics 87
Statistics Offices 87
Climate 87
Constitution and Government
88
National Anthem 88
Recent Elections 89
Current Administration 89
Political Profiles 90
Fernando Henrique Cardoso
90
Marco Antonio de Oliveira Maciel
91
Pedro Sampaio Malan 92
Luiz Felipe Lampreia 92
Local Government 93
Defence 93
Army 94
Navy 94
Air Force 94
International Relations 95
Economy 95
Policy 96
Performance 97

Budget 97
Currency 97
Banking and Finance 98
Major Banks 98
Other Banks 100
Stock Exchanges 100
Chambers of Commerce 101
Business Associations and Other
Organizations 101
Weights and Measures 102
Energy and Natural Resources
102
Environment 102
Environmental Policies 102
Electricity 103
Oil and Gas 104
Minerals 104
Agriculture 105
Forestry 107
Fisheries 107
Industry 107
Top 20 Companies 108
Labour 108
Trade Unions 109
International Trade 109
Imports and Exports 109
Communications 110
Roads 110
Rail 110
Civil Aviation 111
Shipping 112
Telecommunications 112
Postal Services 113
Social Institutions 113
Justice 113
Religion 114
Education 114
Health 115
Health Requirements 115

Culture 116
Broadcasting 116
Radio 116
Television 116
Press 117
Newspapers 117
Magazines 118
News Agencies 118
Libraries 118
Tourism 118
Tourist Organizations 118
Visas 118
Festivals 119
Public Holidays 120
Social Etiquette 120
Diplomatic Representatives 120
Further Reading 121

MEXICO 123

Territory and Population 124
Time Zones 126
Key Historical Events 127
Pre-Columbian 127
Conquest and Colonial
Domination 128
Mexican Independence 129
Revolution, Constitution and
Corruption 130
NAFTA, Zapatista and Modern
Mexico 131
Political and Social Chronology for
the Century 132
Leading Cultural Figures 137
Diego Rivera 137
Octavio Paz 137
Carlos Fuentes 138
Major Cities 139
Mexico City 139
Introduction 139

Tourist Information 140
Financial and Currency 141
Taxis 142
Rail 142
Postal Services 142
Internet Access 142
Landmarks 144
El Zócalo and the Metropolitan
Cathedral 144
Chapultepec Park, Castle and
Zoo 145
El Templo Mayor 145
Museums and Galleries 145
Museo Nacional de Antropología
145
Museo de Arte Moderno
(Museum of Modern Art)
146
Museo de Templo Mayor 146
Palacio de las Bellas Artes 146
Theatre and Opera 147
Opera Nacional 147
Teatro 147
Auditorio Nacional (National
Auditorium) 147
Teatro de la Danza, Unidad
Artistica y Cultural del Bosque
147
Social Statistics 147
Statistics Offices 148
Climate 148
Constitution and Government 149
National Anthem 149
Recent Elections 150
Current Administration 150
Political Profiles 151
Ernesto Zedillo 151
Diódoro Carrasco 152
Rosario Green 153

Enrique Cervantes Aguirre 154
José Aangel Gurría Treviño 155
Local Government 155
Defence 156
  Army 156
  Navy 156
  Air Force 156
International Relations 156
Economy 157
  Policy 158
  Performance 158
  Budget 159
  Currency 159
  Banking and Finance 159
    Major Banks 159
    Stock Exchange 161
  Chambers of Commerce 161
  Weights and Measures 161
Energy and Natural Resources
  162
  Environment 162
  Electricity 163
  Oil and Gas 163
  Minerals 163
  Agriculture 163
  Forestry 164
  Fisheries 164
Industry 164
  Top 20 Companies 165
  Labour 166
  Trade Unions 166
International Trade 167
  Imports and Exports 167
Communications 168
  Roads 168
    Rules of the Road 168
  Rail 168
  Civil Aviation 169
  Shipping 170

Telecommunications 170
Postal Services 171
Social Institutions 171
  Justice 171
  Religion 171
  Education 172
  Health 173
    Health Requirements 173
  Welfare 174
Culture 174
  Broadcasting 174
    Radio 174
    Television 174
  Cinema 175
  Press 175
Tourism 176
  Tourist Organizations 177
  Visas 177
  Festivals 177
  Public Holidays 178
Social Etiquette 178
Doing Business in Mexico 179
Diplomatic Representatives 181
Further Reading   181

BELIZE 183
Key Historical Events 183
Territory and Population 183
Social Statistics 184
Constitution and Government
  185
  Recent Elections 185
  Current Administration 185
  Defence 186
Economy 186
  Performance 186
  Budget 187
  Currency 187
  Banking and Finance 187

Industry 187
Labour 187
International Trade 188
Imports and Exports 188

BOLIVIA 189

Key Historical Events 189
Territory and Population 189
Social Statistics 190
Constitution and Government 191
Recent Elections 191
Current Administration 192
Defence 193
Economy 193
Performance 193
Budget 193
Currency 193
Banking and Finance 193
Industry 194
Labour 194
International Trade 194
Imports and Exports 194

CHILE 196

Key Historical Events 196
Territory and Population 197
Social Statistics 198
Constitution and Government 199
Recent Elections 199
Current Administration 200
Defence 200
Economy 201
Performance 201
Budget 201
Currency 201
Banking and Finance 201
Industry 202
Labour 202

International Trade 202
Imports and Exports 202

COLOMBIA 203

Key Historical Events 203
Territory and Population 204
Social Statistics 206
Constitution and Government 206
Recent Elections 207
Current Administration 207
Defence 208
Economy 208
Performance 208
Budget 208
Currency 209
Banking and Finance 209
Industry 209
Labour 209
International Trade 210
Imports and Exports 210

COSTA RICA 211

Key Historical Events 211
Territory and Population 211
Social Statistics 212
Constitution and Government 212
Recent Elections 212
Current Administration 212
Defence 214
Economy 214
Performance 214
Budget 214
Currency 214
Banking and Finance 215
Industry 215
Labour 215
International Trade 216
Imports and Exports 216

ECUADOR 217

Key Historical Events 217
Territory and Population 217
Social Statistics 220
Constitution and Government
      220
Recent Elections 220
Current Administration 221
Defence 222
Economy 222
  Performance 222
  Budget 222
  Currency 222
  Banking and Finance 223
Industry 223
  Labour 223
International Trade 224
  Imports and Exports 224

EL SALVADOR 225

Key Historical Events 225
Territory and Population
      226
Social Statistics 227
Constitution and Government
      227
Recent Elections 227
Current Administration 228
Defence 228
Economy 228
  Performance 228
  Budget 229
  Currency 229
  Banking and Finance 229
Industry 229
  Labour 229
International Trade 230
  Imports and Exports 230

GUATEMALA 231

Key Historical Events 231
Territory and Population 232
Social Statistics 233
Constitution and Government
      233
Recent Elections 234
Current Administration 234
Defence 234
Economy 235
  Performance 235
  Budget 235
  Currency 235
  Banking and Finance 235
Industry 236
  Labour 236
International Trade 236
  Imports and Exports 236

GUYANA 237

Key Historical Events 237
Territory and Population 237
Social Statistics 238
Constitution and Government
      238
Recent Elections 239
Current Administration 239
Defence 240
Economy 240
  Performance 240
  Budget 240
  Currency 240
  Banking and Finance
      241
Industry 241
  Labour 241
International Trade 241
  Imports and Exports 241

HONDURAS 243

Key Historical Events 243
Territory and Population 243
Social Statistics 244
Constitution and Government
  245
Recent Elections 245
Current Administration 245
Defence 246
Economy 246
  Performance 246
  Budget 246
  Currency 247
  Banking and Finance 247
Industry 247
  Labour 247
International Trade 248
  Imports and Exports 248

NICARAGUA 249

Key Historical Events 249
Territory and Population 250
Social Statistics 251
Constitution and Government
  251
Recent Elections 252
Current Administration 252
Defence 253
Economy 253
  Performance 253
  Budget 253
  Currency 253
  Banking and Finance 254
Industry 254
  Labour 254
International Trade 254
  Imports and Exports
  254

PANAMA 255

Key Historical Events 255
Territory and Population 256
Social Statistics 257
Constitution and Government
  257
Recent Elections 258
Current Administration 258
Defence 259
Economy 259
  Performance 259
  Budget 259
  Currency 259
  Banking and Finance 259
Industry 260
  Labour 260
International Trade 260
  Imports and Exports 260

PARAGUAY 261

Key Historical Events 261
Territory and Population 262
Social Statistics 262
Constitution and Government
  262
Recent Elections 263
Current Administration 263
Defence 264
Economy 264
  Performance 264
  Budget 264
  Currency 264
  Banking and Finance
  264
Industry 265
  Labour 265
International Trade 265
  Imports and Exports 265

PERU 266

Key Historical Events 266
Territory and Population 267
Social Statistics 268
Constitution and Government 268
Recent Elections 269
Current Administration 270
Defence 270
Economy 271
    Performance 271
    Budget 271
    Currency 271
    Banking and Finance 271
Industry 271
    Labour 272
International Trade 272
    Imports and Exports 272

SURINAME 273

Key Historical Events 273
Territory and Population 273
Social Statistics 274
Constitution and Government 275
Recent Elections 275
Current Administration 275
Defence 276
Economy 276
    Performance 276
    Budget 276
    Currency 277
    Banking and Finance 277
Industry 277
    Labour 277
International Trade 278
    Imports and Exports 278

URUGUAY 279

Key Historical Events 279
Territory and Population 280
Social Statistics 281
Constitution and Government 281
Recent Elections 282
Current Administration 282
Defence 283
Economy 283
    Performance 283
    Budget 283
    Currency 284
    Banking and Finance 284
Industry 284
    Labour 285
International Trade 285
    Imports and Exports 285

VENEZUELA 286

Key Historical Events 286
Territory and Population 287
Social Statistics 288
Constitution and Government 289
Recent Elections 290
Current Administration 290
Defence 291
Economy 291
    Performance 291
    Budget 291
    Currency 292
    Banking and Finance 292
Industry 292
    Labour 292
International Trade 293
    Imports and Exports 293

Colour maps fall between pages 146 and 147

ARGENTINA

República Argentina

Capital: Buenos Aires

Area: 2,780,400 sq. km

Population estimate, 2000: 37·03m.

Head of State: Fernando de la Rúa

TERRITORY AND POPULATION

The second largest country in South America, the Argentine Republic is bounded in the north by Bolivia, in the northeast by Paraguay, in the east by Brazil, Uruguay and the Atlantic Ocean, and the west by Chile. The republic consists of 23 provinces and 1 federal district with the following areas and populations as at 30 June 1999:

Provinces	Area (sq. km)	Population	Capital	Population (1991 census)
Federal Capital	200	2,982,146	Buenos Aires	–
Buenos Aires	307,571	13,935,243	La Plata	542,567
Corrientes	88,199	899,903	Corrientes	258,103
Entre Ríos	78,781	1,094,327	Paraná	277,338
Chaco	99,633	931,073	Resistencia	292,350
Santa Fé	133,007	3,040,786	Santa Fé	406,388
Formosa	72,066	487,260	Formosa	148,074
Misiones	29,801	960,436	Posadas	210,755
Jujuy	53,219	587,888	San Salvador de Jujuy	180,102
Salta	155,488	1,033,629	Salta	370,904
Santiago del Estero	136,351	713,648	Santiago del Estero	263,471
Tucumán	22,524	1,265,322	San Miguel de Tucumán	622,324
Córdoba	165,321	3,031,327	Córdoba	1,208,713
La Pampa	143,440	298,613	Santa Rosa	80,592
San Luis	76,748	351,431	San Luis	110,136
Catamarca	102,602	309,130	Catamarca	132,626
La Rioja	89,680	270,702	La Rioja	103,727
Mendoza	148,827	1,572,784	Mendoza	121,696
San Juan	89,651	566,212	San Juan	352,691
Neuquén	94,078	534,516	Neuquén	243,803
Chubut	224,686	433,702	Rawson	19,161
Río Negro	203,013	600,290	Viedma	57,473

| Santa Cruz | 243,943 | 199,497 | Río Gallegos | 64,640 |
| Tierra del Fuego | 21,571 | 134,036 | Ushuaia | 29,166 |

Argentina also claims territory in Antarctica.

The area is 2,780,400 sq. km excluding the claimed Antarctic territory and the population at the 1991 census was 32,615,528 (16,677,548 females); 1997 estimate, 36·1m. giving a density of 13 per sq. km. The official census included the 'sovereign territories of Argentina in the Antarctic': population 3,300.

The UN gives a projected population for 2000 of 37·03m.

In 1998, 89·3% of the population were urban.

In April 1990 the National Congress declared that the Falklands and other British-held islands in the South Atlantic were part of the new province of Tierra del Fuego formed from the former National Territory of the same name. The 1994 Constitution reaffirms Argentine sovereignty over the Falkland Islands.

The population of the principal metropolitan areas in 1995 was: Buenos Aires, 11,802,000; Córdoba, 1,294,000; Rosario, 1,155,000; Mendoza, 851,000; La Plata, 676,128 (1992); Tucumán, 642,473 (1992).

95% speak the national language, Spanish, while 3% speak Italian, 1% Guaraní and 1% other languages.

Time Zones

The standard time in Argentina is GMT –3 hrs.

KEY HISTORICAL EVENTS

Pre-Columbian

Two main indigenous American groups existed in the region of modern Argentina before the European arrival. The Diaguita people lived in the northwest, near Bolivia and the Andes, while the Guarani people lived further to the south and east. Both groups developed the cultivation of maize, thereby constituting the origins of a permanent agricultural civilization in Argentina. The Diaguita successfully prevented the powerful Inca from expanding their empire from Bolivia into Argentina. In addition to these two groups there were numerous nomadic tribespeople in the region.

The successful nature of these indigenous groups accounts for the length of their resistance to Spanish rule and colonization. Although Juan de Solis first landed in Argentina in 1516 and Buenos Aires was founded in 1536, Spanish dominance was not fully established until after Juan de Garay refounded Buenos Aires over 40 years later in 1580 when colonial settlement became possible. It should also be remembered that indigenous resistance was weakened as much by European diseases as by Spanish military aggression.

Spanish Rule

Even after Colonial rule had been established Spain largely neglected Argentina in preference of the riches of Peru, maintaining the regional seat of government in Lima. By the 18th century the King was represented by a viceroy and a trading ban was put on Buenos Aires, preventing it trading with foreign countries, turning it into something of a smuggler's haunt.

When Spain came under Napoleonic French control the British attacked Buenos Aires, first in 1806 and then again in 1807. Both times the colonists repelled the invasions without any help from Spanish forces, an achievement that helped to develop the region's growing sense of independence. In 1810 the first locally elected government was formed in Buenos Aires where nationalists took advantage of the weakness of the Spanish crown to implement the libertarian principles of the American and French Revolutions.

Independence

By 1816 a major division between Argentina and Spain had become apparent. A group of separatists declared the territory's independence on 9 July. One of the group, José de San Martin, crossed the Andes and captured Lima and is regarded as one of the major figures in the independence movement in Spanish South America.

The early days of independence were marked by bitter struggles between the Unitarists, wanting a strong central government, and Federalists, advocating regional control. It was not until 1853 that stable government was finally achieved when the Unitarists, largely representing the interests of Buenos Aires, were able to inaugurate a new constitution. The next 50 years saw a stable period of presidential succession along with impressive economic growth. By the beginning of the 20th century the country had seen 3 decades of yearly growth at 6% and Argentina had become a magnet for European immigration.

The injection of new European blood put pressure on the political system to broaden its representation. The new immigrants, mainly Italian and Spanish, established the new Socialist, Anarchist and Union Civica Radical parties. This latter political group became the main political force and under the leadership of Hipólito Yrigoyen won their first presidential election in 1916.

Peron

The history of modern Argentina is dominated by military coups and autocratic regimes. In Sept. 1930 a coup brought Argentina's first military government to power. Its period of rule lasted until 1943 and is known as the 'Era of Patriotic Fraud'. Although the actual period of autocratic military rule was brief, and gave way to a government of semi-legality based on the Constitution, further elections were dominated by vote-rigging and fraud. This period of military rule oversaw the country's major industrialized development.

Although remaining neutral at the outbreak of the Second World War another coup in 1943 brought General Juan Domingo Peron to power. He chose to side with the allies and before the conflict ended declared war on the axis powers. Peron soon emerged as a military strongman. His regime was autocratic but populist and nationalistic. He won Presidential elections in 1946 and 1951 on the back of the urban working class support that industrialization had created. Peron's political strength was reinforced by his second wife Eva Duarte de Peron. She acted as de facto minister of health and labour and established a national charitable organization which awarded wage increases to the unions.

Peron's increasing authoritarianism led to a coup by the armed forces in 1955 sending him into exile. Although a civilian administration was established, military intervention in Argentine politics persisted until 1966 when another military coup instigated seven years of military dictatorship. A political party had, however, established itself around the Perons and, when elections were again held in 1973, the Peronists emerged as the victors. After Peron's death in 1974 his new wife, Isabelita, succeeded him as President. She became the hemisphere's first woman chief of state until she too was deposed by the military in 1976 and the army's commander-in-chief, General Jorge Videla, became President. Videla's regime, supported by governments throughout the Americas (including the US) implemented what became known as the 'Dirty War'. Driven by an obsessive fear of 'communism' and 'subversive forces' thousands of Argentines disappeared, with most believed to have been tortured and executed.

Galtieri, the Falklands and Modern Argentina

Videla was succeeded as President by General Viola and then in March 1981 by General Leopoldo Galtieri. In April 1982, in an effort to distract attention from domestic failings, Galtieri ordered the invasion of the Falkland Islands, with the intention of reclaiming Las Malvinas (their Spanish name) as national territory. By 21 May more than 5,000 British marines and paratroops had landed on the islands and regained control. This military defeat precipitated the fall of Galtieri and the junta in July 1982. Between Peron's fall in 1955 and the re-establishment of stable democracy in 1983 there had been 5 coups, 3 counter-coups, 2 rigged elections and a series of outrageous human rights violations.

The war in the Falklands helped worsen the country's severe economic crisis. Decades of state intervention, regulation, inward looking policies and generalized subsidies had taken their toll on the country's economy. Presidential elections were held in Oct. 1983 restoring civilian rule under Raúl Alfonsin, leader of the middle-class Union Civica Radical. Despite attempting to redress the finances of the bloated public sector, growing unemployment and four-figure inflation led to a Peronist victory in the 1989 elections and Carlos Menem, a Peronist, became Argentina's new president.

Menem

In Dec. 1990 an attempted military coup was suppressed by commanders loyal to the legitimate government, enabling Menem to continue as president. In Jan. 1991 Menem instigated a major cabinet reshuffle after corruption regarding the country's privatization programme. Menem's new Cabinet oversaw the convertibility plan of Domingo Cavallo, the economy minister, to stabilize the economy.

Menem's period of office has overseen a major economic overhaul with the opening up of the economy, deregulation, greater market orientation, less state interference, an end to subsidies and an all out privatization drive. Despite domestic unrest and opposition-led protests these initiatives have ensured some level of economic stability, giving Menem the political clout to alter the constitution to allow for his re-election for a second, reduced term of four years. This new constitution was adopted in 1994 reinforcing Argentina's commitment to democratic rule. A year later Argentina and the UK signed an agreement to promote oil and gas exploration in the southwest Atlantic thereby helping to defuse a potentially difficult issue. Although the question of the Falkland Islands' sovereignty is still off the agenda, recent years have seen discrete bilateral negotiations with the UK over various matters concerning the islands such as fishing rights and Argentine access. Despite the difficulties and passions aroused by the situation Anglo-Argentine relations have greatly improved under Menem with symbolic visits to London by the Argentine President and by the Prince of Wales to Buenos Aires.

Economic recession throughout South America at the end of 1998 has had its impact on Argentina. By Aug. 1999 unemployment had risen to nearly 15% and unrest and riots in the worst affected regions had dented national confidence. This economic slowdown, along with irritation at certain excesses of the Menem government, has affected the President's public support. Menem has made repeated attempts to alter the constitution to allow him to stand for a third term of office, currently forbidden under the terms of the constitution. Recently the 2 main opposition parties, Frepaso and the UCR, have combined to present a concerted challenge to the Peronists under the banner of the Alliance. In the presidential election held on 24 Oct. 1999, Fernando de la Rúa of the centrist Alliance (a coalition between the traditional middle-class Radical Party and a new grouping made up of dissident Peronists called the Frepaso) won 48·5% of the vote to become the country's first non-Peronist president in 10 years.

POLITICAL CHRONOLOGY FOR THE CENTURY

1904

Manuel Quintana replaces Julio Roca as President.

1906

President Manuel Quintana dies. José Figueroa Alcorta becomes President.

1910

Roque Saenz Pena becomes President.

1914

Saenz Pena dies. Victorino de la Plata becomes President.

1916

Hipólito Yrigoyen becomes the first Radical Party member to be elected president.

1922

Marelo T. de Alvear is elected President.

1928

Hipólito Yrigoyen is re-elected as President.

1930

President Yrigoyen's government comes to a violent end due to a coup d'etat led by General José Felix Uriburu who imposes his own rule as a military dictator.

1932

Agustin P. Justo becomes President.

1938

Roberto M. Ortiz becomes President.

1940

President Ortiz is taken ill. Ramón S. Castillo rules as acting President.

1943

Generals Rawson and Ramírez overthrow the government.

1944

Edelmiro Farrell becomes President with Juan Domingo Peron as his vice-president.

1945

Peron is imprisoned and then freed.

1946

General Juan Domingo Peron takes office with vast popular support.

1955

A new coup d'etat ends the Peronist period of office. A provisional government is established under General Lonardi. General Pedro E. Aramburu becomes President.

1958

Arturo Frondizi becomes President.

1962

Frondizi is overthrown and José M. Guido becomes President.

1963

Arturo Illia becomes President.

1966

A military coup led by General Ongania overthrows Illia and Alejandro Lanusses is made President.

1970

Ongania's government is overthrown and General Roberto Levingston becomes president. Peron returns to Argentina.

1971

Levingston is overthrown and Lanusse is made President again.

1973

Hector Campora becomes president for less than two months before resigning. Raúl Listiri rules for a similar period before Juan Peron returns as President to replace him.

1974

On 1 July Peron dies. His wife Maria Estela (Isabel) Martínez Peron succeeds him.

1976

In a military coup Isabel Peron is overthrown and replaced by Jorge Rafael Videla.

1981

Roberta Viola rules until Dec. when General Leopaldo Fortunato Galtieri overthrows him.

1982

Argentine armed forces seize control of the Falkland Islands (Las Malvinas). The UK sends a task force and British control of the island is re-established. Galtieri resigns and is replaced by Reynaldo Bignone.

1983

Democracy is restored as the military junta abandons its hold on power. President Raúl Alfonsin (UCR) institutes national renewal and democratization.

1989

Hyperinflation forces an early but constitutional transfer of power when Alfonsin resigns. Carlos Menem assumes power.

1995

President Menem wins a second term. MERCOSUR begins to operate, creating a free trade area between Argentina, Brazil, Paraguay and Uruguay with a combined population of over 200m. and a domestic turnover of over US$800bn.

1999

In Aug. Argentinians are allowed to visit the Falklands Islands for the first time since the end of the war. The first flight carrying Argentinian passport holders touches down on 16 Oct. Fernando de la Rúa is elected President with 48·5% of the vote.

CULTURAL CHRONOLOGY FOR THE CENTURY

1900

The first film theatres especially intended for films and news reports are opened in Buenos Aires.

1902

Martin Malharro returns from Paris and exhibits his works, which are the first examples of expressionistic painting seen in Argentina.

1903

Ludovico Saracco's Company is offered the local premiere of Delibes' 'Copelia' with Ida Ronzio.

1908

The Teatro Colon is inaugurated.

1910

The International Exhibition for the Centenary is staged in Buenos Aires and exhibits works by the Nexus group of Argentine painters, which include Fernando Fader. The first Argentine film with professional actors, La Revolución de Mayo (The May Revolution), is released.

1913

Dhiagilev's Ballet Russes tours Argentina with Nijinsky, Karsavina and Bolm bringing modern ballet to Argentina.

1914

The first feature-length Argentine film, 'Amalia', is released.

1917

The world's first feature-length animated film, El Apostol (The Apostle), is made in Argentina. The Ballet Russes returns to Buenos Aires.

1918

Eduardo Sivori, considered one of the main forces in introducing naturalistic art to Argentina, dies.

1921

José Luis Borges sets up a new literary magazine, 'Proa'.

1923

Borges publishes his first collection of poems.

1925

First show by the Ballet Company of the Colon Theatre.

1927

Artists Reinaldo Giudici and Ernesto de la Carcova die.

1930

The foundation of the Theatre of the People gives rise to the Independent Theatre, an artistic movement seeking to fight against commercial theatre.

1935

Fernando Fader, one of the key figures in the development of Argentine art, and Carlos Gardel, the Tango singer, die.

1940s

The film-makers group, Associated Argentine Artists, is formed.

1944

Arturo magazine is published; a manifesto for concrete art.

1948

Very Estima magazine is published. One of its critics, Jorge Romero Brest, becomes one of the leading figures in Argentine contemporary arts.

1950

The Paris Opera Ballet, led by Lifar and Toumonova, tours Argentina. The Neo-humanist group of writers, a response to the new post-war way of thinking, begin to publish their work.

1951

The Bonino gallery is created.

1956

Faustino Brughetti, a contemporary of Malharro whose painting is considered as one of the major forces behind the development of a distinctly Argentine style of painting, dies. Jorge Brest becomes curator of the National Museum.

1957

The Cinema Act is passed leading to the creation of the Institution Nacional de Cinematografia (INC).

1961

Borges shares the Formentor Prize with Samuel Beckett.

1973–75

Argentine cinema achieves record critical and popular success with films such as 'Juan Moreira', 'La Patagonia Rebelde' ('Rebellious Patagonia') and 'La Tregua' ('The Respite'), a film which is nominated for an Oscar. The new military government's censorship affects all cultural art forms detrimentally.

1981

The Teatro Abierto (Open Theatre) starts performing as the military government loosens its pressure on the arts.

1985

Two young dancers, Julio Bocca and Maximiliano Guerra, give ballet huge new popularity.

1986

Jorge Luis Borges dies.

1987

Alicia Alonso's last professional appearance takes place with the Cuban National Ballet at the Colón Theatre.

1996

Alan Parker's film of 'Evita', the story of Evita Peron, is made in Argentina and stars Madonna in the title role.

LEADING CULTURAL FIGURES

Jorge Luis Borges (1899–1986)

Jorge Luis Borges was born on 24 Aug. 1899 in the Palermo district of Buenos Aires. Shortly before the outbreak of the First World War he was taken by his family to Europe and, forced to stay there by the war, completed his education in Geneva. When he returned to Argentina in 1921 he set up a new literary magazine, 'Proa', with the help of other writers. He soon became known as a fine poet and essayist, publishing his first collection of poems in 1923. Borges' early writing helped create the ultraist movement, whose main ideals were the extensive use of metaphor and being 'enemies of rhyme'. His was fiercely concerned with writing as an Argentine, with a distinctly Argentinian dialect and vocabulary.

In the 1930s he began writing short stories which became his main form. His two most famous collections of short stories, 'Fictions' and 'Aleph', came from this early period and were written as essays despite being creative fiction. Between 1955, when Peron was overthrown, and 1973, with Peron's return, he was the director of Argentina's National Library. His works were increasingly translated into English and in 1961 he shared the Formentor Prize with Samuel Beckett. Although his later blindness and the demands of international literary fame began to slow his output, he still managed to publish several collections of short stories and poems in the 1970s. Much of his best poetry dates from this later period.

Borges was married twice, the second time shortly before his death in 1986, to his former student, Maria Kodama.

Carlos Gardel (1890–1935)

Carlos Gardel was the tango's greatest folk hero. To many millions of Latin Americans he is one of the authentic superstars of the 20th century. Born poor and illegitimate in Toulouse, France, he emigrated with his mother to Argentina aged 2. Blessed with a beautiful baritone voice he had already become a famous and much loved singer in Argentina before he took up the tango as his main musical style. It was Gardel, in many ways, who established the tango in the popular imagination of South America at the time. He became the most famous tango singer of all time, mirroring the history of the style itself by rising from humble origins to the height of established, fashionable society. Gardel and his lyricist, Alfredo Le Pera. were killed in a plane crash on 24 June 1935.

CITY PROFILE

Argentina's country code is 54 and its outgoing international code 00.

BUENOS AIRES

Estimated population 2000: 12,431,000 (Source: 1996 World Urbanization Prospects. United Nations Population Division.) Located on the south bank of the River Plate, Buenos Aires is the largest city in Argentina and the largest city in South America outside Brazil. Buenos Aires' first settlement was established by Pedro de Mendoza in 1536. It lasted for five years before a combination of native harassment and hunger forced its abandonment. The city was refounded by Juan de Garay in 1580. Its position as a port facilitated its steady growth to an extent whereby when the Spanish created the Viceroyalty of the River Plate in 1776 Buenos Aires was established as its capital.

The city managed to repel two British invasions in 1806 and 1807, demonstrating its strength and ability to stand on its own. Encouraged by ideas of liberation coming from France its First Junta was formed in May 1810 as a reaction against the trading monopoly imposed by Spain. In July 1816 the United Provinces of the River Plate finally declared their independence from Spain at Tucuman city.

Continued warring with Spain sent Buenos Aires into decline in the middle part of the 19th century. It was at this time that the status of capital was transferred away. However, in 1862, after long years of fighting and civil war, this capital status was re-established. The latter years of the 19th century and early years of the 20th saw immigration from all over the world triple the city's population contributing to a cosmopolitan identity still in evidence today. There is a strongly European feel to the city whose architectural style is closer to Paris than colonial Spain. In addition the city supports a larger population of psychoanalysts per capita than any other city in the world.

Tourist information

Secretaría de Turismo de la Nación: Centro Nacional de Información Turística, Av. Santa Fe 883 PB. Tel: (0)1 312-2232. Web site: www.presidencia.ar/turismo/turis.html

Casa la Provincia de Buenos Aires, Callao 237. Tel: (0)1 317-3587.

Centro Florida, Florida between Paraguay and Av. Cordoba

Centro Diagonal, Florida and Diagonal Roque Saenz Peña

Financial and Currency

American Express Travel Service: Plaza San Martin, Arenales 707, 1061.

Tel: (0)11 4310-3535.

Open Monday to Friday from 9·00–18·00.

Taxis

Taxis are black and yellow. Available ones have a red light on the front, and the fare is metered.

Postal Services

Main Office: Sarmiento 189. Open Monday to Friday from 9·00–19·30.

Internet Access

Cybercafe: Maure 1886, Buenos Aires 1426.

Email: info@cyber.com.ar

Open 24 hours.

16 pentium multimedia machines.

Contacto: Bacacay 1715, Buenos Aires 1406. Tel: (0)1 631-3973.

E-mail: info@contactoweb.com.ar

Open Monday to Thursday from 11.00–20.00, Friday and Saturday from 11·00–2·00 and Sunday from 16·30–23·00.

Cybercafe, music, chat, E-mail, shows and exhibitions.

SSD Internetcenter: Maipu 24, Buenos Aires.

E-mail: ventas@ssdnet.com

Web site: www.pcstudio.com.ar

PCStudio: Uruguay 654 2° 211, Buenos Aires. Tel: (0)11 4371-9763.

E-mail: pcstudio@fibertel.com.ar

Open Monday to Friday from 9.00–22.00.

In a hidden office in the downtown area.

Landmarks

Catedral Metropolitana (Metropolitan Cathedral):

Rivadavia and San Martín.

Tel: (0)1 331-2845

Although the façade of the cathedral was begun in 1822 the building itself dates back over a hundred years earlier. Inside the cathedral are the remains of General José de San Martin, who is regarded as Argentina's Liberator in the War of Independence against Spain. His tomb is permanently guarded by soldiers from San Martin's own regiment, the Grenadiers.

Plaza de Mayo (May Square):
Named after the uprising against Spain on 25 May 1810, the square has become synonymous with national celebration and demonstration. The obelisk (Piramide de Mayo) was erected in the centre of the square in 1912 and commemorates the May revolution. Throughout the late '70s and early '80s the Madres (Mothers) de la Plaza de Mayo held weekly marches to protest at the disappearance of their children under the military government.

Casa Rosada (Presidential Palace): Calle Hipólito Yrigoyen 211. Tel: (0)1 374-9841.
Famous for its first-floor balcony from which Evita Peron rallied the workers, the palace is the official headquarters of the government and is still used by the country's leaders to address crowds although it is no longer the presidential residence. Adjoining the palace is the Museo de la Casa Rosada, which features presidential memorabilia.

Museums and Galleries
Museo Nacional de Bellas Artes (National Museum of Fine Arts):
Av. del Libertador 1473. Tel: (0)1 803-0802.
The museum is Buenos Aires' premier gallery and is housed in the city's former waterworks. Its extensive collection is particularly strong on Argentine artists and includes several major Impressionist paintings. Arguably the highlight of the museum is a room dedicated to the Paraguayan war scenes painted by a soldier, Cándido López. There is a fine collection of contemporary Argentine art in the museum's new wing.

Museo Nacional de Arte Decorativo (National Museum of Decorative Arts): Av. del Libertador 1902. Tel: (0)1 801-8248.
The museum houses a fine collection of decorative arts in a magnificent French classical building. At present the museum also houses

the Museo de Arte Oriental (Museum of Oriental Art) although it is uncertain for how much longer.

Museo de Arte Hispanoamericano Isaac Fernandez Blanco (Museum of Hispano-American Art): Calle Suipacha 1422.
Tel: (0)1 327-0228.
The museum houses an extensive collection of colonial silver, paintings, carvings and other artefacts from colonial Argentina. Housed in the former residence of the architect Martín Noel, which dates from the late 18th century, it also hosts outdoor theatre in its extensive and overgrown garden.

Museo Histórico Nacional (National Historical Museum):
Calle Defensa 1600.
Tel: (0)1 307-4457.
The Lezama homestead, a stately if decaying old mansion, now displays the official history of Argentina from the 16th century to the beginning of the 1900s—in particular artefacts relating to General José de San Martín and his campaigns during the War of Independence in 1810. The museum also contains several paintings by Cándido López, a soldier in the Paraguayan War of the 1870s, whose work displays the same power of visual effectiveness as contemporary primitive painting.

Museo de Arte Moderno (Museum of Modern Art): Calle Defensa 1344.
Tel: (0)1 361-3953.
Recently opened in a converted cigarette factory the museum displays temporary exhibitions of local artists' work.

Theatre and Opera

Teatro Colón (Colón Theatre): Cerrito 618, Buenos Aires 1010.
Tel: (0)1 358924.
Fax: (0)1 111232. E-mail: colon@is.com.ar
The Teatro Colón is one of the world's great opera houses. It opened
in 1908 and has hosted the likes of María Callas, Arturo Toscanini,
Igor Stravinsky, Enrico Caruso and Luciano Pavarotti. The striking
Italianate building with French decoration is the work of several
successive turn-of-the-century architects. With only 2,500 seats the
queues often stretch around the block, especially when an international celebrity is starring. Guided tours of the theatre and museum
are available and provide a glimpse at the building's inner
workshops, 15 metres below the street. The international season runs
from April to Nov.

SOCIAL STATISTICS

Rates, 1997 (per 1,000 population): birth, 19·4; death, 7·6; infant
mortality, 18·8 per 1,000 live births. Estimated life expectancy at
birth, 1995–2000, 69·7 years for males and 76·8 years for females.
Annual growth rate, 1995–2000, 1·3%; fertility rate, 1997, 2·6 births
per woman.

Statistics Offices

INDEC (Instituto Nacional de Estadistica y Censos): Ave. Julio A.
Roca 615, PB, (1067) Buenos Aires. Tel: (0)1 349-9654.
Fax: (0)1 349-9621.
E-mail: ces@indec.mecon.ar Web site: www.indec.mecon.ar

CLIMATE

The climate is warm temperate over the pampas, where rainfall occurs at all seasons, but diminishes towards the west. In the north and west, the climate is more arid, with high summer temperatures, while in the extreme south conditions are also dry, but much cooler. Buenos Aires, Jan. 74°F (23.3°C), July 50°F (10°C). Annual rainfall 37″ (950 mm). Bahía Blanca, Jan. 74°F (23.3°C), July 48°F (8.9°C). Annual rainfall 21″ (523 mm). Mendoza, Jan. 75°F (23·9°C), July 47°F (8·3°C). Annual rainfall 8″ (190 mm). Rosario, Jan. 76°F (24·4°C), July 51°F (10·6°C). Annual rainfall 35″ (869 mm). San Juan, Jan. 78°F (25·6°C), July 50°F (10°C). Annual rainfall 4″ (89 mm). San Miguel de Tucumán, Jan. 79°F (26·1°C), July 56°F (13·3°C). Annual rainfall 38″ (970 mm). Ushuaia, Jan. 50°F (10°C), July 34°F (1·1°C). Annual rainfall 19″ (475 mm).

CONSTITUTION AND GOVERNMENT

On 10 April 1994 elections were held for a 230-member constituent assembly to reform the 1853 constitution. The Justicialist National Movement (Peronist) gained 38·8% of votes cast and the Radical Union 20%. On 22 Aug. 1994 this assembly unanimously adopted a new Constitution. This reduces the presidential term of office from 6 to 4 years, but permits the President to stand for 2 terms. The President is no longer elected by an electoral college, but directly by universal suffrage. A presidential candidate is elected who gains more than 45% of votes cast, or 40% if at least 10% ahead of an opponent; otherwise there is a second round. The Constitution attenuates the President's powers by instituting a *Chief of Cabinet*. The *National Congress* consists of a Senate and a Chamber of Deputies: The Senate comprises 72 members, 3 nominated by each provincial legislature and 3 from the Federal District for 9 years (one-third retiring every 3 years). The Chamber of Deputies comprises 257 members directly elected by universal suffrage (at age 18).

National Anthem

'Oid, mortales, el grito sagrado Libertad' ('Hear, mortals, the sacred cry of Liberty'); words by V. López y Planes, 1813; tune by J. Blas Parera.

RECENT ELECTIONS

In presidential elections held on 24 Oct. 1999, Fernando de la Rúa of the Alliance won 48·5% of the vote, followed by the Peronist's Eduardo Duhalde with 38·1% and Domingo Cavallo of Action for the Republic with 10·1%.

On 6 Aug. 1997 the Radical Union and centre-left Frepaso parties joined together to form the Alliance to fight against the ruling Peronists in the lower house of Congress elections in Oct. 1997. 127 of the 257 seats were up for election. On 26 Oct. 1997 the Justicialist Party (JP/Peronists) suffered its first legislative defeat since 1983. The Alliance (including smaller parties) received 36·5% of votes cast and in the 10 provinces where no coalition existed the two parties separately collected an additional 9·6%, bringing the opposition tally to 46·1%. The JP received nearly 36% of votes cast, losing 12 seats and its absolute majority in Congress (it remains the largest single political bloc). As a result of the election the JP had 119 seats and the Alliance 107 (111 including smaller parties). The remainder of the seats were contested on 24 Oct. 1999, the Alliance winning 63 seats, the Peronists 50, Action for the Republic 9 and other parties 8. The standing of the parties following the election was: Alliance, 124; JP, 101; Action for the Republic 12. Other parties have 3 seats or fewer.

CURRENT ADMINISTRATION

President: Fernando de la Rúa, b. 1937 (Alliance; sworn in 10 Dec. 1999).

Vice-President: Carlos Alvarez.

The Cabinet comprised in Jan. 2000:

Ministerial Coordinator: Rodolfo Terragno. *Defence:* Ricardo López Murphy. *Economy and Finance:* José Luis Machinea. *Infrastructure and Housing:* Nicolas Gallo. *Education and Culture:* Juan José Llach. *Foreign Relations:* Adalberto Rodríguez Giavarini. *Interior:* Frederico Storani. *Justice:* Ricardo Gil Lavedra. *Labour and Social Security:* Alberto Flamarique. *Public Health:* Hector Lombardo. *Social Welfare and Environment:* Mejide Graciela Fernandez.

POLITICAL PROFILES

Dr Fernando de la Rúa (1937–)

Fernando de la Rúa became President of the Argentine Republic on 24 Oct. 1999.

Born on 15 Sept. 1937 de la Rúa attended the Liceo Militar General Paz school in Córdoba before going to law school at the Universidad de Córdoba. Having graduated, aged 21, he joined the UCR (Radical Civic Union) and served as an advisor to the Ministry of the Interior during Dr Arturo's Illia's constitutional presidency (1963–66). Having been elected as a senator in 1973 he served as a legislator in the Upper Chamber until the military coup of 1976. In 1983 he was nominated as a pre-candidate for the National Presidency and, following the primaries, he came top of the senator's ballot with 60% of the vote, enabling him to become a senator. He won two further senatorial ballots before being removed from his position by an agreement among the minorities in the Electoral College in 1989.

In 1991, after a second overwhelming victory in the partisan primaries, he was elected as President of the UCR's Capital Committee and nominated as the candidate for National deputy, a position he won convincingly. Having won a fourth election for National Senator in 1992 he became the first Head of Government of Buenos Aires with a convincing 40% of the vote. Three years later he won a landmark Presidential election victory as candidate for *Alianza para el Trabajo, la Justicia y la Educación* (known as the *Alianza*), winning over 48% of the votes. His government took office on 10 Dec. 1999.

De la Rúa has promised to tackle the country's social problems of unemployment and a widening gap between rich and poor. He has also said he will follow many of the key economic policies introduced by the outgoing President, Carlos Menem. His first moves have been to introduce large spending cuts and plans to combat tax evasion.

De la Rúa is married to Inés Pertiné and has 3 children.

Carlos Alberto Alvarez (1948–)

Carlos Alberto Alvarez is the Vice-President of the Argentine Republic.

Alvarez was born on 26 Dec 1948. Having obtained a degree in History from the University of Buenos Aires (UBA) he served as an advisor to the National Senate's Commission of Regional Economics (1983–89), a position he held whilst also being director of the magazine 'UNIDOS' (1985–89). He was later elected National Deputy for the Federal Capital representing the Justicialist Party.

In disagreement with Carlos Menem's policies he resigned his position and left the Justicialist Party in 1990. In an attempt to create a new political front he formed an independent parliamentary bloc with 7 other legislators, forming the 'Group of Eight'. In the same year he formed the MODEJUSO party (Movement for Democracy and Social Justice) and a year later founded the Frente Grande with other progressist parties.

In 1993 he was elected as a National Deputy for the Federal Capital and, having gained an overwhelming victory in the election, was able to become a member of the Constituent Assembly that later amended the constitution. At the end of 1994 he founded FREPASO (Front of Common Unity), a collection of progressist and socialist parties. He was second in the national election for the Vice President in May 1995 with over 5m. votes.

In 1997 he won legislative elections representing the Alliance for Work, Justice and Education (an alliance between FREPASO and UCR (Radical Civic Union) thereby becoming National Deputy for Buenos Aires with 57% of the vote. Accompanying Fernando de la Rúa he became Vice President of Argentina in 1999 with 48% of the vote.

He is married to Liliana Chiernajowsky and has 4 children.

José Luis Machinea (1946–)

José Luis Machinea is the Minister of the Economy and Finance for the Argentine Republic.

Born on 5 Oct. 1946, he attended the Colegio Don Bosco before graduating in economics from the Universidad Católica Argentina in 1968. From 1970 he served as an advisor to the Directorate of Economic Policy of the Ministry of the Economy and later as a chief analyst at the Centre of Monetary and Banking Studies at the Central Bank (1974–78). By 1983 he had become Manager of Research and Economic Statistics at the same organization.

From 1985–86 he served as Under Secretary for Economic Policy at the Ministry of the Economy and later became President of the Central Bank. From Feb. 1992 to March 1993 he served as the Director of Research at Fundación UIA's Institute for Industrial

Development. Fernando de la Rúa appointed him Minister of Economy and Finance in 1999.

Adalberto Rodríguez Giavarini

Adalberto Rodríguez Giavarini is the Minister of Foreign Relations for the Argentine Republic.

Giavarini is an economist with extensive macroeconomic, fiscal and monetary training. After graduating from the University of Buenos Aires in 1971 he became Chief Economist for the National Atomic Energy Commission, a position he held until 1974. The following year he became Chief Co-ordinator for the commission's technical team.

From 1975 he served as the Director of Management Control for the General Association of Public Enterprises, a position he held until he was appointed Budget Under Secretary at the Ministry of the Economy (1983–85) and then Planning Secretary at the Ministry of Defence (1986–89).

In 1995 Giavarini was elected as a National Deputy for the UCR (Radical Civic Union), a position he resigned from to become Secretary of Economy and Finance for the Government of the City of Buenos Aires in Aug.1996. In June 1998 he was appointed as the representative to international credit agencies and institutions for the government of the City of Buenos Aires.

Outside of politics Giavarini is a member of the UIA's (Argentine Industrial Union) Academic Council and a member of CARI (Argentine Council for Foreign Affairs). In addition he has published several works on various issues and has been a regular guest columnist for major national and international media.

Ricardo López Murphy (1951–)

Ricardo López Murphy is the Minister for Defence for the Argentine Republic.

Born on 10 Aug. 1951 he graduated in economics from Universidad de La Plata. He has served as Chief Economist at FIEL (Latin American Economic Research Foundation) and as an academic advisor to IAEF (Argentine Finance Executives Institute).

He has been the National Director of Research and Fiscal Analysis for the Finance Secretariat of the Ministry of the Economy and an advisor to the President of the Central Bank. In addition he has been a consultant and advisor to Uruguay's Central Bank and a consultant to the International Monetary Fund, the UN Program for Development, the World Bank, the IDB and CEPAL.

Ricardo López Murphy has co-written several books and published numerous articles.

Carlos Menem (1930–)

Dr Carlos Saul Menem is the former President of the Argentine Republic.

He was born in Anillaco in the province of La Rioja on 2 July 1930. The son of immigrant parents he was educated in his native province before attending the Law School at the Universidad de Córdoba. After graduating as a lawyer in 1955 he returned to La Rioja and defended political prisoners of the then military government.

6 years after having been arrested for political activism he was elected provincial congressman within his native town of Anillaco (1962). However, he was unable to carry out his duties due to another military coup. In March 1973 he was elected governor of his province for the first time and 3 years later was arrested by the military that had overthrown Estela Peron's civilian government. He remained in prison for nearly five years until his release in February 1981. With the restoration of democracy Menem was re-elected as governor of La Rioja and then again in 1987.

On 9 July 1988 Dr Menem was confirmed as the Justicialist Party's presidential candidate for the national elections and, on 14 May

1989, was duly elected President. The Constitutional Reform carried out in 1994 allowed Carlos Menem to run as presidential candidate once again, enabling him to win another term of office in May 1995. He stepped down from his position as President when the term ended with the elections of Oct. 1999. He plans to stand again in the 2003 elections from which the constitution cannot bar him.

He is married to Zulema Fatima Yoma.

Carlos Ruckauf (1944–)

Dr Carlos Federico Ruckauf is the Governor of the Province of Buenos Aires.

He was born on 10 July 1944 in the province of Buenos Aires. Having studied Law at the National University of Buenos Aires he has held several public service posts including Under-secretary at the Department of Social Security, President of the Justicialist Party of the Federal Capital province, Ambassador to Italy, Interior Minister and Vice-President (during Carlos Menem's presidency). At the 1999 elections he won a close race to win the Governorship of the Province of Buenos Aires—the second most important post in Argentine politics and where a third of the Argentine population live.

He is married with three sons.

LOCAL GOVERNMENT

23 provincial gubernatorial elections were held Aug.–Dec. 1991. Peronists won 14 governorships.

DEFENCE

Conscription was abolished in 1995. In 1998 defence expenditure totalled US$5,157m. (US$147 per capita), representing 1·8% of GDP.

Army

There are 5 military regions. In 1999 the Army was 40,000 strong. The trained reserve numbers about 250,000, of whom 200,000 belong to the National Guard and 50,000 to the Territorial Guard.

There is a paramilitary gendarmerie of 18,000 run by the Ministry of Defence.

Navy

The Argentinian Fleet (1999) included 3 diesel submarines, 6 destroyers and 7 frigates. Total personnel was 20,000 including 2,000 in Naval Aviation and 2,800 marines. Main bases are at Buenos Aires, Puerto Belgrano (HQ and Dockyard), Mar del Plata and Ushuaia.

The Naval Aviation Service has some 31 combat aircraft in 1999 including Super-Etenard strike aircraft and 8 armed helicopters; however, the only aircraft carrier, the 'Veinticinco de Mayo', is currently inactive.

Air Force

The Air Force is organized into Air Operations, Air Regions, Materiel and Personnel Commands. There were (1999) 10,500 personnel and 125 combat aircraft including Mirage 5 and Mirage III jet fighters. In addition there were 27 armed helicopters.

INTERNATIONAL RELATIONS

Argentina is a member of the UN, OAS, Inter-American Development Bank, LAIA, Mercosur, IOM and the Antarctic Treaty, and is set to apply for membership of the OECD. Diplomatic relations with Britain broken since the 1982 Falklands War were re-opened in 1990. Praising Argentina's 'call to peace', in Nov. 1997 US President Clinton announced his intention to give the country 'major non-NATO ally' status. The alignment with US foreign policy comes after years of anti-American sentiment and a policy of neutrality.

ECONOMY

Although Argentina has developed a diversified industrial base it is still known primarily for its agricultural exports such as grain, oilseeds and meat products. When Carlos Menem became president in 1989 the country was in the grip of massive inflation, reaching 200% per month, huge external debts and sharply falling output. To combat this the government pursued policies of trade liberalization, deregulation and privatization. Radical monetary reforms were introduced which tied the peso to the US dollar. This helped to curb inflation which plummeted in the following years. The Mexican peso crisis provoked a brief recession in 1995 leading to a new series of reforms to help bolster the domestic banking system.

The Menem government's handling of the economy saw considerable success in the late 1990s. Figures for 1997 indicate that GDP per capita came to US$8,985, making Argentina the wealthiest country in Latin America on a per capita basis. Growth in the economy has been led by investment and export, with consumption expenditures falling behind. The latest Argentinian GDP figures show that 57·2% came from the service sector, 35·5% from the industrial sector and 7·3% from the agricultural sector. In 1996 Argentina's top 5 exports were: fuels, fats and oils, food by-products, cereals and vehicles. Together these 5 made up 48·5% of total merchandise exports. It is estimated that in 1997 foreign investment in Argentina totalled over US$6bn., an increase of 24% on 1996.

GDP growth declined sharply in 1998 due to the Russian and Brazilian financial crises. Investment fell sharply in the second half of the year after a 26% rise in 1997. The IMF felt that the banking system has been successful in weathering the turmoil in international markets. Argentina's unemployment problem is, however, acute, standing at 14·5% in Oct. 1999. The executive board of the IMF 'commended the authorities for their prudent economic management, which has helped the economy withstand the recent turmoil affecting emerging market countries, and welcomes the progress made in a number of structural areas'.

Services contributed 61% of GDP in 1997, industry 33% and agriculture 7%.

Policy

In 1990 the government introduced a programme privatizing some 40 public enterprises. An economic plan entering into force on 1 April 1991 guaranteed the convertibility of the currency, lowered interest rates and opened the economy to foreign imports. Agricultural export taxes were abolished in March 1991. Argentina suffered a severe recession in 1995 but since then privatization and deregulation have improved the economy's prospects into the medium term. Tax evasion and fraud remain a major occurrence but tighter controls are being instituted. In Feb. 1998 the IMF approved a 3-year US$2·8bn. extended fund facility for Argentina. The accord set a target for the 1998 fiscal deficit of US$3·5bn., just over 1% of GDP, against the 1996 US$4·5bn. target.

Performance

The economy grew by 4·4% in 1996, after falling 4·6% in 1995, and was estimated to have grown by 8·6% in 1997. It grew again in 1998, by 2·9%, but was forecast to shrink by 3·3% in 1999, mainly as a result of the recession in Brazil which started in 1998 and the devaluation of the Brazilian *real* in Jan. 1999. Consumer spending is recovering gradually from the 1995 recession. GDP per capita has more than tripled since 1989, to US$9,010 in 1997, and was forecast to rise still further to US$9,520 in 1998.

Budget

The financial year commences on 1 Jan. Estimated revenue in 1998 was US$56bn. and expenditure US$60bn.

Currency

The monetary unit is the *peso* (ARP) which replaced the austral on 1 Jan. 1992 at a rate of 1 peso = 10,000 australs. Inflation was 0·3% in 1997 and was estimated at 0·8% in 1998. For 1999 deflation of 1% was forecast. Gold reserves were 360,000 troy oz in Feb. 1998. In 1999 foreign exchange reserves were estimated at US$20·0bn. Total money supply was 22,263m. pesos in Feb. 1998.

Banking and Finance

In 1998 there were 17 government banks, 87 private banks and 23 other financial institutions. Bank and non-bank total monetary resources totalled US$67,449m. as at Dec. 1996. The *Governor* of the Central Bank is Pedro Pou. Convertibility regulations of April 1991 require the Central Bank to back the entire currency in circulation with its foreign currency reserves. The current account balance in 1999 was forecast to be US$–16·0bn.

There is a stock exchange at Buenos Aires.

Major Banks

Banco Bansud: Sarmiento 447, 1041 Buenos Aires.

Tel: (0)1 329-7800. Fax: (0)1 325-5641.

Web site: www.bansud.com

One of Argentina's major private banks providing commercial and
retail services through its branch network.

Banco de Galicia y Buenos Aires: TTE. Gral Juan D. Peron 407,
1038 Buenos Aires.

Tel: (0)1 329-6000. Fax: (0)1 329-6100.

Web site: www.bancogalicia.com.ar

In terms of assets and liabilities and branch network size Banco
Galicia is the largest private bank in Argentina's financial system.

Banco del Suguia: 25 de Mayo 160, 5000 Cordoba. Tel: (0)51 200200.

Fax: (0)51 200280. Web site: www.bancosuquia.com

Commercial bank with 8 branches in Argentina and representative
offices throughout Latin America, North America, Europe and the Far
East.

Banco Frances: Reconquista 165/199, 1000 Buenos Aires.

Tel: (0)1 346-4310. Fax: (0)1 953-8009.

Web site: www.bancofrances.com.ar

A private commercial bank that provides general banking services to
corporate and retail customers.

Banco Rio de la Plata: Bartolome Mitre 480, 1002 Buenos Aires.

Tel: (0)1 341-1081. Fax: (0)1 341-1074.

Web site: www.bancorio.com.ar

Provides general banking services to the corporate and financial
sectors.

Stock Exchanges

Bolsa de Comercio de Buenos Aires: Sarmiento 299, 2nd floor, Buenos Aires 1353. Tel: (0)1 317-8980. Fax: (0)1 317-2676.

Bolsa de Comercio de Rosario: Cordoba 1402, Rosario, Santa Fe 2000. Tel: (0)41 213471. Fax: (0)41 241019.

Bolsa de Comercio de La Plata: Calle 48, 515, La Plata, Buenos Aires 1900. Tel: (0)21 141266.

Chambers of Commerce

American Chamber of Commerce in Argentina: Viamonte 1133, Piso 8, 1053 Buenos Aires. Tel: (0)1 371-4500. Fax: (0)1 371-8400.

Camara de Comercio Internacional, Argentina: 1003 Buenos Aires. Tel: (0)1 331-8051. Fax: (0)1 331-8055. E-mail: karplus@dialup.com.ar

Anglo-Argentine Chamber of Commerce: Piso 10, Avenida Corrientes 457, 1043 Buenos Aires. Tel: (0)1 394-2318. Fax: (0)1 394-2282.

Argentine-Brazilian Chamber of Commerce: Montevideo 770, Piso 12, 1019 Buenos Aires. Tel: (0)1 811-4503.

Argentine-Canadian Chamber of Commerce: Cuba 2665, Piso 2, 1428 Buenos Aires. Tel: (0)1 343-6268.

French-Argentine Chamber of Commerce: Av. Pte RS Pena 648, 9A, 1085 Buenos Aires. Tel: (0)1 331-6650.

German-Argentine Chamber of Commerce: Florida 537, Piso 19, 1005 Buenos Aires. Tel: (0)1 393-5404.

Weights and Measures

The metric system is legal.

ENERGY AND NATURAL RESOURCES

Electricity

Electric power production (1998) was 76,200m. kWh (7,453m. kWh nuclear). In 1997 there were 2 nuclear reactors in use. Installed capacity in 1998 was 21·76m. kW; consumption per capita in 1996 was 1,541 kWh.

Oil and Gas

Crude oil production (1998) was 49·15m. cu. metres. Reserves were estimated at some 416m. cu. metres in 1997. The oil industry was privatized in 1993. Natural gas extraction (1998) 38,631m. cu. metres. Reserves were about 684,000m. cu. metres in 1997. The main area in production is the Neuquen basin in western Argentina, with over 40% of the total oil reserves and nearly half the gas reserves.

Minerals

An estimated 215,000 tonnes of washed coal were produced in 1996. Other minerals (with estimated production in 1997) include gold (2,289 kg), silver (52,250 kg), tungsten, beryllium, clays (3·94m. tonnes), marble, lead (13,760 tonnes of metal), zinc (33,357 tonnes of metal), borates (422,556 tonnes), bentonite (104,880 tonnes), iron ore (3,388 tonnes of metal in 1996) and granite. Production from the US$1·1bn. Alumbrera copper and gold mine, the country's biggest mining project, in Catamarca province in the northwest, started in late 1997. In 1993 the mining laws were reformed and state regulation was swept away creating a more stable tax regime for investors. In Dec. 1997 Argentina and Chile signed a treaty laying the legal and tax framework for mining operations straddling the 5,000 km border, allowing mining products to be transported out through both countries.

Agriculture

In 1996 there were 25·0m. ha of arable land and 2·2m. ha of permanent crops. The agricultural population was 3·82m. in 1995, of whom 1·49m. were economically active. 1·7m. ha were irrigated in 1997.

Livestock (1998): cattle, 47,075,156; sheep, 22,408,681; pigs, 3,341,652; horses, 1,994,241. In 1997 wool production was 45,120 tonnes; milk (in 1998), 9,450m. litres.

Crop production (in 1,000 tonnes) in 1998–99: wheat, 10,700; sugarcane, 18,193; corn, 14,000; potatoes, 3,412 (1997–98); soybeans, 18,500; sunflower seed, 6,600. Cotton, vine, citrus fruit, olives and yerba maté (Paraguayan tea) are also cultivated.

Forestry

The woodland area was 44,975,115 ha in 1994. Production in 1996 included 1·71m. cu. metres of sawn wood, 6.6m. tonnes of round logs and 63,000 tonnes of tannin. Timber production totalled 13·19 cu. metres in 1997.

Fisheries

Fish landings in 1998 amounted to 1,117,300 tonnes, almost exclusively from sea fishing.

INDUSTRY

Production (1998 in tonnes): paper, 1,159,000; crude iron, 3,660,000; crude steel, 4,210,000; primary aluminium, 186,702; Portland cement, 7,092,000; synthetic rubber, 54,005; polyethylene, 279,538; sugar, 1,749,000; oleaginous oils, 4,867,000. Motor vehicles produced totalled 353,074; tractors, 3,513; tyres, 9,190,000. Industrial production in 1999 was forecast to be down 5·4% on the 1998 total.

Top 10 Companies

Rank	Company	Market Capital ($1m.)
1	YPF	9,142·7
2	Telefonica de Argentina	6,907·5
3	Telecom Argentina	5,857·1
4	Pérez Companc	3,430·3
5	CEI Citicorp Holdings	1,594·1
6	Transportadora Gas del Sud	1,589·0
7	Banco Galicia	1,461·7
8	Banco Rio de la Plata	1,275·0
9	Siderca	1,200·0
10	Banco Frances	1,194·4

Labour

The labour force in 1996 totalled 13,809,000. 2·12m. persons were registered unemployed at July 1996. Unemployment, which had been 18·4% in 1995, was down to 11·0% of the workforce in 1998, but had risen to 14·5% by Oct. 1999.

Trade Unions

Confederación General del Trabajo da la Republica Argentina:
Azopardo 802, Codigo Postal 1107, Buenos Aires.

Tel (0)11 4343-1883. Fax: (0)11 4343-1883.

E-mail: secgral@cgtra.org.ar Web site: www.cgtra.org.ar

The body to which most Argentinian unions are affiliated.

INTERNATIONAL TRADE

External debt was US$123,221m. in 1997.

Imports and Exports

Foreign trade (in US$1m.):

	1993	1994	1995	1996	1997	1998
Imports	16,784	21,590	20,122	23,762	30,450	31,404
Exports	13,118	15,839	20,963	23,811	26,431	26,441

Principal exports in 1997 (in US$1m.) were food products and live animals, (10,180), machinery and transportation equipment (4,008), fuels, mineral lubricants and related products (3,092) and manufactured goods (3,788).

Principal imports in 1997 (in US$1m.) were machinery and transportation equipment (14,897), manufactured goods (7,278), chemical products (4,892) and food products and live animals (1,315).

In 1998 imports (in US$1m.) were mainly from Brazil (7,055), USA (6,227), Germany (1,876), Italy (1,605), France (1,584) and Japan (1,453); exports went mainly to Brazil (7,949), USA (2,211), Chile (1,864), Netherlands (1,100), Uruguay (843) and Spain (839).

In 1997 exports grew by 7%, but imports rose by 27%.

The trade balance deteriorated to a deficit of almost US$4·9bn. in 1997, and around US$5·0bn. in 1998, but was projected to rise back to US$4·9bn. in 1999.

COMMUNICATIONS

Roads

In 1998 there were 38,371 km of motorways and national and provincial highways. The 4 main roads constituting Argentina's portion of the Pan-American Highway were opened in 1942. Vehicles in use in 1996 totalled 5,414,000, of which 4,459,000 were passenger cars, 943,000 trucks and vans, and 12,000 buses and coaches. In 1997, 4,718 people were killed in road accidents.

Rail

There is a major international rail service between Buenos Aires and Asuncion in Paraguay. In addition there are direct links with Bolivia, Brazil and Chile. The internal rail service has suffered in recent years due to underfunding and recent privatization. The rail network numbers some 33,000 km of track connecting Buenos Aires with most commercial areas of the country.

In 1998 railways carried 18,838,000 tonnes of freight and 480,138,000 passengers.

The metro and light rail network in Buenos Aires extends to 46 km.

Civil Aviation

Argentina's international airport is **Ezeiza Ministro Pistarini** (EZE) International Airport, located 42 km from the centre of Buenos Aires. There is a bus service to the city operating every 30 minutes between 5am and 9pm. For domestic flights there is a connecting bus service to **Jorge Newbery** airport, known locally as Aeroparque, which flies to **Cordoba** (COR) and destinations throughout Argentina.

The national carrier, Aerolíneas Argentinas, is 15% state-owned. In 1998 services were also operated by Aeroflot, Aeroperú,

Air France, Alitalia, ALTA, American Airlines, Austral, Avianca, British Airways, Canadian Airlines International, Cubana, Ecuatoriana, Iberia, KLM, Lan-Chile, Lloyd Aéreo Boliviano, Lufthansa, Malaysia Airlines, Mexicana, Pluna, SAS, South African Airways, Swissair, Transbrasil, Transportes Aereos del Mercosur, United Airlines, VASP and Varig.

In 1996 Aerolíneas Argentinas flew 85·4m. km, carrying 4,165,700 passengers (2,161,300 on international flights).

Shipping
The merchant shipping fleet totalled 595,000 GRT in 1995, including oil tankers totalling 107,000 GRT.

Telecommunications
The telephone service Entel was privatized in 1990. The sell-off split Argentina into 2 monopolies, operated by Telefonica Internacional de España, and a holding controlled by France Telecom and Telecom Italia. There are also 2 independent cellular operators. The number of lines in service in 1997 totalled 6,824,425. In June 1997 there were approximately 170,000 Internet users. In 1997 there were 2·01m. mobile phone subscribers, 1,400,000 PCs in use (39 per 1,000 persons) and 70,000 fax machines.

Telephone numbers have recently been modified. The digit 4 has to be placed before dialling any number. For long distance calls another digit—which changes according to the region—also has to be dialled (1 for Buenos Aires and its outskirts, 2 for the Southern part of the country and 3 for the North). Although IDD is available it is not extensively used. Local calls can be made from public call boxes identifiable by a blue sign outside. Reduced tariffs are available between 20·00–8·00. In addition fax facilities are widespread and available in most large hotels.

Postal Services

Airmail to Europe takes between five and ten days, surface mail takes around 20–25 days. There are close to 6,000 post offices throughout the country open from 8·00–20·00 Monday to Friday and 8·00–14·00 on Saturday.

SOCIAL INSTITUTIONS

Justice

Justice is administered by federal and provincial courts. The former deal only with cases of a national character, or those in which different provinces or inhabitants of different provinces are parties. The chief federal court is the Supreme Court, with 5 judges whose appointment is approved by the Senate. Other federal courts are the appeal courts, at Buenos Aires, Bahía Blanca, La Plata, Córdoba, Mendoza, Tucumán and Resistencia. Each province has its own judicial system, with a Supreme Court (generally so designated) and several minor chambers. The death penalty was re-introduced in 1976 for the killing of government, military police and judicial officials, and for participation in terrorist activities. The total prison population in 1997 was 6,177.

The police force is centralized under the Federal Security Council.

Religion

The Roman Catholic religion is supported by the State; affiliation numbered 31·06m. in 1997. There were 2·66m. Protestants of various denominations in 1997, and 520,000 Muslims. There were 275,000 Latter-day Saints (Mormons) in 1998.

Education

Adult literacy was 96·5% in 1997 (males, 96·6%; females, 96·5%). In 1996, 1,116,951 children attended pre-school institutions, 5,250,329 primary schools, 2,594,329 secondary schools and 391,778 tertiary colleges. Numbers of teachers in 1994–95: pre-school, 63,751; primary, 277,064; secondary, 228,289; tertiary, 40,160.

In 1996, in the public sector, there were 33 universities; 1 technical university; and university institutes of aeronautics, military studies, naval and maritime studies and police studies. In the private sector, there were 15 universities; 7 Roman Catholic universities; 1 Adventist university; universities of business administration, business and social science, the cinema, notarial studies, social studies, and theology; and university institutes of biomedical science, health and the merchant navy. In 1996 there were 790,775 university students and 128,478 academic staff.

In 1994 total expenditure on education came to 3·8% of GNP and represented 14% of total government expenditure.

Health

Free medical attention is obtainable from public hospitals. In 1996 there were 7,243 beds available in public health care institutions.

Health Requirements

There are no required inoculations for visitors to Argentina although precautions against cholera are advisable. The effectiveness of the cholera vaccination is somewhat doubtful but it may be appropriate for anyone working or travelling for more than 3 months in less than sanitary conditions where medical facilities are unavailable. There is a malaria risk, primarily in the benign vivax form, in pockets of the provinces of Salta, Jujuy, Misiones and Corrientes. The Argentinian Tourist Board recommends protection in the form of 300 mg of chloroquine prophylaxis administered weekly.

Tap water is safe to drink although outside of main cities and towns drinking water may be contaminated. Pasteurised milk and dairy products are safe for consumption. For travellers visiting the northeastern forest areas a yellow fever vaccination is recommended. Rabies is present and for those at high risk vaccination is advisable. Hepatitis A and gastro-enteritis are widespread and there is some risk of viral hepatitis and anthrax. Like most Latin American countries there is the risk of AIDS from unprotected sex or from used needles or syringes.

Welfare

Until the end of 1996 trade unions had a monopoly in the handling of the compulsory social security contributions of employees, but private insurance agencies are now permitted to function alongside them.

CULTURE

Broadcasting

There are state-owned, provincial, municipal and private radio stations overseen by the Secretaria de Comunicaciones, the Comité Federal de Radiodifusión, the Servicio Oficial de Radiodifusión (which also operates an external service and a station in Antarctica) and the Asociación de Teleradiodifusoras Argentinas. There were 23,800,000 radio sets in 1996 and 10,300,000 TV receivers (colour by PAL) in 1997.

Cinema

In 1997 there were 598 cinemas with an audience of approximately 26,565,000.

Press

In 1995 there were 190 daily newspapers with a combined circulation of 4,700,000, a rate of 135 per 1,000 inhabitants.

The main newspapers are: **Diario Los Andes, Diario Ambito Financiero, Clarin, La Nueva Provincia, Diario HOY, Brief, Diario Rio Negro, La Nación, La Voz del Interior, Pagina/12** and **Tiempo Fueguino.** The **Buenos Aires Herald** is an English language newspaper with a daily circulation of 25,000.

Tourism

In 1998, 4,859,867 tourists visited Argentina, providing receipts of US$5·36bn. There were 7,738 hotels providing 428,872 beds.

Tourist Organization

Secretaria de Turismo de la Nación: Calle Suipacha 1111, 1368 Buenos Aires.

Web site: www.sectur.gov.ar/homepage.htm

The official tourist board is **ArTour**: Web site: www.artour.com

Visas

A passport valid for 6 months is required by all visitors except nationals of Argentina, Bolivia, Brazil, Chile, Paraguay and Uruguay. No visas are required by EU nationals—including the UK—Australia, Canada, USA or New Zealand provided that the stay is no longer than 90 days.

Festivals

Jan: **Sea Festival**: At Mar del Plata.

Chaya Festival: Celebration of the chaya musical instrument in La Rioja.

Folklore Festivals: Across the country with large festivals in Diamante (Entre Rios), Intendente Alvear (La Pampa) and Cosquin (Cordoba).

Feb: **Carnival**: Pre-Lent carnivals across the country.

April: **Holy Week** (Semana Santa): Nationwide.

Aug: **Snow Festivals**: At Rio Turbio (Santa Cruz) and Bariloche.

Sept: **Chamamé Music Festival**: Local celebration of music at Corrientes.

Nov: **Tradition Week**: Traditional gaucho shows at San Antonio de Areco.

Dec: **Gaucho Festival**: Traditional celebration of gauchos at Gral. Madaria (Buenos Aires).

Public Holidays 2000

1 Jan.	New Year's Day.
20 April	Maundy Thursday.
21 April	Good Friday.
24 April	Easter Monday.
1 May	Labour Day.
25 May	National Day (Anniversary of the 1810 Revolution).
10 June	Day to celebrate sovereignty over the Malvinas.
9 July	Independence Day.
18 Aug.	Death of General José de San Martin.
9 Oct.	Day of the Americas (Columbus Day).
8 Dec.	Immaculate Conception.
25 Dec.	Christmas Day.

Social Etiquette

Most normal European courtesies are adhered to in Argentina. Visitors should expect to shake hands on greeting and departing and it is quite common to take a dish of home-made food to a meal. On the whole dress is casual although in a formal situation appropriate attire should be worn. The Falklands war is still a sensitive subject for most Argentinians and its mention, particularly from British visitors, should be with the utmost discretion. Even its name, Falklands/Malvinas, is a politically sensitive issue.

Although tipping is theoretically outlawed, in most cases a 10% tip is still expected, particularly in bars or taxis. Some hotels add a 25% service charge in which case any tip should be minimal.

DIPLOMATIC REPRESENTATIVES

Of Argentina in Great Britain (65 Brook St., London, W1Y 1YE)
Ambassador: Rogelio Pfirter.
Of Great Britain in Argentina (Dr Luis Agote 2141/52, 1425 Buenos Aires)
Ambassador: William Marsden, CMG.
Of Argentina in the USA (1600 New Hampshire Ave., NW, Washington, D.C., 20009)
Ambassador: Diego Guelar.
Of the USA in Argentina (4300 Colombia, 1425 Buenos Aires)
Ambassador: Vacant.
Of Argentina to the United Nations
Ambassador: Fernando Enrique Petrella.
Of Argentina to the European Union
Ambassador: Juan Uranga.

FURTHER READING

INDEC. *Statistical Yearbook of Argentina*
Bethell, L. (ed.) *Argentina since Independence.* CUP, 1994
Biggins, Alex, *Argentina.* [Bibliography] ABC-Clio, Oxford and Santa Barbara (CA), 1991

Lewis, P., *The Crisis of Argentine Capitalism.* North Carolina Univ.
  Press, 1990
Manzetti, L., *Institutions, Parties and Coalitions in Argentine Politics.*
  Univ. of Pittsburgh Press, 1994
Rock, D., *Argentina 1516–1982.* London, 1986
Shumway, N., *The Invention of Argentina.* California Univ. Press, 1992
Wynia, G. W., *Argentina: Illusions and Realities.* 2nd ed. Hoddesdon,
  1993
National statistical office: Instituto Nacional de Estadística y Censos
  (INDEC). Av. Presidente Julio A. Roca 609, 1067 Buenos Aires.
Director: Dr Hector E. Montero.
Website: http://www.indec.mecon.ar/default.htm

BRAZIL

República Federativa do Brasil

Capital: Brasília (Federal District)

Area: 8,547,395 sq. km

Population estimate, 2000: 169·2m.

Head of State: Fernando Henrique Cardoso

TERRITORY AND POPULATION

Brazil is bounded in the east by the Atlantic and on its northern, western and southern borders by all the Latin American countries except Chile and Ecuador. The area is 8,547,395 sq. km including 55,457 sq. km of inland water. Population as at censuses of 1991 and 1996:

Federal Unit and Capital	Area (sq. km)	Census 1991	Census 1996
North	3,869,639		
Rondônia (Porto Velho)	238,513	1,132,692	1,229,306
Acre (Rio Branco)	153,150	417,718	483,593
Amazonas (Manaus)	1,577,820	2,103,243	2,389,279
Roraima (Boa Vista)	225,116	217,583	247,131
Pará (Belém)	1,253,165	4,950,060	5,510,849
Amapá (Macapá)	143,454	289,397	379,459
Tocantins (Palmas)	278,421	919,863	1,048,642
North-East	1,561,177[1]		
Maranhão (São Luís)	333,366	4,930,253	5,222,183
Piaui (Teresina)	252,378	2,582,137	2,673,085
Ceará (Fortaleza)	146,348	6,366,647	6,809,290
Rio Grande do Norte (Natal)	53,307	2,415,567	2,558,660
Paraíba (João Pessoa)	56,585	3,201,114	3,305,616
Pernambuco (Recife)	98,938	7,127,855	7,399,071
Alagoas (Maceió)	27,933	2,514,100	2,633,251
Sergipe (Aracajú)	22,050	1,491,876	1,624,020
Bahia (Salvador)	567,295	11,867,991	12,541,675
South-East	927,287		
Minas Gerais (Belo Horizonte)	588,384	15,743,152	16,672,613
Espírito Santo (Vitória)	46,184	2,600,618	2,802,707

Rio de Janeiro (Rio de Janeiro)	43,910	12,807,706	13,406,308
São Paulo (São Paulo)	248,809	31,588,925	34,119,110
South	577,214		
Parana (Curitiba)	199,709	8,448,713	9,003,804
Santa Catarina (Florianópolis)	95,443	4,541,994	4,875,244
Rio Grande do Sul (Porto Alegre)	282,062	9,138,670	9,634,688
Central West	1,612,078		
Mato Grosso (Cuiabá)	906,807	2,027,231	2,235,832
Mato Grosso do Sul (Campo Grande)	358,159	1,780,373	1,927,834
Goiás (Goiânia)	341,290	4,018,903	4,514,967
Distrito Federal (Brasília)	5,822	1,601,094	1,821,946
Total	8,547,395	146,825,475	157,070,163

[1]Including disputed areas between states of Piauí and Ceará (2,977 sq. km).

Population density, 18 per sq. km. The 1996 census showed 77,442,865 males and 79,627,298 females. The urban population comprised 79·6% in 1997.

The UN gives a projected population for 2000 of 169·2m.

The official language is Portuguese.

Population of principal cities (1996 census):

São Paulo	9,839,066	Porto Alegre	1,288,879
Rio de Janeiro	5,551,538	Manaus	1,157,357
Salvador	2,211,539	Belém	1,144,312
Belo Horizonte	2,091,371	Goiânia	1,003,477
Fortaleza	1,965,513	Guarulhos	972,197
Brasília	1,821,946	Campinas	908,906
Curitiba	1,476,253	São Gonçalo	833,379
Recife	1,346,045	Nova Iguaçu	826,188

Osasco	622,912	Niterói	450,364
Campo Grande	600,069	Uberlândia	438,986
João Pessoa	549,363	São João de Meriti	434,323
Jaboatão	529,966	Cuiabá	433,355
Contagem	492,214	Soroca ba	431,561
São José dos Campos	486,167	Aracaju	428,194
Ribeirão Preto	456,252	Juiz de Fora	424,479
Feira de Santana	450,487	Londrina	421,343
São Luis	780,833	Santos	412,243
Maceió	723,142	Joinville	397,951
Duque de Caxias	715,089	Campos dos Goytacazes	389,547
São Bernardo do Campo	660,396	Olinda	349,380
Natal	656,037	Diadema	323,116
Teresina	655,473	Porto Velho	294,227
Santo André	624,820		

The principal metropolitan areas (census, 1996) were São Paulo (16,583,234), Rio de Janeiro (10,192,097), Belo Horizonte (3,803,249), Porto Alegre (3,246,869), Recife (3,087,967), Salvador (2,709,084), Fortaleza (2,582,820), Curitíba (2,425,361) and Belém (1,485,569).

Time Zones

Brazil spans several time zones. The standard Brazilian time is GMT –3 hrs (GMT –2 in summer). In the Amazon, except for Acre, it is GMT –4 hrs (GMT –3 in summer). In Acre State it is GMT –4 hrs throughout the year.

KEY HISTORICAL EVENTS

Pre-Columbian

Before the Portuguese discovery and occupation of the present-day Brazilian region there was a population of indigenous Americans that numbered some 2·5m. at the beginning of the 16th century. This population was fragmented into a number of smaller tribes, the largest of which was the Tupi-Guarani, a deeply spiritual people who survived their sub-tropical environment through pruning and clearing just enough land for their crops.

The first Europeans the indigenous peoples came into contact with were exiled criminals, or degredados, who lived amongst them, learning their language and methods for farming, hunting and survival. Later Jesuit missionaries attempted to convert the native people with limited success. Although some were converted the majority rebelled or escaped areas of Jesuit influence.

Portuguese Exploration

The first Portuguese contact with Brazil was by Pedro Alvares Cabral who left Lisbon in 1500 with orders to travel along the Cape of Good Hope route discovered by the Portuguese navigator Vasco da Gama in 1497–98. In an attempt to avoid storms that could have wrecked his voyage he set a course more westerly than da Gama's and was carried still farther westward by currents, landing him in a place he named Terra da Vera Cruz (Land of the True Cross)—an area later renamed Terra do Brasil (Land of Brazil).

Although the official reason for Portuguese exploration was religious—the conversion of the natives to the true faith—the greater impetus was to find a direct all-water trade route with Asia and thereby break Italian domination in that field.

Early Portuguese economic activity in Brazil revolved around the exploitation of the huge timber (Brazilwood) resources. This was soon superseded by the sugarcane and, to a lesser extent, tobacco plantations that sprang up in the interior of the country in the16th and 17th centuries. As these industries came to dominate the colonies' economy more and more the need for large-scale labour became more pressing. Where the indigenous people proved unsuitable or unavailable, largely due to ill health from the newly introduced European diseases, millions of Africans were enslaved and shipped to the region, adding a further element to Brazil's ethnic makeup.

It was not long before the Portuguese set about conquering the vast Brazilian interior. Early excursions were made by bandeirantes, men pursuing private enterprise and dreams of vast wealth. It was these men who, in forging waterways and paths into the interior, discovered the first gold in the region at Minas Gerais in 1695. This opened up a whole new resource for exploitation by the Portuguese crown.

In 1807 Napoleon's invasion forced the Portuguese royal family to flee Portugal and take refuge in Rio, declaring it the temporary capital of the Portuguese Empire. In 1816 King João VI ascended to the Portuguese throne yet refused to return to Lisbon until revolts demanded his presence there five years later. In his absence his son, Pedro, became Brazil's Regent.

Brazilian Independence

Pedro's reign as Regent ran into trouble when he battled the Cortes, the Portuguese parliamentary body's, demand for him to return to Portugal. In Sept. 1822 the Cortes decided to reduce his powers. Pedro's response was to push for independence, unsheathing his sword on the banks of the Ipiranga River and proclaiming 'independence or death'. On 1 Dec. 1822 he was crowned Constitutional Emperor and Perpetual Defender of Brazil. The United States recognized Brazil's independence in May 1824, soon followed, in 1825, by the acceptance of Portugal itself.

Pedro II and the Creation of the Republic

Pedro was forced to abdicate in 1831 following a disastrous war with Argentina and a rampant money crisis deepened by his promises to free the slaves. He left his five-year old son Pedro II as the ruler in waiting. In 1840 Pedro II ascended the throne and proceeded to establish himself as leader, free of all political influences, by 1847. He ruled for nearly 50 years, initiating the beginnings of the gradual abolition of slavery by outlawing the slave trade in 1854.

In 1889 General Manuel Deodoro da Fonseca led a military revolt which forced Pedro's abdication. A republic was proclaimed, headed by Fonseca, which instigated the separation of church and state. In Feb. 1891 Brazil officially became a Federal Republic with Fonseca elected as its first President.

Vargas

Over the course of the first part of the 20th century Brazilian political fortunes fluctuated as several leaders attempted to make their mark. In 1929 Getulio Vargas lost the presidential election prompting a military junta to seize power from the legitimately elected government and make Vargas leader. During his period of rule some areas such as São Paulo saw considerable industrial development helping Brazil to reach a competitive level of modern economic development. In the 1940s the first steel plant was built in the state of Rio de Janeiro at Volta Redonda with US Eximbank financing.

By 1954 Vargas had become a constitutional President directly elected by the people. However, he became indirectly implicated in the attempted murder of a journalist who had publicly called him a communist. The High Command demanded his resignation and Vargas responded by shooting himself through the heart bringing to an end 25 years of uninterrupted rule.

Economic Crisis and Military Rule

Juscelino Kubitschek, popularly known as JK, was elected as President in 1956. Promising '50 years progress in five' he brought 40 years inflation in four. A big spender, he built roads and hydro-electric plants. The creation of Brasília, supposed to be the catalyst for development of Brazil's huge interior, was initiated under his presidency.

Janio Quadros became the next president in 1961 on a wave of public euphoria. But when he decorated Che Guevara in a public ceremony, he1 upset the right wing military. A few days later Quadros resigned after only six months in office. João Goulart, his vice-president, took over. His leftist policies led to his overthrow by the military in 1964. This was followed by 20 years of single party rule and censored press.

Brazil's military regime was not as brutal as those of Chile or Argentina, but at its height, around 1968 and 1969, the use of torture was widespread. The generals benefited from the Brazilian economic miracle in the late '60s and '70s when the economy was growing by more than 10% each year. Brazil became one of the biggest industrial nations in the world, but uncoordinated growth made bureaucracy, corruption and inflation explode.

In 1980 a militant working-class movement sprung up under the charismatic leadership of a worker called Lula. The popular opposition, together with economic problems, forced the military slowly to announce the so-called 'abertura' (opening)—a slow process of returning democratic government.

Tancredo Neves, leader of the main opposition party (the Partido do Movimento Democratico Brasiliero—PMDB) surprised his military opponents by winning the 1985 elections, but tragically died shortly before assuming power. José Sarney, his vice-president, took over. Although initially there was some doubt as to Sarney's fitness to rule he successfully guided the country through the difficult transition from military to civilian rule as well as overseeing the drafting and implementation of a new democratic constitution. Despite this political success the country drifted into economic chaos with a new finance minister every three months, and foreign debt reaching Cr$115,000m.

Recent History

In 1989 Fernando Collor de Mello, governor of a forgotten state in the northeast, won a hard-fought victory over the Labour Party candidate, Lula. One of the main promises of the incoming government was to cut inflation and attack corruption. When he assumed control in March 1990 Collor took drastic measures. In an attempt to reduce inflation caused by excess liquidity in the market, he confiscated 80% of every bank account worth more than US$1,200, promising to release it 18 months later with interest. He announced the privatization of state-owned companies and the opening of Brazilian markets to foreign competition and capital.

By 1992 few promises had been met, most of the popular goodwill was gone and Collor found his government shaken by scandals and corruption linked directly to his family. Inflation was heading into astronomical figures once again. The parliament, under public pressure, forced an impeachment. Itamar Franco, Collor's vice-president, took office until elections were held in Oct. 1994.

Fernando Henrique Cardoso, former finance minister responsible for the 'Plano Real', the economic plan to end inflation, was elected president for the Partido da Social Democracia Brasiliera, formed in 1990 by PMDB dissidents. He instituted an economic revolution that included a radical privatization programme and a lowering of trade barriers. In 1997–98 economic turbulence in the Far East spread to Brazil, which had to be kept afloat by IMF loans. In Jan. 1999, the real was devalued, thereafter losing 35% of its value against the dollar in two months. Despite these major economic difficulties Cardoso's government's economic performance has been reasonably sound. Politically, however, little has been done to tackle the social problems afflicting Brazilian society: the country's corruption riddled political system and its country's huge social inequalities. It perhaps augers well, however, that Cardoso has managed to build up a certain amount of public trust, winning the Oct. 1998 presidential election with more votes than the rest of the candidates put together.

POLITICAL AND SOCIAL CHRONOLOGY FOR THE CENTURY

1902
Rodrigues Alves replaces Campos Salles as president.
1906
Affonso Penna becomes president.
1909
Nilo Peçanha becomes president.
1910
Hermes da Fonseca becomes president.
1914
Wenceslau Braz becomes president. Contestado rebellion in south challenges colonial-dominated system.
1917
Brazil declares war on Germany and joins allied powers.
1918
Delfim Moreira becomes president.
1919
Epitacio Pessoa becomes president.
1922
Tenente (Lieutenants') Movement begins with Copacabana revolt. Arthur Bernardes becomes president.

1926

Washington Luis becomes president.

1929

Getulio Vargas loses the presidential election.

1930

The world depression causes coffee to reach its lowest price in history. The economic crisis that follows leads to a military coup in which there are 5 presidents in as many months, as Washington Luis, Menna Barreto, Isaias Noroha and Augusto Fragoso all hold the post. General Getulio Vargas finally establishes a government.

1932

São Paulo rebellion brings civil war.

1934

Vargas wins a second term as President and introduces a new constitution, which, among other things, gives the vote to women.

1937

Shortly before the presidential elections Vargas declares a state of emergency, dissolves Congress and installs extraordinary powers which enable him, in effect, to head a dictatorship that lasts until 1945.

1942

Brazil joins in the Second World War on the allied side. Construction begins on Brazil's first major steel mill.

1944

A 25,000 strong expeditionary forced is sent to fight alongside the Americans in Italy.

1945

The military deposes Vargas.

1946

Gaspar Dutra becomes president on a wave of popular support. He is Brazil's first civilian leader for 15 years. A new democratic constitution is approved.

1947

Brazil breaks diplomatic relations with the Soviet Union.

1951

Getulio Vargas is constitutionally elected as president.

1954

In the midst of a political crisis and controversial allegations, Vargas commits suicide and Café Filho takes over as a caretaker leader.

1955

Carlos Coimbra becomes president for 3 days until Nereu Ramos takes over.

1956

Juscelino Kubitschek becomes president and instigates a new nationalist and developmentalist political emphasis, economic openness and the creation of Brasília.

1958

Brazil wins the football World Cup for the first time.

1960

Brasília is inaugurated as the new capital of Brazil.

1961

Janio Quadros is elected as President on a wave of public euphoria but lasts only 6 months before resigning having decorated Che Guevara in a public ceremony. His vice-president João Goulart takes over but only after Congress approves a parliamentary system, which curtails his presidential powers.

1962

Brazil retains the football World Cup.

1963

João Goulart wins a second term as president and a national plebiscite restores full presidential powers.

1964

João Goulart is overthrown by the military due to his Marxist sympathies. Castello Branco takes over as a military dictator in a one-party state on a wave of anti-Communist feeling.

1965

Second Institutional Act bans all existing political parties and imposes legal guidelines for new parties.

1966

Third Institutional Act replaces direct election of governors with indirect elections by state assemblies and substitutes presidential appointees for mayors of capital cities.

1967

Arthur da Costa e Silva takes over as president but still as a head of the military dictatorship. A new constitution is instigated.

1968

Fifth Institutional Act gives Costa e Silva dictatorial powers.

1969

Costa e Silva resigns due to ill health. Aurelio Tavares, Augusto Radamaker and Marcio Mello rule as a military junta until Emilio Medici becomes president. The economy is growing at over 10% a year but human rights violations are widespread.

1970

Brazil wins the football World Cup for the third time, the first team ever to do this.

1973

Real growth, as measured by GDP, reaches 14%.

1974

Ernesto Geisel becomes president and proposes a period of political liberalization.

1975

Brazil signs nuclear energy accord with the Federal Republic of Germany.

1977

Divorce is legalised. Brazil renounces its military alliance with the USA.

1979

João Figueiredo is inaugurated as president and begins the process of opening up the political system to eventual restoration of political rights and democracy.

1980

The charismatic worker, Lula (Luis Inacio da Silva), starts a militant working-class opposition movement.

1982

Democratic elections, the first since 1965, are held for the positions of the state governors.

1985

Tancredo Neves, the head of the opposition, wins the presidential election but becomes ill and dies. The Vice-President José Sarney becomes president in his place and heads Brazil's first civilian government for 21 years.

1988

A new 'Citizen constitution' is approved.

1990

Fernando Collor becomes president having defeated Lula in an election.

1992

Collor resigns the presidency amidst allegations of corruption. Itamar Franco takes over office. The first global summit on environmental issues, the Earth Summit, is held in Rio de Janeiro. The destruction of the Brazilian Rain Forest is a major issue.

1994

Congress approves constitutional reform reducing the presidential term of office to 4 years. A new currency, the real, is introduced, at parity with the US$. Fernando Enrique Cardoso wins the Oct.

presidential elections. Brazil wins the football World Cup for the fourth time (their first in 24 years).

1995

Fernando Cardoso assumes the presidential office. Ex-president Collor is acquitted of corruption.

1998

Brazil's economy is hit by crisis, rocking the world stock markets. Cardoso wins his second presidential term.

LEADING CULTURAL FIGURES

Emiliano Di Cavalcanti (1897–1986)

Di Cavalcanti is the master of contemporary Brazilian art. His work is famed for its sensuality, melancholy and tenderness and it has been called the artistic portrait of the Brazilian soul. He began his career as a caricaturist and illustrator. In 1919 he illustrated Manuel Bandeira's 'Carnaval' and published a collection of his drawings in 'Midnight Puppets' in 1921. Inspired by the English artist Aubrey Beardsley he illustrated Oscar Wilde's 'The Ballad of Reading Gaol' and his exciting modern style began to gain critical approval.

Di Cavalcanti was a self-taught painter with impressionist tendencies who was developing a natural and impulsive expressionism born from the need to satirize, combat and demolish the anachronistic forms of conventional art. In 1923 he visited Europe and studied Picasso's art. Di Calvalcanti absorbed numerous different influences helping him develop his own original style, which he translated into the nudes he painted on his return.

Lúcio Costa (1902–98)

Lúcio Costa was born in 1902. In 1936 he was put in charge of the team responsible for the Ministry of Education headquarters in Rio de Janeiro, today the Palace of Culture. In the process he contacted the French architect Le Corbusier, a figure who would be a great influence in Costa's later designs. Costa went on to design a scheme for the University City in Rio de Janeiro, the Casa do Brasil in Paris and, with Oscar Niemeyer, the Brazilian pavilion at the World Fair in New York. He received the São Paulo Biennial Award for the apartment buildings he projected in the Guinle Park in Rio in the early 1950s. With President Juscelino Kubitschek's election victory in 1956 Costa submitted a plan for the competition to design a new capital for Brazil and his scheme, submitted on five medium sized cards with no technical drawings, was chosen.

His designs for Brasília had in mind the creation of a city that would be a work of art; a model of a more human, socially just and beautiful world. In recent years he has been recognized as a funda-mental figure in the study of urban design and planning.

Oscar Niemeyer (1907 –)

Oscar Niemeyer became world famous as an architect for his bold, innovative and uncompromisingly modern designs for the buildings of Brazil's capital city, Brasília. Niemeyer graduated from the National Belas Artes School in Rio de Janeiro in 1934. Two years later he participated in the Ministry of Health and Education project, today the Palace of Culture, which was adapted from the designs of Le Corbusier. However, it was not until his designs for the new district of Pampulha in Belo Horizonte that his particular modern style began to really show itself. The São Francisco church he designed was startlingly original. In 1946 he was invited to help in the development of the United Nations building in New York and, in conjunction with Le Corbusier, designed the organization's present headquarters. Soon after this Niemeyer joined the communist party, a move that preju-diced him in the eyes of the Brazilian and North American governments and which for a time prevented any public commissions. His career became dependent on private commissions.

In 1956 Niemeyer was chosen to lead the team to turn Lucio Costa's designs for Brasília into reality. Rejecting older concepts of functionality and utility Niemeyer strove to capture the innovative spirit of the new city and the latent symbolism of the capital status along with the creation of simple forms of incontestable beauty.

Leaving Brazil in 1964 he opened representative offices in several foreign countries. He soon picked up important projects including the Mondadori in Milan, the headquarters of the French communist party in Paris and the urban plan for the Algarve in Portugal. He articulated his ideas and conceptions in several published books and articles. He has recently completed the Memorial da America Latina and the Latin American Parliament in São Paulo.

Heitor Villa-Lobos (1887–1959)

Villa-Lobos is considered the most important and significant composer of the Brazilian Nationalistic movement of the first half of this century. Born in Rio de Janeiro he learnt music from his father who was a highly cultured amateur musician. This early musical start meant Villa-Lobos had turned professional by the turn of the century, earning his living playing the cello as a café musician. In 1905 he made his first trip to Brazil's northeastern states to collect the folk music that would make his music so vibrant and original. On his return to Rio he studied at the National Institute of Music although his compositional style never conformed to any academic conventions.

His music first began to attract attention in 1915 when he was able to stage a concert. His reputation soon grew so that by 1923 he had attracted enough official favour to win a government grant to study in Paris. On his return in 1930 he was made the director of music education in Rio itself, allowing him to design a complete system of musical instruction based upon the country's rich musical culture. In

1944 he travelled to the USA to conduct his works. It was to be the start of a distinguished period of international critical and popular acclaim. He died in his home town of Rio de Janeiro on 17 Nov. 1959. He will ultimately be remembered for breaking from traditional western classical music and creating a music representative of the people of his country and its traditions.

MAJOR CITIES

The country code in 55. The outgoing call code is 00.

SÃO PAULO

Estimated population 2000: 17,711,000 (Source: 1996 World Urbanisation Prospects. United Nations Population Division.) São Paulo is located 55 km from Brazil's Atlantic Coast on a plateau 760 metres above sea level. The city was founded by the Jesuits José de Anchieta and Manuel da Nobrega, who set up a mission by the Rio Tiete in 1554 to convert the local Indians, the Tupi-Guarani. The town settlement attracted traders and adventurers looking for mineral wealth further inland. As more and more people settled there, the town grew in importance, becoming the seat of regional government in 1681.

The city was known as 'a cidade de barro' (the mud city) until the 1870s as most of its buildings were built from clay and packed mud. It remained a relatively sleepy, small town until the development of the coffee trade in the region in the late 19th century. As plantation owners moved in so the infrastructure grew as railway lines, water, gas and electricity operations developed—aided by the availability of plentiful hydroelectric power. By the end of the century the region had become the largest exporter of coffee in the world and related industrial and commercial growth soon followed. Exports and imports flowed through the coastal port of Santos forging the city's position as the nation's industrial powerhouse. This lead to a population explosion as immigrants arrived to meet the requirements of commercial operations that were outgrowing the capacity of the established city.

São Paulo is still Brazil's leading industrial centre, the largest city in South America and one of the largest in the world. It is three times the size of Paris, covering over 1,500 sq. km. It accounts for 33% of Brazil's total exports and 40% of its imports. Modern São Paulo numbers some 20,000 industrial plants of all types and sizes and around 2,000 banking agencies. The various waves of immigration into the city have left São Paulo with an extensive multi-cultural legacy including the largest Japanese community outside of Japan and sizeable Arabic and Italian communities. In addition there has been a huge amount of foreign investment in the city, particularly from German companies such as Volkswagen, Mercedes-Benz, Audi and Siemens.

Tourist Information

CIT Terminal Turístico de Compras 25 de Março: (In front of 'Palacio das Indústrias').

CIT República—República Subway Station. Tel: (0)11 231-2922.

Financial and Currency

American Express Travel Service: Alameda Santos, 1.437. Hotel Sheraton Mofarrej, 01419–001. Tel: (0)11 251-3383. Hours: Monday to Friday 9·30–17·30. Closed Holidays: Jan. 1, 25, Carnival, Good Friday, April 21, May 1, Corpus Christi, Sept. 7, Oct. 12, Nov. 2, 15, Dec. 25.

Post Services

Main Office: Praça Correio. (at the corner of Av. São João)

Internet Access

Des Arts Cybercafe: Rua Pedro Humberto 9, Itaim Bibi, São Paulo–SP.
Tel: (0)11 829-7828/829-2850.
Web site: www.netpoint.com.br/desarts/caracol.gif

C@fe com Leinternet: 1555 Rua Fradique Countinho, São Paulo.
Tel: (0)11 867-0739.
Fax: (0)11 867-0739. E-mail: artagent@that.com.br
Web site: www.midia.com/café
3 computers, a printer and a scanner available.

Rail

There are four main stations in São Paulo:
Barra Funda: Rua Mario de Andrade 74—Barra Funda Subway
Station.
Tel: (0)11 702-1400.
Departure point for the Tren da Prata (Silver Train) to Rio.

Luz Station: Praça da Luz, 01—Luz Subway Station.
Tel: (0)11 225-0040.
For state commuter trains northeast or southeast of the city.

Julio Prestes Station: Praça Julio Prestes, 148—Campos Eliseos.
Tel: (0)11 220-8862.
For commuters to the west of the city.

Roosevelt Station: Praça Agente Cicero—Bras.
Tel: (0)11 942-1132.
For commuters east of the city.

Landmarks

Cathedral of the Sé: Praça da Sé, Downtown—Sé Subway
Station.

Started in 1913 in a Gothic style, the cathedral took 4 decades to
complete. It is the biggest church in São Paulo with 92 metre towers,
a 30 metre cupola and room for 8,000 people.

About 800 tonnes of rare ivory have been used in the interior, and
its Italian organ is the biggest in South America.

Its crypt is a church in itself and includes works by the sculptor
Francisco Leopoldo and the mausoleum of chieftain Tibiriçá—the
head of the Guaianazes tribe that lodged the first Jesuits in Planalto
de Piratininga thereby making the foundation of São Paulo
possible.

São Bento Monastery and Basilica: Largo São Bento,
Downtown—São Bento Subway Station.

The present abbey is the fifth such building on the site of the
residence of the first couple to live in the São Paulo area: the Indians
Tibiriçá and Bartira.

The patroness of the church is Our Lady of Assumption and the
Basilica has an eclectic style, with elements of neo-gothic.
Particularly of interest among the many decorative features are the
impressive baroque crucifix, dated 1777, the Portuguese image of
Our Lady of Conception, from the 17th century, and the icon of the
Kasperovo's Virgin dated 1893. This latter item was brought by
Russian fugitives from the socialist revolution, and is incrusted with
rubies, turquoise and six thousand pearls from the Black Sea.

In the church are the remains of important people from Brazilian
history.

Praça da República and Edificio Italia:
Tree-lined square. Nearby is the city's tallest building, the Edificio

Italia, on the corner of Av. Ipiranga and Av. São Luis. There is a restaurant on top with a sightseeing balcony.

Memorial da América Latina: Avenida Mario de Andrade 664—next to Barra Funda metro station. Tel: (0)11 823-9611. Open Tuesday to Sunday from 9·00–18·00.

Designed by Oscar Niemeyer, the architect behind Brasília, and built in 1989 the memorial is one of the city's largest cultural centres. It contains a relief map of central and South America under a glass floor as well as the Library of the Americas, an auditorium that seats over 1,500 people and a permanent exhibition of Latin American art and craftwork.

Museums and Galleries

MASP: Avenida Paulista, 1578. Tel: (0)11 251-5644.

E-mail: atemasp@yahoo.com

Web site: www2.uol.com.br/masp

Open from Tuesday to Friday 13·00–17·00 and Saturday and Sunday from 14·00–18·00.

Located in São Paulo's new financial centre, at Avenida Paulista, MASP is the most important museum of Western Art in the Latin America. The modern museum building, purpose-built by the Italian architect Lina Bo Bardi, contains some 3,487 works, including 850 paintings by major artists from all periods from the Middle Ages to the first decades of this century. The collection includes works by Bosch, Rembrandt, Poussin, Van Gogh, Renoir and Degas among others.

MASP receives temporary exhibitions from Europe and United States. It also stages music, conferences and lectures.

MAC (Museu de Arte Contemporânea): Rua de Reitoria, 160. By bus (Butantan–USP)—República Subway Station.

Tel: (0)11 818-3039. Fax: (0)11 212-0218.

E-mail: infomac@edu.usp.br Web site: www.usp.br/mac/

Open from Tuesday to Saturday, 12·00–18·00 and Sunday from

10·00–18·00.

MAC was established in 1963 from donations from the Modern Art

Museum and private collections. It comprises nearly 5,000 works from

the most diverse contemporary artistic movements. There are valuable

works by international artists including Modigliani, Picasso, Chagall,

Matisse, Miró and many others. Most of the works by foreign artists are

on display in the University of São Paulo's main building. There are in

addition major works by Brazilian artists including Tarsila do Amaral, Di

Cavalcanti, Anita Malfatti, João Câmara and Wesley Duke Lee. Entry is

free.

Museu de Arte Moderna: Marquise of Ibirapuera Park.

Tel: (0)11 251-5644.

Open from 11·00–18·00 and on Thursdays from14·00–20·00.

The oldest museum of modern art in the country. It has about 2,000

works, almost all Brazilian from the 1920s. The collection includes

paintings and sculptures by Tarsila do Amaral, Di Cavalcanti, Alfredo

Volpi, Brecheret, Amilcar de Castro, Tomie Ohtake, Baravelli and other

artists.

Paulista Museu: Independence Park. By bus (Maria Estela) in Praça da

República—República Subway. Tel: (0)11 215-4588.

Open from Tuesday to Sunday, from 9.00–16.45.

The magnificent building, in neo-classic renaissance style, located

at the back of Independence Park lends the museum the air of a

European palace. Inaugurated in 1895, the collection consists of an

historical estate including weapons, religious pieces, furniture, objects

and personal jewels belonging to famous residents of São Paulo and

artefacts used by 'bandeirantes' and Indians.

Its vast garden contains a replica of the Palace of Versailles by the landscape designer Arsênio Puttemans.

Museu de Arte Sacra de São Paulo (Museum of Sacred Art):
Avenida Tiradentes, 676. Tiradentes Subway Station.
Tel: (0)11 227-7694.
Open from Tuesday to Sunday, from 13·00–17:00.

The Museum of Sacred Art is contained in the 'Mosteiro da Luz', the oldest example of colonial architecture in São Paulo. It is organized from the estate of the Archdiocesan Miter of São Paulo. There are at least 640 pieces on exhibition, from a total of 11,000 that make up the estate of the museum. Among these pieces, there are clay images of the 17th century, cuts, baroque oratory, silver plates and European goldsmithery—brought during the colonization—as well as furniture and works by Francisco Xavier de Brito and Aleijadinho. Built in 1774, the building has been restored recently and preserves all its original characteristics. Entry is free.

MIS (The Museum of Image and Sound): Avenida Europa, 158.
By bus at Rua Augusta (Pinheiros, Cidade Universitária)—
Consolação Subway Station.
Tel: (0)11 280-0896.
Open daily from 14·00–22·00.

The first Brazilian museum of audio-visual documentation was opened in 1970. MIS conserves motion pictures, photographs, sound recordings, old photographic cameras and motion picture cameras, in addition to gramophones and other phonographic appliances. As well as films, there are about 150,000 photos and 10,000 slides. Entry is free.

Theatre and Opera

Teatro Municipal: Praça Ramos de Azevedo, s/n, 01307–000 São Paulo. República Subway Station.

Tel: (0)11 222-8698. Fax: (0)11 223-5021.

Conceived in neo-baroque style and inspired by the Paris opera house, the Municipal is the premier theatre in the city. Built between 1903 and 1911 by Ramos de Azevedo, the building was recently restored and preserves many of its original characteristics. It has been the scene of some of the most important cultural and artistic events in the city. With 1,585 seats, it has staged important events such as the Modern Art Week, in 1922, the ballet seasons of the IV Centenary Ballet and important International Theatre Festivals. It is the permanent home for the Municipal Symphony Orchestra, the São Paulo City Ballet, the Lyric Chorus and São Paulo Chorus and the String Quartet.

Teatro Alfa-Real: R. Bento Branco de Andsade Filho, 722—Santo Amaro, São Paulo.

Tel: (0)11 518-17333. Fax: (0)11 518-17176.

E-mail: institut@alfa-real.com.br

Stages opera with capacity for over 1,200 people.

Other theatres include the **Aliania Francesca** (R. Gen. Jardim 182, Vila Buarque), the **Italia** (Avenida Ipiranga 344), the **Cacilda Becker** (R. Tito 295, Lapa), the **Paiol** (R. Amaral Gurgel 164, Santa Cecilia) and the **Ruth Escobar** (R. dos Ingleses 209, Bela Vista).

RIO DE JANEIRO

Estimated population 2000: 10,556,000 (Source: 1996 World Urbanization Prospects. United Nations Population Division.) Although the status of capital was transferred from Rio de Janeiro to Brasília in 1960 the city remains the cultural capital of Brazil. Rio was discovered by Gonçalo Coelho in 1502, 2 years after the discovery of Brazil itself. The name Rio de Janeiro was chosen by Lemos mistakenly thinking he was in a river (rio)—it was actually a bay—in the month of January (Janeiro).

The first settlers in the bay area arrived with Admiral Villegaignon in 1555 with the intention of establishing a colony of French Calvinists. The French settlement was, however, badly organized and weakly lead by Villegaignon giving the Portuguese the impetus to invade. Mem de Sá was sent from Portugal to expel them and, despite achieving this, his nephew, Estacio de Sá, was forced to return in 1564 to expel the French once again. After a two year struggle between the two sides de Sá finally expelled the French and established his own settlement thereby founding the city of Rio.

Early economic activity in the colony centred on the production of sugarcane and whaling. Slaves from Africa and the indigenous Indian population were introduced to do the work. With the discovery of gold in the neighbouring Minas Gerais State Rio was used as the destination port for the gold expeditions. As a result the city's population began to grow significantly. In an effort to boost security the Portuguese built forts throughout Brazil including 6 in Rio itself. Despite these measures there were numerous attacks made on the city. The French made raids in 1710 and again in 1711 when René Duguay-Trouin, with a large fleet, sacked the city for two months in an attempt to extract a ransom before being expelled.

By the end of the 19th century Rio had undergone a population explosion. The growth of industry encouraged major internal migration, particularly from the African ex-slaves who had been freed in 1888. This was coupled with large-scale European immigration from Portugal, Italy and Germany. The first shanty town (favela) soon sprang up on Providencia Hill after black soldiers who had fought in Bahia were not accepted back into the city on returning home. Today Rio is Brazil's second largest city (after São Paulo), a major service industry centre and a major producer of foodstuffs, building materials, electrical equipment, chemicals, pharmaceuticals and textiles. It is also the capital of the state of Rio de Janeiro. Rio's major industry is, however, leisure. It is unrivalled as the nation's liveliest city with its world famous beaches thronging with sun worshippers. A significant part of the population live in shanty-towns in appalling conditions. Little is done to address the problem and corruption in local government is endemic.

Tourist Information

Embratur: R. Uruguaiana 174, 8th floor, Centro, São Paulo.

Tel: (0)21 509-6017.

Web site: www.embratur.gov.br

The national tourist organization offices for information on all aspects of Brazil.

Riotur: R. da Assembleia 10, 9th floor.

Tel: (0)21 217-7575. Fax: (0)21 531-1872.

E-mail: riotur@rio.rj.gov.br Web site: www.rio.rj.gov.br/riotur

Small information desk for city tourism.

Other information stands are to be found at Pao de Acucar (the cable-car station), at the international airport and at the main bus station.

Financial and Currency

American Express: Av. Atlântica 1702, Copacabana (at the Copacabana Palace Hotel), Zip: 22021–000.

Tel: (0)21 548-2148. Hours: Monday to Friday 9:00–17.30.
Saturday 9:00–13.00.

Taxis

Rio has an extensive taxi fleet which includes yellow metered cabs that can be hailed in the streets, as well as a series of special taxis operated by licensed companies which can be found at the airports, hotels or booked by phone. From the international airport and the main shopping centres most of the special taxis work on a fixed fare by area which is paid in advance at the company's counter above which the fare price must be displayed.

Postal Services

Main Offices: Rua Primeiro do Marco (corner of Rosario), Centro.
Av. N. S. de Copacabana 540, Copacabana.
Rua Visconde de Piraja 452, Ipanema.
Av. Ataulfo de Paiva 822, Leblon.

Internet Access

@Café Cybercafe: Av. das Americas 4666 lj 125/126—
Barrashopping Rio de Janeiro, RJ 22631–450.
Tel: (0)21 431-9727. Fax: (0)21 431-9840.
E-mail: cybercafe@arrobacafe.com.br
Web site: www.internethouse.com.br
Open daily from12.00–02.00.

Café with 2 links of 128 Kb and 11 stations connected 24 hours a day.

Internet House: 195, Nossa Senhora de Copacabana Avenue, shop 106—Copacabana, Rio de Janeiro, 22020–000.
Tel: (0)21 542-3348. Fax: (0)21 542-3348.
E-mail: cybercafe@internethouse.com.br
Web site: www.comprio.com.br

Open from Monday to Saturday from 9.00–20.00.

Café with 9 computers linked to each other, in close proximity to the beach.

Comp Rio: Rua da Assembléia 10 SS114, Rio de Janeiro, RJ 20119–900.

Tel: (0)5521 531-1382. Fax: (0)5521 533-4372.

E-mail: info@comprio.com.br

Web Site: www.imagelink.com.br

Open from Monday to Friday from 9.00–19.00.

Located in the heart of the business area. Microsoft Office tools and printers available.

Image Link: Rua Visconde de Piraja, 207/216, Rio de Janeiro, RJ 22410–001.

Tel: (0)21 522-5850. Fax: (0)21 522-5850.

E-mail: mailto:suporte@imagelink.com.br

Web site: www.infotecrio.com.br/internet_cafe.html

Open from Monday to Friday from 9.00–1800.

Internet provider with a few internet connected computers available to rent.

Internet C@fé: Rua da Assembléia, 10 Lj. 112, Rio de Janeiro 20011–000.

Tel: (0)5521 531-1201. Fax: (0)5521 531-1201

Email: internet_cafe@infotecrio.com.br

Open from Monday to Friday from 9.00–19.00 and Saturday from 9.00–13.00.

Offers internet access, E-mail and fax facilities.

Landmarks

Catedral Metropolitana (Metropolitan Cathedral): Av. Chile, Rio de Janeiro. Tel: (0)21 240-2669.

Controversially unfinished after 12 years' work when it was consecrated in 1976, it was eventually completed in 1979. Built in a striking modernist style reminiscent of the Mayans, everything about the church is imposing.

Pão de Açúcar (Sugar Loaf):

Rising 1,300 metres high the mountain offers stunning views of the city, the Corvocado mountain and the legendary Copacabana and Ipanema beaches. The view is particularly impressive at sunset. The first wooden cable-car to carry visitors was constructed in 1912 but has since been replaced by a far more modern version. For the more adventurous it is possible to climb the mountain although this takes about two days.

Monumento Cristo Redentor (Christ the Redeemer)—On Corcovado, Rio de Janeiro. Tel: (0)21 285-2533 (for Cosme Velho train).

Standing an impressive 730 metres high on top of the Corcovado Mountain the Monumento Cristo Redentor dominates the city. The statue is the instantly recognisable symbol of both Rio and Brazil. It is visible from all over the city and when illuminated at night is particularly inspiring. The statue itself is 36 metres high and is easily accessible from the Cosme Velho railway station at the base of Corcovado.

Museums and Galleries

Museu Historico Nacional: Praça Marechal Âncora—Near to Praça XV, 20.021–200, Rio de Janeiro–RJ. Tel: (0)21 240-2092. Fax: (0)21 220-6290.

Open Tuesday to Friday from 10·00–17·30 and Saturday and Sunday from 14·00–18·00.

The National Museum of History, created in 1922, is one of the most important museums in Brazil with 287,000 items including the largest collection of coins in Latin America. Renovated in 1987, the permanent exhibition is divided into thematic modules, intended to illustrate the economic and social aspects of the history of Brazil.

Museu de Arte Moderna (Museum of Modern Art): Av. Infante Dom Henrique 85 (Parque Brigadeiro Eduardo Gomes, Flamengo), Rio de Janeiro.
Tel: (0)21 210-2188.

Opened in 1958 to the designs of architect Afonso Eduardo Reidy, the Museum of Modern Art, or MAM, has been a showcase for the best and most famous modern Brazilian artists. Despite being badly damaged by a fire in 1978 the museum still has a fine permanent collection and includes workshops and research centres. The striking modernist style of the centre is loved by some whilst detested by others.

Museu da Chácara do Céu: Rua Murtinho Nobre 93 (Santa Tereza), Rio de Janeiro.
Tel: (0)21 232-1386.
Open every day except Mondays.

Formerly the home of Raymundo de Castro Maia, a leading Brazilian industrialist, the museum displays the impressive private art collection he built up with his fortune. The collection features works by great European modern artists such as Picasso, Matisse, Dali and Monet as well as the works of famous Brazilian artists such as Portinari, Di Cavalcanti and Volpi.

Museu Nacional de Belas Artes (National Fine Arts Museum):
Av. Rio Branco 199, Rio de Janeiro. Tel: (0)21 240-0068.
First opened in 1937 the collection features over 20,000 paintings
and sculptures. The main purpose of the museum is to offer an
overview of the development of Brazilian culture over the centuries.
In addition to works by Brazilian artists there are many fine pieces
from international artists. The striking building the collection is
housed in was built in 1908 in the style of the Louvre. It was originally
used to house the Brazilian National Academy of Fine Arts.

Espaço Cultural dos Correios (Cultural Corridor): Rua Visconde
Itaboraí 20, Rio de Janeiro. Tel: (0)21 563-8770.
Open every day except Mondays.
 Housed in the former Bank of Brazil building this cultural complex
comprises six floors of art, historical archives, information and
performance areas.

Theatre and Opera
Teatro Municipal: Av. Rio Branco, 20040 Rio de Janeiro.
Tel: (0)21 210-2463.
 The city's premier opera house has a busy and varied programme.
The house itself has room for over 2,300 spectators.

Metropolitan: Avenida Ayrton Senna 3000/1005, Barra da Tijuca,
Rio de Janeiro. Tel: (0)21 238-3773.
 South America's largest performance centre featuring evening
concerts by Brazilian and international artists.
 There are around 40 working theatres in Rio although a knowledge
of Portuguese is essential.

BRASILIA

Estimated population 2000: 1,985,000 (Source: 1996 World Urbanization Prospects. United Nations Population Division.) Although the creation of a new Brazilian capital in an inland area had been considered since the 18th century it was not until 1956 that the design and construction of 'Brasília', a name suggested by José Bonifacio as long ago as 1823, began. The process of shifting the capital from Rio was long and drawn out. In 1891 Article 3 of the Republic of Brazil's first written constitution outlined the creation of a new capital. In 1892 the Comissão Exploradora do Planalto Central, the so-called 'Cruls Mission', was appointed, and 2 years later earmarked an area of 14,400 sq. km for the new capital. In 1922 the foundation stone of the future capital was laid near the city of Planaltina, on the outskirts of the present day Federal District.

In 1956, having won an election on the promise of implementing Article 3 of the constitution, President Juscelino Kubitschek established NOVACAP, the Company to Urbanize the New Capital of Brazil. A year earlier the New Federal Capital Locating Commission selected the area for the construction of the new city. The site was centrally located in Brazil 1015 km from São Paulo, 1148 km from Rio de Janeiro and 2120 km from Belem. The nearest railway line was 125 km away, the nearest paved road was over 600 km away and the nearest airport some 190 km from the planned location. Despite the infrastructural and geographical obstacles Brasília was operational as a capital city in just 4 years.

The competition to design the master plan for the city was won by the Brazilian architect and urban planner, Lúcio Costa. His design was submitted on five medium sized cards with no technical drawings and became known as the Pilot Plan. The government buildings were designed by the Brazilian architect chosen to head NOVACAP, Oscar Niemeyer, in a striking modern style, and the landscape designer

Roberto Burl Marx chose the plant varieties and layout of the open spaces. Brasília was officially inaugurated on 21 April 1960 when the government and officials moved in. The construction of the city has continued to develop ever since with the University of Brasília inaugurated in 1962, the TV Tower that dominates the city's skyline completed in 1967, the Cathedral opening in 1970, the City Park inaugurated in 1978, the Central bank building opening in 1981 and the subway scheduled to begin operations in 1999. The construction of the city, however, created a debt of over US$2bn. In 1987 UNESCO declared Brasília a world heritage site.

Despite being the capital of one of the largest and most important countries in the world Brasília itself has become more famous as an urban representation of the ideologies and theories that formed it. Brasília was built from the modernist ideas of Le Corbusier who believed that planned urban development could produce an ideal city that could act as a catalyst to the development of an ideal society. The whole plan for the city incorporated Le Corbusier's recommendations for the separation of areas for different purposes—residential, professional, governmental and recreational—as well as the creation of major road and motorway schemes to make car accessibility extensive and easy. Brasília remains a potent symbol of the strengths and flaws inherent in the modernist ideology of urban development affecting cities all around the world.

Tourist Information
Secretariat of Tourism for the Federal District (SETUR/DF):
Tel: (0)61 325-5713. Fax: (0)61 225-5706.
E-mail: gdfsetur@conectanet.com.br

There are information desks at the Centro de Convenções, near the TV Tower, at Catetinho and at Praça dos Três Poderes, near the Congress.

Financial and Currency

Banco do Brasil agency at the airport:

Closed on Sundays. This bank exchanges your VISA and Mastercard travellers with a fee that varies from a minimum of US$5 to a maximum of US$20. Tel: (0)61 365-1183.

American Express Travel Service: Buriti Turismo Ltda (R), Cls 402 Bloco A Lojas 27/33, 70236–510. Tel: (0)61 225-2686. Open Monday to Friday from 8·30–19·00 and Saturday from 9·00–12·00.

Aps/Beltur (R), Cls 410, Bloco 'A', Loja 29, 70276–510. Tel: (0)61 244-5577.

Open Monday to Friday from 8·00–19·00 and Saturday from 9·00–13·00.

There are over 30 other places in the city where you can exchange currency.

Internet Access

Liverpool Coffee Shop: CLS 108, Bloco A, Loja 23, Distrito Federal Brasília, 70347–510. Tel: (0)61 443-2286.

Web site: www.liverpoolmidia.com.br/

Landmarks

Catedral Metropolitana: Located on the Esplanada dos Ministerios. Tel: (0)61 224-4073.

Its architect, Oscar Niemeyer, designed its circular shape to represent the crown of thorns. Inside are 3 aluminium angels, suspended from the domed, stained-glass ceiling, designed by the sculptor Alfredo Scesciatte. The cariollos outside was a gift from the Spanish government.

Television Tower

Dominating Brasília's skyline is the Television Tower. It has a free observation platform 75 metres up, a bar and souvenir shop. Construction started in 1965 and the tower was opened in March 1967. Designed by Lucio Costa himself it is one of the few major buildings in the city not designed by Oscar Niemeyer.

Juscelino Kubitschek Memorial: Tel: (0)61 226-7860. Tuesday to Sunday from 9·00–17·45.

This memorial to the man who conceived and built Brasília, Juscelino Kubitschek, was designed by Oscar Niemeyer. Inside the monument is Kubitschek's tomb and a collection about his life and the construction of Brasília, with more than 3,000 works. It has an auditorium for lectures, concerts, and movie exhibitions.

Praça dos Tres Poderes

The city's main square is surrounded by the Congress buildings, the Palacio do Planalto (the President's office), the Palacio da Justica and the Panteao Tancredo Neves. 19 tall ministry buildings line the Esplanada dos Ministerios, west of the Praça, which culminates in 2 towers, linked by a walkway to form the letter 'H', representing Humanity.

Museums and Galleries

Museum of Art of Brasília (Museu de Arte de Brasília): Located near the Alvorada Palace and the Arena Theatre, SHTN—lt. 2 A. Tel: (0)61 325-6242. Tuesday to Sunday from 13·00–19·00.

The museum has a permanent exhibition of paintings, prints, and sculptures by Brazilian artists. Its collection holds more than 700 works.

Museum of North-eastern Art and Tradition (Museu de Arte e Tradição do Nordeste): Located at the Casa do Ceará, SGAS Q. 910, lts. F and G. Tel: (0)61 272-3833.

Monday to Friday from 9·00–11·00 and from 13·00–17·00.

Permanent exhibits of handicrafts characteristic of the northeast of Brazil. There is a small shop that sells typical products from the region.

Historical Museum of Brasília (Museu Histórico de Brasília): Located on the Praça dos Três Poderes.

Tel: (0)61 321-9843.

Open daily from 9·00–18·00.

The museum shows pictures and videos on the history of the transfer and foundation of the Capital of the country. It offers special professional guided visits for schools.

Catetinho Museum (Museu do Catetinho): Located at km 0 of the BR 040 highway.

Tel: (0)61 380-1921

Tuesday to Sunday from 9·00–17·00.

The name of the museum is an allusion to the Catete Palace in Rio de Janeiro. The Catetinho was the first official presidential residence in Brasília and holds the first design for the city by Oscar Niemeyer. The museum shows furniture and objects used by President Juscelino Kubitschek and is surrounded by a very pleasant wooded area.

Currency Museum of the Central Bank (Museu de Valores do Banco Central): Setor Bancário Sul, Q. 3, Bl. B, 1º subsolo (In the basement of the Central Bank Headquarters).

Tel: (0)61 414-1449.

Tuesday to Friday from 10·00–17·30 and Saturday from 14·00–18·00.

The museum has four halls with permanent exhibits: the Strong Hall, with gold items and the history of pan mining in the country; the Brazil Hall, with old coins; the Coin Hall, which shows the technology used for making coins; and the World Hall, showing coins from 55 countries

Theatre and Opera

Claudio Santoro National Theatre (Teatro Nacional Claudio Santoro): Located at Setor Bancário Norte, Via N2.

Tel: (0)61 325-6240.

Major theatre complex with 3 theatres: the Villa Lobos with 1,307 seats, the Martins Penna with 399 seats and the Alberto Nepomuceno with 95 seats.

Brasília Arena Theatre (Concha Acustica de Brasília): Located near Lake Paranoá, at Setor de Hotéis Norte. Open arena with capacity for 8,000 people.

Dulcina Theatre (Teatro Dulcina): Tel: (0)61 226-0182. Theatre with a capacity for 458 people.

Further Information

Brunn, Stanley D. and Williams, Jack F., *Cities of The World*. HarperCollins College Publishers, New York 1993.

Epstein, David, *Brasília, Plan and Reality*. Berkeley: University of California Press, 1973.

Holston, James, *The Modernist City*. The University of Chicago Press, Chicago, 1989.

Shoumatoff, Alex, *The Capital of Hope*. Coward, McCann & Geoghegan, Inc., New York, 1980.

Spade, Rupert, *Oscar Niemeyer*. Simon and Schuster, New York, 1971.

Underwood, David, *Oscar Niemeyer and Brazlian Free-Form Modernism*. George Braziller, Inc., New York, 1994.

SOCIAL STATISTICS

1998 estimates: births, 3,451,000 (rate of 20·9 per 1,000 population); deaths, 1,404,000 (8·5 per 1,000 population). Life expectancy was 66·85 years in 1998 (63·2 years for males and 70·6 for females). 1996 growth rate, 1·4%; infant mortality (1997), 37 per 1,000 live births; fertility rate, 1997, 2·3 children per woman.

Statistics Offices

IBGE (Instituto Brasileiro de Geografia e Estatística):
Web site: www.ibge.gov.br

CLIMATE

Because of its latitude, the climate is predominantly tropical, but factors such as altitude, prevailing winds and distance from the sea cause certain variations, though temperatures are not notably extreme. In tropical parts, winters are dry and summers wet, while in Amazonia conditions are constantly warm and humid. The northeast *sertão* is hot and arid, with frequent droughts. In the south and east, spring and autumn are sunny and warm, summers are hot, but winters can be cold when polar air-masses impinge. Brasília, Jan. 72°F (22·3°C), July 68°F (19·8°C). Annual rainfall 63″ (1,603 mm). Belém, Jan. 78°F (25·8°C), July 80°F (26·4°C). Annual rainfall 102″ (2,315 mm). Manaus, Jan. 79°F (26·1°C), July 80°F (26·7°C). Annual rainfall 110″ (2,842 mm). Recife, Jan. 80°F (26·6°C), July 77°F (24·8°C). Annual rainfall 94″ (2,474 mm). Rio de Janeiro, Jan. 83°F (28·5°C), July 67°F (19·6°C). Annual rainfall 67″ (1,758 mm). São Paulo, Jan. 75°F (24°C), July 57°F (13·7°C). Annual rainfall 71″ (1,800 mm). Salvador, Jan. 80°F (26·5°C), July 74°F (23·5°C). Annual rainfall 90″ (2,315 mm). Porto Alegre, Jan. 75°F (23·9°C), July 62°F (16·7°C). Annual rainfall 67″ (1,775 mm).

CONSTITUTION AND GOVERNMENT

The present Constitution came into force on 5 Oct. 1988, the eighth since independence. The *President* and *Vice-President* are elected for a 4-year term and are not immediately re-eligible. To be elected candidates must secure 51% of the votes, otherwise a second round of voting is held to elect the President between the two most voted candidates. Voting is compulsory for men and women between the ages of 18 and 70, and optional for illiterates, persons from 16 to 18 years old and persons over 70. A referendum on constitutional change was held on 21 April 1993. Turn-out was 80%. 66·1% of votes cast were in favour of retaining a republican form of government, and 10·2% for re-establishing a monarchy. 56·4% favoured an executive presidency, 24·7% parliamentary supremacy.

A constitutional amendment of June 1997 authorizes the re-election of the President for one extra term of 4 years.

Congress consists of an 81-member *Senate* (3 Senators per federal unit) and a 513-member *Chamber of Deputies*. The Senate is two-thirds directly elected (50% of these elected for 8 years in rotation) and one-third indirectly elected. The Chamber of Deputies is elected by universal franchise for 4 years. There is a *Council of the Republic* which is convened only in national emergencies.

Constituição da Republica Federativa do Brasil. Brasília, 1988

Baaklini, A. I., *The Brazilian Legislature and Political System.* London, 1992

Martinez-Lara, J., *Building Democracy in Brazil: the Politics of Constitutional Change.* London, 1996

National Anthem

'Ouviram do Ipiranga. . .' ('They hear the river Ipiranga'); words by J. O. Duque Estrada; tune by F. M. da Silva·

RECENT ELECTIONS

At the presidential elections of 4 Oct. 1998, Fernando Henrique Cardoso was re-elected President by 53·1% of votes cast against 4 other candidates, his closest rival, Luiz Inacio Lula da Silva, backed by a coalition of the left, obtaining 31·7%. Cardoso thus became the first Brazilian president to win a second successive term in office. Turn-out was 80%.

Parliamentary elections were also held on 4 Oct. 1998 for both the Chamber of Deputies and the Senate.

In the elections to the Chamber of Deputies the government coalition gained 347 seats (Liberal Front, 106; Brazilian Social Democratic Party, 99; Party of the Brazilian Democratic Movement, 82; Progressive Party, 60); their ally the Brazilian Labour Party gained 31 seats and the opposition gained 135 (Workers' Party, 58; Democratic Labour Party, 25; others, 52).

In the Senate elections the Party of the Brazilian Democratic Movement won 27 of the 81 seats; Liberal Front, 20; Brazilian Social Democratic Party, 16; Workers' Party, 7; Progressive Party, 5; Socialist Party, 3; Democratic Labour Party, 2; Socialist People's Party, 1.

CURRENT ADMINISTRATION

President: Fernando Henrique Cardoso, b. 1931 (Social Democrat; sworn in 1 Jan. 1995, re-elected 4 Oct. 1998).

Vice-President: Marco Maciel.

In Jan. 2000 the government comprised:

Minister of Justice: José Carlos Dias. *Foreign Affairs:* Luiz Felipe Palmeira Lampreia. *Finance:* Pedro Sampaio Malan. *Transport:*

Eliseu Lemos Padilha. *Development, Industry and Commerce:* Clovis Carvalho. *Agriculture:* Marcus Vinicius Pratini de Moraes. *Education:* Paulo Renato Souza. *Culture:* Francisco Corrêa Weffort. *Labour and Employment:* Francisco Oswaldo Neves Dornelles. *Social Security:* Waldeck Vieira Ornélas. *Health:* José Serra. *Mines and Energy:* Rodolpho Tourinho Neto. *Communications:* João Pimenta de Veiga Filho. *Science and Technology:* Ronaldo Mota Sardenberg. *Environment:* José Sarney Filho. *Budget and Management:* Martus Antônio Rodrigues Tavares. *Sports and Tourism:* Rafael Valdomiro Greca de Macedo. *Agricultural Reform:* Raul Jungmann. *National Integration:* Fernando Bezerra.

POLITICAL PROFILES

Fernando Henrique Cardoso (1931–)

Fernando Henrique Cardoso has been the President of the Federal Republic of Brazil since 1 Jan. 1995. The candidate of the alliance PSDB/PFL/PTB/PPB, he was re-elected by an absolute majority (53·06%), on 4 Oct. 1998.

Born in Rio de Janeiro, he is married with three children.

A sociologist, he was a member of the Brazilian Senate. First elected Senator, for the State of São Paulo, from the Movimento Democrático Brasileiro (MDB) in 1978, he was re-elected from the Partido do Movimento Democrático Brasileiro (PMDB) in 1986. One of the founding members of the Partido da Social Democracia Brasileira (PSDB) at the beginning of 1988, he was the party's leader in the Senate until Oct. 1992. He was Minister of Foreign Affairs (from Oct. 1992 to May 1993) and the former President Itamar Franco's Minister of Finance from May 1993 to March 1994.

A former Professor Catedrático of Political Science, he is now Emeritus Professor at the University of São Paulo. He has previously

been an Associate Director of Studies at the École des Hautes
Études en Sciences Sociales, and visiting professor at the Collège
de France and at the University of Paris-Nanterre. He has also taught
at Cambridge, where he was elected Simon Bolivar Professor, and at
the Universities of Stanford and Berkeley. He is a member of the
Institute for Advanced Study at Princeton and holds honorary
degrees from Rutgers (the State University of New Jersey) as well as
from the Universities of Notre Dame (South Bend, Indiana), Central of
Caracas (Venezuela), of Porto and Coimbra (Portugal), the Free
University of Berlin, Lumière Lyon 2, Bologna, Cambridge and
London. He is an Honorary Foreign Member of the American
Academy of Arts and Sciences.

Some of his books are translated in English: São Paulo, Growth
and Poverty (et alii, 1978), Dependency and Development in Latin
America (with E. Faletto, 1979), The New Global Economy in the
Information Age (with M. Carnoy, M. Castells and S. S. Cohen, 1993).

Marco Antonio de Oliveira Maciel (1940–)

Marco Maciel is the leader of the PFL in the Senate and the Vice-
President of the Federative Republic of Brazil.

Born in Recife, Marco Maciel was educated at the Colegio
Nobrega and the Law Faculty in Recife, Harvard University and
Pernambuco University. He practised as a lawyer until becoming the
Assistant Secretary in the Pernambuco State Government in 1964.
From 1967–71 he was the State Deputy and Government Leader in
the Pernambuco Legislative Assembly. In 1971 he became the
Federal deputy (for the ARENA party) in Pernambuco, a position he
held until 1979. He was the Governor of Pernambuco State
(1979–82) and its Federal Senator for the PDS Party from 1982. He
became Brazil's Minister for Education in 1985, Minister-Chief of Staff
of the President (1986), PFL National President (1987) and the
Government Leader in the Senate (1991–92).

He received the Cross of Merit from the Federal Republic of Germany in 1979, the Legion of Honour from France in 1978 and the National Order of Merit from France in 1985. Marco Maciel is married to Anna Maria Ferreira Maciel and has three children.

Pedro Sampaio Malan (1948–)

Pedro Sampaio Malan has been the Brazilian Minister for Finance since 1995.

Born in Petropolis, Rio de Janeiro he graduated with a degree in electrical engineering from the Catholic University of Rio de Janeiro in 1965. He also has a PhD in economics from the University of Berkeley, California.

He entered the Ministry of Finance in 1966 and became a Senior Research Member in the Institute of Applied Economic Research and of the National Economic Development Council of the Ministry of Finance. He has also held senior posts with the United Nations in New York, the World Bank and the InterAmerican Bank for Development.

He was appointed as the President of the Brazilian Central Bank by the President of Brazil in Sept. 1993, a position he held until becoming Minister for Finance. He is 51 years old and married.

Luiz Felipe Lampreia (1941–)

Luiz Felipe Lampreia is the Brazilian Minister for Foreign Affairs. Born in Rio de Janeiro, he studied Sociology at the Pontifical Catholic University in Rio and Economics at Columbia University in New York. In 1963 he graduated from the Brazilian Foreign Service academy (the Rio Branco Institute) and has been a career diplomat since then.

He served at the Brazilian Missions to the United Nations in New York and Geneva before becoming economic advisor in the Office of the Minister for External Relations in 1974. From 1977–79 he was Press Secretary and Spokesman for the Ministry for External

Relations, becoming Minister Counsellor at the Brazilian Embassy in Washington in 1979. He held various diplomatic and government positions before becoming the Brazilian Ambassador to Portugal in 1990. In 1992 he became the Secretary General of the Ministry of External Relations, becoming Acting Minister for external relations in the summer of 1993. Later that year he became Brazil's permanent representative to the United Nations in Geneva, a position he held until his appointment as Minister for External Relations at the end of 1994. He is married to Lenir Lampreia and has five daughters.

LOCAL GOVERNMENT

Brazil consists of 27 federal units (26 states and 1 federal district). Each has its distinct administrative, legislative and judicial authorities, and its own constitution and laws, which must, however, agree with federal constitutional principles. The governors and members of the legislatures are elected for 4-year terms. The country is subdivided into 5,507 municipalities, each under an elected mayor and municipal council, and then further sub-divided into districts. The Federal District is the national capital, inaugurated in 1960; it is divided into 12 administrative Regions, the first Region being Brasília. Gubernatorial elections were held for all 27 federal units etc. in Oct.–Nov. 1994. Municipal elections were held on 30 Oct. 1996 and, for municipalities with at least 0·2m. electors, on 15 Nov. 1996.

DEFENCE

Conscription is for 12 months, extendable by 6 months.

In 1998 defence expenditure totalled US$18,053m. (US$108 per capita), the most in Latin America. In 1985 expenditure was just US$5,515m.

Army

There are 7 military commands and 11 military regions. Strength, 1999, 189,000 (40,000 conscripts). There is an additional potential first-line 1,115,000 of whom 400,000 are subject to immediate recall. There is a second-line reserve of 225,000 and a paramilitary Public Police Force of some 385,000.

Navy

The principal ship of the Navy is the 20,200-tonne Light Aircraft Carrier *Minas Gerais*, formerly the British *Vengeance*, completed in 1945 and purchased in 1956. There are also 4 diesel submarines and 14 frigates including 4 bought from the UK in 1995 and 1996. Fleet Air Arm personnel only fly helicopters.

Naval bases are at Rio de Janeiro, Recife, Belém, Floriancholis and Salvador, with river bases at Ladario and Manaus.

Active personnel, 1999, totalled 52,000 (3,200 conscripts), including 13,900 Marines and 1,150 in Naval Aviation.

The Brazil navy is preparing to buy 20 McDonnell Douglas A-4 Skyhawk fighter-bombers from Kuwait for US$70m. (£43m.) as part of a long-term project to increase its ability to protect military and civilian shipping. The jets will be the Brazilian navy's first fixed-wing aircraft and will be operated from its single aircraft carrier, the Minas Gerais.

Air Force

The Air Force is organized in 6 zones, centred on Belém, Recife, Rio de Janeiro, São Paulo, Porto Alegre and Brasília. Personnel strength (1999) 50,000 (5,000 conscripts). There were 274 combat aircraft in 1999, including Mirage F-103s and F-5Es, and 29 armed helicopters.

INTERNATIONAL RELATIONS

Brazil is a member of the UN, OAS, Inter-American Development Bank, LAIA, Mercosur and the Antarctic Treaty.

ECONOMY

Historically Brazil's economy is marked by a succession of cycles, each of them based on the exploitation of a single export commodity: timber (brazilwood) in the first years of colonisation; sugarcane in the 16th and 17th centuries; precious metals (gold and silver) and gems in the 18th century and coffee in the 19th and early 20th century. After the First World War industrialization increased rapidly so that by the outbreak of the Second World War Brazil had reached a level of modern economic performance. The industrialization process from the 1950s to the 1970s led to the expansion of important sectors of the economy such as the automobile industry, petrochemicals and steel. Brazil's economy expanded markedly throughout the 1970s fuelled by capital infusion from US, European and Japanese banks. In the early 1980s, however, a sudden increase in interest rates in the world economy precipitated Latin America's debt crisis. This high debt burden and spiralling inflation led to the introduction of a series of stringent economic measures in the late '80s, aimed at monetary stabilization. In the 1990s successive governments have overseen the opening up of Brazil's economy. Privatization has accelerated, especially in the steel and fertilizer industries, and policies of trade liberalization and deregulation have been pursued in an attempt to encourage new foreign investment.

More dynamic and diversified than it once was, until recently the Brazilian economy was performing impressively. In 1994 industry was responsible for 38·1% of economic output, agriculture for 10% and services accounted for 51·9%. From 1988 to 1992 Brazilian exports earned in excess of US$33bn. In 1998 the economy was hit by the adverse impact of the Asian and Russian economic crises; however, the economy in 1999 has performed significantly better than expected. Real GDP, which had stagnated in 1998, began to recover and even grew in the first and second quarters of 1999. The external trade deficit declined to US$618m. in the first half of 1999 from US$6·6bn. for 1998 as a whole. The IMF has been pleased with the Brazilian government's handling of the economy saying: 'Following a brief unsettled period at the beginning of the year, when the exchange rate regime was changed, the Brazilian authorities have maintained a firm monetary policy stance in the last few months'.

The European Union absorbs almost 26% of Brazilian exports, North America around 22% (the USA is the largest individual trading partner), Asia 16%, MERCOSUR 14%, the rest of ALADI 10% and the Middle East 4% with the remaining exports distributed over a variety of smaller markets.

Agriculture accounted for 8% of GDP in 1997, industry 35% and services 57%.

Policy

In 1991 a National Reconstruction Plan was introduced to promote growth and investment and reduce the role of the state. State monopolies in ports, communications and fuels were reduced and agricultural and industrial subsidies ended. A sixth economic plan was introduced in 1993 to cut spending and accelerate privatization. Since Oct. 1994 the government has authorized privatization of the energy, electricity, petrochemicals and telecommunications sectors. The programme is the largest privatization drive in the world. After an initial stage in which steel, petrochemical, fertilizers and mining industries were privatized, the programme was headed by roads, railways, sea ports, electricity and telecommunications in 1997. During 1990–95, 22 state-owned and 19 partly state-owned companies were privatized. The Real Plan (*Plano Real*), a monetary and economic stability programme, was launched in July 1994. In Nov. 1997 the government announced a package of proposed spending cuts and tax rises worth R$20,000m. to reduce the long-standing fiscal and balance-of-payments deficits.

Revenue from privatization since 1991 has exceeded US$18m.

In 1997 the Asian financial crisis put the *real* under pressure, forcing up interest rates to 50%. A US$18bn. package of tax rises and spending cuts was intended to cut the budget deficit by 2·5% of GDP. Even so, Brazil's borrowing requirement had climbed from 4·5% of GDP in 1997 to 7·8% in 1998. In Nov. 1998 the IMF announced a US$41bn. financing package to help shore up the Brazilian economy.

Performance

Real GDP growth was 17% from 1994 through 1998, equal to an annual average growth rate of 3·3%. 1998 was the sixth consecutive year of GDP growth. In 1999 growth was 0·9%. In March 1999 an IMF agreement introduced a tight monetary policy with an emphasis on reducing the ratio of debt to GDP.

Budget

1995–96 (in R$1,000): revenue was 229,722,437 and expenditure 173,992,572. Internal federal debt, July 1996, was R$176,478m. Internal states and municipalities (main securities outstanding), R$49,672m.

Currency

The unit of currency is the *real* (equal to 100 *centavos*) which was introduced on 1 July 1994 to replace the former *cruzeiro real* at a rate

of 1 real (R$1) = 2,750 cruzeiros reais (CR$2,750). The *real* was
devalued in Sept. 1994, March 1995, June 1995 and Jan. 1999.
Inflation fell from 2,500% in 1993 to 22% in 1995 and 11·1% in 1996,
and was −1·8% in 1998, with a forecast of a rise of 7·4% in 1999. In
Feb. 1998 foreign exchange reserves were US$56,656m. and gold
reserves 3·22m. troy oz. Total money supply in Jan. 1998 was
R$45,056m.

Banking and Finance

On 31 Dec. 1964 the Banco Central do Brasil (*President*, Armínio
Fraga Neto) was founded as the national bank of issue.

The Bank of Brazil (founded in 1853 and reorganized in 1906) is a
state-owned commercial bank; it had 3,125 branches in 1995
throughout the republic. On 31 Dec. 1996 deposits were R$33,604m.
In 1994 there were 6 public-sector banks and 24 banks controlled by
state governments.

There are 9 stock exchanges of which Rio de Janeiro and São
Paulo are the most important. All except São Paulo are linked in the
National Electronic Trading System (Senn).

Lees, F. A. *et al.* (eds.) *Banking and Financial Deepening in Brazil.*
London, 1990

Major Banks

Banco Bradesco: Cidade de Deus, Vila Yara, Osasco, São Paulo
06029–900.
Tel: (0)11 7084-5376. Fax: (0)11 7083-2564.
Web site: www.bradesco.com.br
A multiple service bank employing over 60,000 staff.

Banco do Brasil: 502 Rua Mario Veloso, JD. São Luiz, Montes Claros,
MG 39401–063.
Tel: (0)38 212-1223. Fax: (0)38 333-8535.

Web site: www.bancobrasil.com.br

The largest financial institution in Latin America with a network of 4,443 service outlets in Brazil and 37 abroad.

Banco do Estado de São Paulo: 6 Praça Antonio Prado, São Paulo, SP 01010–010.

Tel: (0)11 259-6622. Fax: (0)11 258-1216. Web site: www.banespa.com.br

BANESPA is one of the major Brazilian financial institutions, with 1,362 branches, offering a variety of banking services. It also runs a network of foreign exchange branches throughout Brazil.

Banco Itau: 176 Rua Boa Vista, São Paulo, SP 01014–919.

Tel: (0)11 237-3000.

Fax: (0)11 277-1044. Web site: www.itau.com.br

One of Brazil's major financial institutions, with over 1,700 branches in Brazil and abroad, employing over 40,000 staff.

Banco Real: Bela Vista, 1374–3 Andar, Av. Paulista, São Paulo, SP 01310–916.

Tel: (0)11 3174-9601. Fax: (0)11 3174-0977.

Web site: www.real.com.br

Engages in commercial lending, banking services, retail and corporate clients and international trade financing operations. The bank has 2,755 branches.

Unibanco Uniao de Bancos Brasileiros: 891–2 Andar, Av. Euzebio Matoso, São Paulo, SP 05423–901.

Tel: (0)11 867-4322. Fax: (0)11 815-5084.

A multi-bank combining in one entity, a variety of financial activities and employing some 30,000 staff.

Other Banks

Banco Crefisul: 143 Rua Alvares Penteado, São Paulo 01012–904.
Tel: (0)11 232-1022.
Fax: (0)11 606-1550.

Banco do Nordeste do Brasil: 1 Praça Murilo Borges, Fortaleza,
CE 60025–210.
Tel: (0)85 255-4000. Fax: (0)85 255-4685.

Banco Mercantil do Brasil: 680–15 Andar, Rua Rio de Janeiro, Belo
Horizonte, MG 30160–912.
Tel: (0)31 239-6163. Fax: (0)31 271-2392.

Banco Mercantil Finasa São Paulo: 1450 Av. Raulista, São Paulo,
SP 01310–917.
Tel: (0)11 252-2121. Fax: (0)11 284-3312.

Banco Sudameris Brasil: 1000, Av. Paulista, Bela Vista,
São Paulo 01310–912. Tel: (0)11 3170-9225. Fax: (0)11 3170-9202.
Web site: www.sudameris.com.br

Stock Exchanges

Securities and Exchange Commission—CVM: Rua Sete de Setembro,
111 / 26º a 34º andar, 21059–900 Rio de Janeiro–RJ.
Tel: (0)21 292-5117. Fax: (0)21 242-4016.

Commodities & Futures Exchange: Praça Antonio Prado, 48,
01010–901 São Paulo–SP. Tel: (0)11 232-5454. Fax: (0)11 232-7537.

Rio de Janeiro Stock Exchange—BVRJ: Praça XV de Novembro,
20, 20010–010 Rio de Janeiro–RJ. Tel: (0)21 271-1839.
Fax: (0)21 221-2151.

São Paulo Stock Exchange—BOVESPA: Rua XV de Novembro,
275, 010013–001 São Paulo–SP. Tel: (0)11 233-2000.
Fax: (0)11 239-4981.

Chambers of Commerce
American Chamber of Commerce in Brazil:
04717–004 São Paulo.
Tel: (0)11 246-9199. Fax: (0)11 246-9080.

Camara do Comercio do Brasil: São Paulo. Tel: (0)12 321-8484.
Fax: (0)12 321-8484. E-mail: personal@iconet.com.br

French Chamber of Commerce in Brazil: 5423 São Paulo, Brazil.
Tel: (0)11 867-8166. Fax: (0)11 211-6920.

International Chamber of Commerce in Brazil: 6 andar, 30140–060
Belo Horizonte, Minas Gerais. Tel: (0)31 213-1550.
Fax: (0)31 213-1552. Web site: www.camint.com.br

The British Chamber of Commerce: Avenida Rio Blanco 181/2007,
20030–002 Rio de Janeiro–RJ.
Tel: (0)21 262-5926. Fax: (0)21 240-1058.
E-mail: bccibri@britcham.com.br

The British Chamber of Commerce: PO Box 1621, Rua Barao de
Itapentininga 275, 04548–005 São Paulo-SP. Tel: (0)11 866-9307.
Fax: (0)11 3044-1655. E-mail: britcham@britcham.com.br

Business Associations and Other Organizations
Brazilian Bureau for Micro and Small Enterprises—SEBRAE:
SEPN 515, Bloco C, lote 3, 70770–530 Brasília–DF.
Tel: (0)61 348-7100. Fax: (0)61 347-7604.

Brazilian Technical Standards Association—ABNT:

Av. 13 de Maio, 13/28º andar, 20031–000 Rio de Janeiro–RJ.
Tel: (0)21 210-3122. Fax: (0)21 532-2143/240-8249.

Brazilian Foreign Trade Association—AEB:

Av. General Justo, 335/4º andar, 20021–130 Rio de Janeiro–RJ.
Tel: (0)21 240-5048. Fax: (0)21 240-5463.

Federation of Foreign Trade Chambers—FCCE:

Av. General Justo, 307/6º andar, 20021–130 Rio de Janeiro–RJ.
Tel: (0)21 297-0011. Fax: (0)21 240-1622.

Brazilian Association of Trading Companies—ABECE:

Rua da Quitanda, 191–6º andar, 20091–000 Rio de Janeiro–RJ.
Tel: (0)21 253-1225. Fax: (0)21 253-7278.

Weights and Measures

The metric system has been compulsory since 1872.

ENERGY AND NATURAL RESOURCES

Environment

Brazil has the world's biggest river system and about a quarter of the world's primary rainforest. Current environmental issues are deforestation in the Amazon Basin, air and water pollution in Rio de Janeiro and São Paulo (the world's third-largest city), and land degradation and water pollution caused by improper mining activities. Contaminated drinking water causes 70% of child deaths.

Environmental Policies

The deforestation of the Amazon rain forest has been a major source of national as well as international concern. The activities of ranchers and developers led to an alarming rate of forest clearing in the '70s and '80s. Recently more effective government policy has reduced this rate. Two thirds of the country is still covered by forest although it is estimated that 15% of the total forest has been cleared. Another major environmental problem has been desertification, which occurs through the degradation of the soils and vegetation of drylands. Several large areas of the northeast came close to becoming arid in the early 1990s.

In urban areas the main environmental dangers have come from air pollution due to massive congestion. Recently, however, this problem has received greater governmental attention. Sanitation has been another urban threat, particularly in middle-sized cities where lesser resources have made it more difficult to cope with the squalor of outdated and inadequate systems.

As far as environmental policy goes, with the help of considerable international investment Brazil has made large steps since the 1980s. In 1992 the Earth Summit was held in Rio de Janeiro where the host nation negotiated sustainable development agreements including the conventions on climate and biodiversity. An Environment Ministry was also created in 1992 and helped to instigate the National Environmental Plan (Plano Nacional do Meio Ambiente—PNMA), supported by a loan of US$117m. from the world bank and the Pilot Program for the Conservation of the Brazilian Rain Forests, supported by a grant of US$258m. from the G–7 and the EC. In addition The Global Environmental Facility (GEF), created in 1990, set aside US$30m. for Brazil.

Electricity

Hydro-electric potential capacity was estimated at 255,000 MW per year in Dec. 1990, of which 41% belonged to the Amazon hydro-electric basin. Installed capacity (1995) 55,512 MW, of which 50,687 MW were hydro-electric. There is 1 nuclear power plant, supplying some 0·2% of total output. Production (1997) 291,630m. kWh (268,560m. kWh hydro-electric). Consumption per capita in 1996 was 1,660 kWh.

Oil and Gas

There are 13 oil refineries, of which 11 are state-owned. Crude oil production (1996), 45,605,631 cu. metres. In 1997 domestic production of 1m. bbls. a day met 55% of demand. The state petroleum company Petrobrás was negotiating joint ventures with up to 70 interested foreign companies to develop some of its oilfields, many off-shore. Crude oil reserves were estimated at 11,600m. bbls. in 1997.

Gas production (1996) 9,167,427,000 cu. metres. One of the most significant developments recently has been the construction of the 3,150-km Bolivia-Brazil gas pipeline, one of Latin America's biggest infrastructure projects, costing around US$2bn. (£1·2bn.). The pipeline runs from the Bolivian interior across the Brazilian border at Puerto Suárez-Corumbá to the far southern port city of Porto Alegre. Gas from Bolivia began to be pumped to São Paulo in 1999.

Minerals

The chief minerals are bauxite, gold, iron ore, manganese, nickel, phosphates, platinum, tin and uranium. Brazil is the only source of high-grade quartz crystal in commercial quantities; output, 1992, 38,148 tonnes raw, 27,275 tonnes processed. It is a major producer of chrome ore: output, 1996, 861,845 tonnes. Other minerals, with 1996 output in tonnes, are mica, 7,000 processed; zirconium, 26,326; beryllium 6,138; graphite, 842,721; and magnesite, 1,270,015. Along the coasts of the states of Rio de Janeiro, Espírito Santo and Bahia are found monazite sands containing thorium. Manganese ores of high content are important: output, 1996, 3,715,910 tonnes; Output, 1996 (in tonnes) of bauxite, 11m. Output,

1996 (in tonnes), mineral salt, 3,870,000; tungsten ore, 37,058; lead (1992), 334,426; asbestos (1992), 3,895,805; coal (1992), 9,241,099. Primary aluminium production in 1989 was 888,000 tonnes. Deposits of coal exist in Rio Grande do Sul, Santa Catarina and Paraná. Total reserves were estimated at 5,190·2m. tonnes in 1988.

Iron is found chiefly in Minas Gerais, notably the Cauê Peak at Itabira. The government is opening up iron-ore deposits in Carajás, in the northern state of Pará, with estimated reserves of 35,000m. tonnes, representing a 66% concentration of high-grade iron ore. Total output of iron ore, 1996, mainly from the Vale do Rio Doce mine at Itabira, was 180m. tonnes. Brazil is the second largest producer of iron ore after China.

Production of tin ore was 20,304 tonnes in 1996; output of barytes, 1996, 44,361 tonnes, and of phosphate rock (1992), 15·5m. tonnes. Gold is chiefly from Pará (18,837 kg in 1992), Mato Grosso (18,009 kg) and Minas Gerais (23,120 kg); total production (1992), 80,543 kg processed. Silver output (processed in 1992) 20,042 tonnes. Diamond output in 1992 was 1,285,402 carats (157,805 carats from Minas Gerais, 1m. carats from Mato Grosso).

Agriculture

In 1995, 30·22m. people depended on agriculture. There were 4·86m. farms in 1995. There were 53·3m. ha of arable land in 1997 and 12·0m. ha of permanent crops. 3·17m. ha were irrigated in 1997. Production (in tonnes):

	1996	1997
Bananas (1,000 bunches)	561,932	595,344
Beans	2,822,340	2,989,637
Cassava	24,583,971	24,310,049
Castor-beans	43,391	95,860
Coconut (1,000 fruits)	1,011,705	1,015,359

Cocoa	256,751	285,029
Coffee	2,685,641	2,342,635
Cotton	1,011,080	835,561
Grapes	733,585	900,979
Maize	32,185,179	34,601,865
Oranges (1,000 fruits)	109,324,530	114,891,259
Potatoes	2,702,942	2,756,618
Rice	9,989,839	9,293,498
Sisal	129,247	145,049
Soya	23,562,279	26,430,782
Sugarcane	325,929,067	337,255,203
Wheat	3,359,447	2,440,863
Tomatoes	2,674,833	2,602,038

Harvested coffee area, 1996, 1,989,890 ha, principally in the states of Minas Gerais, Espírito Santo, São Paulo and Paraná. Harvested cocoa area, 1996, 683,544 ha. Bahia furnished 82% of the output in 1994. 2 crops a year are grown. Harvested castor-bean area, 1996, 121,178 ha. Tobacco output was 470,888 tonnes in 1996, grown chiefly in Rio Grande do Sul and Santa Catarina.

Rubber is produced chiefly in the states of Acre, Amazonas, Rondônia and Pará. Output, 1996 (preliminary), 53,437 tonnes (natural). Brazilian consumption of rubber in 1996 was 150,676 tonnes. Plantations of tung trees were established in 1930; output, 1995, 993 tonnes.

Livestock, 1996: cattle, 165m.; pigs, 36·6m.; sheep, 18m.; goats, 12·2m.; horses, 6·3m.; mules, 1·95m.; asses, 1·3m.; chickens, 810m. Livestock slaughtered for meat in 1994 (in 1,000): cattle, 15,512; pigs, 14,575; sheep and lambs, 763; goats, 729; poultry, 1,447,525. Livestock products, 1995: milk, 16,474m. litres; wool, 24,959 tonnes; honey, 18,123 tonnes; hen's eggs, 18,252m.

Forestry

With forest lands covering 5,511,000 sq. km in 1995, only Russia had a larger area of forests. In 1995, 65·2% of the total land area of Brazil was under forests, down from 66·7% in 1990. In 1990 the total area under forests was 5,639,000 sq. km. The loss of 128,000 sq. km of forests between 1990 and 1995 was the biggest in any country in the world over the same period, and more than twice the area lost in Indonesia, the country with the second biggest reduction in forest area. Nevertheless, an independent study commissioned by NASA found that the rate of deforestation was on the decline and stated that the government had been extremely active since 1990 in reducing the rate of illegal deforestation. In 1996 the government ruled that Amazonian landowners could log only 20% of their holdings, instead of 50%, as had previously been permitted. Timber production in 1997 was 220·31m. cu. metres. In 1997 the government's environmental agency, Ibama, levied fines of nearly US$11m. on illicit loggers.

Fisheries

The fishing industry had a 1997 catch of an estimated 750,000 tonnes (72% sea fishing and 28% inland).

INDUSTRY

The main industries are textiles, shoes, chemicals, cement, lumber, iron ore, tin, steel, aircraft, motor vehicles and parts, and other machinery and equipment. The National Iron and Steel Co. at Volta Redonda, State of Rio de Janeiro, furnishes a substantial part of Brazil's steel. Total output, 1997: crude steel, 26,154,000 tonnes. Cement output, 1997, was 38,097,000 tonnes. Output of paper, 1994, was 5,653,517 tonnes. Production of rubber tyres for motor vehicles (1994), 33,820,000 units; motor vehicles (1997), 2,058,724.

Top 20 Companies (FT 1998)

Rank	Company	Market Capital ($1m.)
1	Eletrobras	11,323·6
2	Petrobras	8,059·1
3	Telesp	7,341·3
4	Telesp Part	7,034·1
5	Bradesco	5,859·3
6	Itaubanco	5,335·5
7	Vale Rio Doce	4,804·9
8	Brasil	4,452·3
9	Embratel Par	3,269·0
10	Cemig	2,958·9
11	Brahma	2,842·9
12	Tele Centro Sul	2,234·4
13	Souza Cruz	1,943·1
14	Telesp Celular	1,890·8
15	Eletropaulo	1,863·0
16	Itausa	1,756·2
17	Paul F. Luz	1,621·6
18	Unibanco	1,411·8
19	Copel	1,359·2
20	Inepar	1,325·6

Labour

The workforce in 1997 numbered 69,331,507, of whom 16,770,675 worked in agriculture and 13,864,785 worked in industry (including the construction industry). A constitutional amendment of Oct. 1996 prohibits the employment of children under 14 years. In 1999 there was a minimum monthly wage of R$136. In May 1999 an estimated 7·7% of the workforce was unemployed (7·6% in 1998).

Trade Unions

There are three major affiliated groups of trade unions:
Confederação General dos Trabalhadores: Rua Castro Alves 284,
Aclimação, São Paulo SP 01532–000. Tel: (0)11 279-6577.
Fax: (0)11 270-2167. E-mail: cgt@cgt.com.br

Central Unica dos Trabalhadores: Rua Caetano Pinto 575, São Paulo
SP 03041–000. Tel: (0)11 242-9411. Fax: (0)11 242-9610.
E-mail: sri@cut.org.br   Web site: www.cut.org.br

Fôrça Sindical: Palacio do Trabalhador, Rue Galvao Bueno 780,
13 andar, São Paulo SP 01506–000. Tel: (0)11 277-5877.
Fax: (0)11 277-5877. E-mail: secgeral@fsindical.org.br

INTERNATIONAL TRADE

In 1990 Brazil repealed most of its protectionist legislation. Import
tariffs on some 13,000 items were reduced in 1995. Since 1991 direct
foreign investment on equal terms with domestic has been permitted.
Foreign investment reached an annual average of US$21.6bn. in
1997–98, much of it as a result of the privatization programme. In
1991 the government permitted an annual US$100m. of foreign debt
to be converted into funds for environmental protection. Total foreign
debt, 1997, US$193,663m. (the highest of any country in the world).

Imports and Exports

Imports and exports for calendar years in US$1m.:

	1994	1995	1996	1997
Imports	35,997	53,783	56,947	65,007
Exports	43,558	46,506	47,762	52,987

Estimate for 1997 trade deficit: US$783m.

Principal imports in 1996 were (in US$1m.): machinery and electrical equipment, 15,671; chemical products, 6,840; transport equipment, 5,512; crude oil, 2,576; foodstuffs, 3,459; coal and coke, 755; fertilizers, 860; cast iron and steel, 792.

Principal exports in 1996 were (in 1,000 tonnes): soya, 3,646; iron, manganese and other ores, 987; coffee, 833; orange juice, 1,180; sugar, 5,989; tobacco, 282; cocoa beans, 33; (in US$1m.) transport equipment, 3,720; machine tools, 187.

Main export markets, 1998: USA, 17·8%; Argentina, 13·2%; Germany, 5·2%; Netherlands, 5·4%; Japan, 4·3%. Main import suppliers: USA, 22·2%; Argentina, 13·2%; Germany, 8·6%; Japan, 5·3%; Italy, 5·2%.

COMMUNICATIONS

Roads

There were (1996 estimate) 1,980,000 km of roads, of which 116,000 km were highways. Less than 10% of roads are paved. In 1997 there were 15m. cars and 1·1m. active trucks. Some 56% of freight is carried by truck.

Rail

There is a limited international rail service with Argentina, Bolivia and Chile. In addition there is a limited service between the major cities and towns. Daytime and overnight trains link São Paulo with Rio de Janeiro. There has been a decline in the long-distance rail service in recent years along the 18 major regional networks.

Public railways are operated by two administrations: the Federal Railways (RFFSA) formed in 1957, and São Paulo Railways (Fepasa) formed in 1971, which is confined to the state of São Paulo. They are in process of being privatized: all 6 branches of the RFFSA network were under private management by the end of Aug. 1997. RFFSA had a route-length of 22,069 km (65 km electrified) in 1994, and Fepasa 4,344 km (1,044 km electrified). An RFFSA subsidiary, CBTU (the Brazilian Urban Train Company), runs passenger services in some cities, while others are in the hands of the local authorities. Principal gauges are metre (24,720 km) and 1,600 mm (5,419 km). Passenger-km travelled in 1995–96 came to 14·5bn. and freight tonne-km to 136·44bn.

There are several important independent freight railways, including the Vitoria à Minas (898 km in 1993), the Ferroeste (238 km), the Carajas (1,076 km in 1991) and the Amapa (194 km). There are metros in São Paulo (44 km), Rio de Janeiro (23 km), Belo Horizonte (14 km), Porto Alegre (28 km) and Brasília (38·5 km).

Civil Aviation

There are three international airports in Brazil:

Brasília International (BSB) is located 11 km south of the city. There are regular buses to and from the city centre.

Rio de Janeiro (GIG) is located 21 km north of the city. Airport buses to the city centre operate from 5·30–21·00.
Web site: www.aviationbr.com/gig

São Paulo (GRU) is located 25 km northeast of the city. There is an airport bus service to the city centre that runs every 30 minutes during the day and every hour during the evening.

The 3 main airlines are Viação Aérea Rio Grande do Sul (Varig), with 49% of the domestic market, Transbrasil and Viação Aérea São Paulo (Vasp; 38% state-owned). In 1996 Varig flew 199.9m. km, carrying 9,945,900 passengers; Vasp flew 79.9m. km, carrying 3,987,000 passengers; and Tranbrasil flew 56·0m. km, carrying 2,978,600 passengers. In 1998 Brazil was also served by Aeroflot, Aerolíneas Argentinas, Aeromexico, Aeroperú, Air France, Alitalia, American Airlines, Avianca, Brasil Central, British Airways, Canadian Airlines International, Continental Airlines, Cubana, Delta Air Lines, Ecuatoriana, Iberia, JAL, KLM, Korean Air, Lan-Chile, Lloyd Aéreo Boliviano, Lufthansa, MEA, Nordeste, Olympic Airways, Pluna, Rio-Sul Servicos Aereos Regionais, SABENA, SAS, South African Airways, Spanair, Swissair, TAAG, TAP, Transportes Aereos del Mercosur, Transportes Aereos Regionais, United Airlines and Yagon Airways.

Brazil's busiest airport is São Paulo (Guarulhos), which handled 12,205,872 passengers in 1996 (6·45m. in 1992), followed by Rio de Janeiro International, with 5,202,997 passengers in 1996.

Shipping

Inland waterways, mostly rivers, are open to navigation over some 43,000 km. Santos and Rio de Janeiro are the 2 leading ports; there are 19 other large ports. During 1996, 26,387 vessels entered and cleared the Brazilian ports; 336·3m. tonnes of cargo were loaded and unloaded. In 1997 Santos handled 0·85m. container units. In 1995 the merchant fleet comprised 249 vessels totalling 10·22m. DWT, representing 1·55% of the world's total fleet tonnage. 16 vessels (14·67% of tonnage) were registered under foreign flags. Total tonnage registered, 5·3m. GRT, including oil tankers, 2·12m. GRT, and container ships, 192,777 GRT.

Telecommunications

Full IDD services are available throughout the country. Public telephone boxes take telephone cards although older boxes may require tokens called 'fichas'. International calls are expensive. In addition fax facilities are available in main post offices in major cities and in some large hotels.

The state-owned telephone system was privatized in 1998. There were 17,038,900 telephone main lines in 1997 (106·6 per 1,000 inhabitants), but 2·4m. people were on the waiting list for a line. Mobile phone services were opened to the private sector in 1996. By the end of 1997 there were 4·4m. mobile phone subscribers. There were approximately 1·3m. Internet users in May 1998. In 1997 PCs numbered 4·2m. (26 per 1,000 persons) and there were 500,000 fax machines. There were still 28,000 telex subscribers in 1996, although telex usage has declined considerably in recent years.

Postal Services

There is a good and reliable postal system in Brazil. Airmail to Europe takes 4 to 6 days whilst surface mail takes around 4 weeks. Brazil's 11,000 post offices are open from 9·00–13·00 Monday to Saturday.

In 1995 there were 10,905 post offices, equivalent to 1 for every 14,300 persons. A total of 6,009,791,111 items were handled in 1996.

SOCIAL INSTITUTIONS

Justice

There is a Supreme Federal Court of Justice at Brasília composed of 11 judges, and a Supreme Court of Justice; all judges are appointed by the President with the approval of the Senate. There are also Regional Federal Courts, Labour Courts, Electoral Courts and Military Courts. Each state organizes its own courts and judicial system in accordance with the federal Constitution.

In Dec. 1999 President Cardoso created the country's first intelligence agency (the Brazilian Intelligence Agency) under civilian rule. It replaced informal networks which were a legacy of the military dictatorship, and will help authorities crack down on organized drug gangs.

The prison population was 0·13m. in 1996. In 1995 there were 511 prisons. In 1997 a further 55 were under construction.

Religion

Brazil is the largest Roman Catholic country in the world. In 1997 about 76% of the population, an estimated 115,500,000 people, declared Roman Catholicism as their religion (including syncretic Afro-Catholic cults having spiritualist beliefs and rituals). This strong Catholic heritage is descended from the zeal of the Portuguese missionaries motivated by their call to spread Christianity to the 'infidel' indigenous populations. Despite the huge number of committed Roman Catholics and the undoubted influence the Roman church has in public and official life, there has been no official state religion in any of the constitutions of the republican period. Roman Catholic estimates in 1991 suggest that 90% were baptised Roman Catholic but only 35% were regular attendees. In 1991 there were 338 bishops and some 14,000 priests. There are numerous sects, some evangelical, some African-derived (e.g. *Candomble*).

In recent years there has been rapid growth in the following of Protestant churches in Brazil. The number of followers of evangelical churches was estimated in 1997 to be about 37m., around 22% of Brazil's total population (of these 13m. belong to the Assembly of God). In 1997 it was estimated that there were some 7,200,000 followers of other religions.

Education

Elementary education is compulsory from 7 to 14. Adult literacy was 84·0% in 1997 (male, 84·1%; female, 83·9%). There were 50,646 literacy classes in 1993 with 1,584,147 students and 75,413 teachers. In 1996 there were 77,740 pre-primary schools with

4,270,376 pupils and 219,517 teachers; 195,767 primary schools, with 33,131,270 pupils and 1,388,247 teachers; 15,213 secondary schools, with 5,739,077 pupils and 326,827 teachers; and 851 higher education institutions, with 1,661,034 students and 141,482 teachers.

The tertiary education sector includes 114 universities (53 private, 37 federal, 20 state and 4 municipal), 85 private and 3 municipal college faculty federations, and 671 other higher education institutions (514 private, 80 municipal, 57 state and 20 federal).

Extensive education reforms are under way to increase the average length of schooling, which in 1997 was 5½ years.

In 1995 total expenditure on education came to 5·2% of GNP.

Health

In 1992 there were 49,676 hospitals and clinics (22,584 private), of which 7,430 were for in-patients (5,316 private). In 1993 there were 222,658 doctors, 160,000 dentists and (1992) 57,047 pharmacists.

Health Requirements

No vaccination certificates are required to enter Brazil unless the traveller is arriving from a country affected by yellow fever (e.g. certain parts of Africa and South America). A yellow fever vaccination is strongly recommended for anyone intending to visit rural areas in Acre, Amazonas, Goias, Maranhao, Mato Grosso, Mato Grosso do Sul, Para, Rondonia and Tocantins States and the territories of Amapa and Roraima. Although a cholera vaccination is no longer required as a condition of entry, as its effectiveness is dubious, precautions should be taken as cases of the disease are still recorded.

There is a malaria risk below 900 metres in Acre, Amazonas, Maranhao, Mato Grosso, Para, Rondonia and Tocantins States and in the territories of Amapa and Roraima as well as on the outskirts of

Manaus and Porto Velho throughout the year and appropriate precautions should be taken. All water should be regarded as potentially contaminated and should be boiled or sterilized before consumption. Similarly unpasteurised milk and dairy products made from unboiled milk should be avoided. Rabies is still present and for those at high risk vaccination before arrival is advisable. Bilharzia is a danger from snakes and leeches. Avoid swimming and paddling in fresh water.

CULTURE

Broadcasting

In 1995 there were 2,033 radio and 119 television stations (colour by PAL). In 1996 there were 70m. radio and 50·5m. television receivers.

Radio

The government broadcasts on all national radio stations for an hour each night. Radio Nacional, the government's overseas radio service, transmits information and cultural programmes to Europe, the Americas, Africa and parts of Asia. The Brazilian Radio Broadcasting Company became the Brazilian Communications Company in 1988 and is commonly known as Radiobras.

Television

The majority of television programming is run by private enterprise. The 5 leading television networks (with station numbers for 1995) are:

Rede Globo de Televisão:	81 stations.
Sistema Brasiliero de Televisão:	77 stations.
Rede Bandeirantes:	63 stations.
Rede Manchete:	36 stations.
TV Record:	12 stations.

There has been major developing of cable television in the main Brazilian cities in the last few years. Most cities also receive the educational channel, **TV Educativa**.

Press

Newspapers
The leading newspapers, with circulations are:
Folha de São Paulo: Daily circulation: 540,000. Sunday circulation: 1·2m.
São Paulo liberal, centre-left newspaper.

O Estado de São Paulo: Daily: 320,000. Sunday: 650,000.
São Paulo, independent.

O Globo: Daily: 280,000. Sunday: 525,000.
Rio de Janeiro newspaper with conservative outlook.

Jornal do Brasil: Daily: 116,000. Sunday: 160,000.
Rio de Janeiro. Catholic leaning paper with conservative outlook.

Gazeta Mercantil: Daily: 100,000.
São Paulo business paper.

Correio Braziliense: Daily: 50,000. Sunday:100,000.
Brasília.

Jornal de Brasília: Daily: 22,000. Sunday: 26,000.
Brasília.

The **Brazil Herald** (circulation 18,000) incorporating the Daily Post is the only daily English language newspaper.

Magazines

The leading news and current affairs titles with circulations are: **Veja** (1,207,521), **Visão** and **IstoE** (491,752). The leading business title is **Exame** (188,000). The leading illustrated general interest title is **Manchete** (130,000). All except Manchete are São Paulo based magazines.

The leading domestic news agencies are: Rio de Janeiro-based **Agencia Globo** and **Agencia JB**, the Brasília-based **Agencia ANDA** and **Empresa Brasiliera de Noticias** and the São Paulo-based **Agencia Estado** and **Agencia Folha**.

Libraries

In 1993 Brazil had a National Library with 5·28m. volumes, and in 1994 a total of 2,739 public libraries.

Tourism

In 1997, 2,995,000 tourists visited Brazil. 657,942 were Argentinian, 224,577 US citizens, 200,423 Uruguayan, 102,106 German, 90,716 Paraguayan, 84,001 Italian, 63,900 Chilean, 59,502 Spanish, 55,257 French, 52,183 Portuguese, 38,520 UK citizens, 33,505 Swiss and 30,219 Japanese. Receipts totalled US$2·47bn.

Tourist Organizations

The official Brazilian Tourist Board is **Embratur:** Rua Mariz e Barros 13, Rio de Janeiro 20270. Tel: (0)21 273-2212. Fax: (0)21 273-9290. Web site: www.embratur.gov.br/

Visas

All Australian, Canadian, American and Japanese visitors require a passport valid up to 6 months from the date of entry and a visa to visit Brazil. With the exception of France all EU nationals can enter Brazil for tourism purposes of up to 90 days without a visa. All EU nationals travelling for business purposes do need a visa except for UK nationals who will be granted an appropriate business visa on arrival provided they hold a return or onward ticket and proof of sufficient funds to cover the duration of their stay.

Festivals

Jan: **Torneio de Repentistas:** In Olinda and Pernambuco.

Festa de São Lazaro: In Salvador and Bahia.

New Year and Festa de Iemanja: In Rio de Janeiro.

Procissão do Senhor Bom Jesus dos Navegantes: In Salvador and Bahia.

Feb: **Rio Carnival:** The largest and most extravagant of all the Latin American pre-Lent celebrations.

Grande Vaquejada do Nordest: In Natal, Rio Grande de Norte.

Festa de Iemanja: In Salvador, Bahia.

March: **Procissão do Encontro:** Salvador, Bahia.

April: **Drama da Paixão de Cristo:** Brejo da Madre de Deus, Pernambuco.

June: **Festas Juninas and Bumba Meu Boi:** Nationwide, particularly São Luis, Belem and the states of Pernambuco and Rio.

July: **Festa do Divino:** Diamantina, Minas Gerais.

Regato de Jangadas Dragao do Mar: Fortaleza, Ceara.

Missa do Vaqueiro: Serrita, Pernambuco.

Aug: **Festa de Iemanja:** Itamaraca, Pernambuco,

Cavalhada: Caete, Minas Gerais.

Oct: **Festa da Nossa Senhora Aparecida:** Aperacida, São Paulo.

Nov: **Festa do Padre Cícero:** Juazeiro do Norte, Ceara.

Dec: **Festa de Santa Barbara:** Salvador, Bahia.

Festa de Iemanja: Belem, Para and João Pessoa, Paraiba.

Celebração de Fim de Ano y Festa de Iemanja:
Rio de Janeiro.

Public Holidays 2000

1 Jan.	New Year's Day/International Peace Day.
4–7 March	Carnival.
21 April	Good Friday.
21 April	Tiradentes.
1 May	May Day.
22 June	Corpus Christi.
7 Sept.	Independence Day.
12 Oct.	Our Lady Aperecida, patron saint of Brazil.
2 Nov.	All Souls' Day.
15 Nov	Proclamation of the Republic Day.
25 Dec.	Christmas Day.

Social Etiquette

In general social conventions follow the normal European models of handshaking, politeness and traditional courtesies. Offers of tea or coffee are frequent and should be accepted with gratitude. It is polite to bring flowers or a similar gift to meals. It should be remembered that the Catholic Church is highly respected in the community and should not be mocked or derided. Tipping is widespread and 10–15% should be added to most bills.

DIPLOMATIC REPRESENTATIVES

Of Brazil in Great Britain (32 Green St., London W1Y 4AT)
Ambassador: Sergio Silva do Amaral.

Of Great Britain in Brazil (Setor De Embaixadas Sul, Quadro 801,
Conjunto K, CP70.408-900, Brasília, DF *or* Av. das Nações, CP07-
0586, 70.359, Brasília, DF)
   Ambassador: Roger Bridgland Bone, CMG.
Of Brazil in the USA (3006 Massachusetts Ave., NW, Washington,
D.C. 20008)
   Ambassador: Rubens Antonio Barbosa.
Of the USA in Brazil (Av. das Nações, Lote 03, Quadra 801, CEP:
70403-900, Brasília, D.F.)
   Ambassador: James Derham.
Of Brazil to the United Nations
   Ambassador: Gelson Fonseca Junior.
Of Brazil to the European Union
   Ambassador: Clodoaldo Hugueney.

FURTHER READING

Instituto Brasileiro de Geografia e Estatística. *Anuário Estatístico do
   Brasil.—Censo Demográfico de 1991.—Indicadores IBGE.*
Monthly *Boletim do Banco Central do Brasil.* Banco Central do
   Brasil. Brasília. Monthly
Baer, W., *The Brazilian Economy: Growth and Development.* 4th ed.
   New York, 1995
Burns, E. B., *A History of Brazil.* 2nd ed. Columbia Univ. Press, 1980
Dickenson, John, *Brazil.* [Bibliography] 2nd ed. ABC-Clio, Oxford
   and Santa Barbara (CA), 1997
Eakin, Marshall C., *Brazil: The Once and Future Country.* New York,
   1997
Falk, P. S. and Fleischer, D. V., *Brazil's Economic and Political Future.*
   Boulder (CO), 1988

Font, M. A., *Coffee, Contention and Change in the Making of Modern Brazil.* Oxford, 1990

Guirmaraes, R. P., *Politics and Environment in Brazil: Ecopolitics of Development in the Third World.* New York, 1991

Mainwaring, S., *The Catholic Church and Politics in Brazil, 1916–86.* Stanford Univ. Press, 1986

Stepan, A. (ed.) *Democratizing Brazil: Problems of Transition and Consolidation.* OUP, 1993

Welch, J. H., *Capital Markets in the Development Process: the Case of Brazil.* London, 1992

For other more specialized titles see under CONSTITUTION AND GOVERNMENT *and* BANKING AND FINANCE, *above.*

National library: Biblioteca Nacional, Avenida Rio Branco 219　39, Rio de Janeiro, RJ.

National statistical office: Instituto Brasileiro de Geografia e Estatística (IBGE), Rua General Canabarro 666, 20.271-201 Maracanã, Rio de Janeiro, RJ.

Website: http:/www.ibge.gov.br/

MEXICO

Estados Unidos Mexicanos
(United States of Mexico)

Capital: Mexico City

Area: 1,967,183 sq. km

Population estimate, 2000: 98·88m.

Head of State: Ernesto Zedillo

TERRITORY AND POPULATION

Mexico is bounded in the north by the USA, west and south by the Pacific Ocean, southeast by Guatemala, Belize and the Caribbean Sea, and northeast by the Gulf of Mexico. It comprises 1,967,183 sq. km (759,529 sq. miles), including uninhabited islands (5,073 sq. km) offshore.

Population at recent censuses: 1970, 48,225,288; 1980, 66,846,833; 1990, 81,249,645. Estimate, 1995, 91,158,290; (46,257,791 females). 1997 est., 95·5m.; density, 49 per sq. km. In 1997, 73·8% of the population were urban.

The UN gives a projected population for 2000 of 98·88m.

Area, population and capitals of the Federal District and 31 states:

	Area (Sq. km)	Population (1990 census)	Population (1995 counting)	Capital
Federal District	1,499	8,235,744	8,489,007	Mexico City
Aguascalientes	5,589	719,659	862,720	Aguascalientes
Baja California	70,113	1,660,855	2,112,140	Mexicali
Baja California Sur	73,677	317,764	375,494	La Paz
Campeche	51,833	535,185	642,516	Campeche
Coahuila	151,571	1,972,340	2,173,775	Saltillo
Colima	5,455	428,510	488,028	Colima
Chiapas	73,887	3,210,496	3,584,786	Tuxtla Gutiérrez
Chihuahua	247,087	2,441,873	2,793,537	Chihuahua
Durango	119,648	1,349,378	1,431,748	Victoria de Durango
Guanajuato	30,589	3,982,593	4,406,568	Guanajuato
Guerrero	63,794	2,620,637	2,916,567	Chilpancingo
Hidalgo	20,987	1,888,366	2,112,473	Pachuca de Soto
Jalisco	80,137	5,302,689	5,991,176	Guadalajara
México	21,461	9,815,795	11,707,964	Toluca de Lerdo
Michoacán	59,864	3,548,199	3,870,604	Morelia
Morelos	4,941	1,195,059	1,442,662	Cuernavaca

Nayarit	27,621	824,643	896,702	Tepic
Nuevo Léon	64,555	3,098,736	3,550,114	Monterrey
Oaxaca	95,364	3,019,560	3,228,895	Oaxaca de Juárez
Puebla	33,919	4,126,101	4,624,365	Puebla de Zaragoza
Querétaro	11,769	1,051,235	1,250,476	Querétaro
Quintana Roo	50,350	493,277	703,536	Chetumal
San Luis Potosí	62,848	2,003,187	2,200,763	San Luis Potosí
Sinaloa	58,092	2,204,054	2,425,675	Culiacán Rosales
Sonora	184,934	1,823,606	2,085,536	Hermosillo
Tabasco	24,661	1,501,744	1,748,769	Villahermosa
Tamaulipas	79,829	2,249,581	2,527,328	Ciudad Victoria
Tlaxcala	3,914	761,277	883,924	Tlaxcala
Veracruz	72,815	6,228,239	6,737,324	Jalapa Enríquez
Yucatán	39,340	1,362,940	1,556,622	Mérida
Zacatecas	75,040	1,276,323	1,336,496	Zacatecas

The official language is Spanish, the mother tongue of over 92% of the population, but there are some indigenous language groups (of which Náhuatl, Maya, Zapotec, Otomi and Mixtec are the most important) spoken by 5,282,347 persons over 5 years of age (1990 census).

The populations (1995 Census) of the largest cities (150,000 and more) were:

Mexico City[1]	16,674,160	Torreón[1]	870,651
Guadalajara[1]	3,461,819	San Luis Potosí[1]	781,964
Monterrey[1]	3,022,268	Mérida[1]	779,648
Puebla[1]	1,561,558	Tampico-Cd. Madera[1]	718,906
Léon[1]	1,174,180	Culiacán Rosales	696,262
Toluca de Lerdo[1]	1,080,081	Mexicali	696,034
Ciudad Juárez[1]	1,011,786	Acapulco de Juárez	687,292
Tijuana	991,592	Querétaro[1]	679,757

Cuernavaca[1]	672,307	Cardenas	302,508
Aguascalientes[1]	637,303	Tepic	292,780
Chihuahua[1]	627,662	Nuevo Laredo	275,060
Ahome[1]	604,679	Poza Rica[1]	273,148
Coatzacoalcos[1]	593,888	Monclova[1]	253,585
Saltillo[1]	583,326	Uruapán	250,794
Morelia[1]	578,061	Pachuca[1]	249,036
Orizaba[1]	567,185	Tapachula	244,855
Veracruz[1]	560,200	Victoria	243,960
Hermosillo	559,154	Carmen	233,423
Villahermosa[1]	533,598	La Piedad[1]	229,716
Durango	464,566	Zacatecas	226,265
Irapuato	412,639	Salamanca	221,125
Oaxaca[1]	394,068	Zamora[1]	214,938
Tuxtla Gutierrez	386,135	Cuautla[1]	207,267
Xalapa[1]	370,430	Campeche	204,533
Matamoros	363,487	Chetumal	202,046
Mazatlan	357,619	Tehuacan	190,468
Celaya	354,473	Colima[1]	187,081
Cajeme	345,222	La Paz	182,418
Reynosa	337,053	Fresnillo	176,885
Tlaxcala[1]	336,637	Chilpancingo	170,368
Ensenada	315,289	Lázaro Cárdenas	155,366
Cancun	311,696	San Juan del Rio	154,922

[1]Metropolitan Area.

Time Zones

There are 3 time zones in Mexico. The majority of the country is on 6 hours behind GMT all year round. Baja California Sur and the northwest coastal states of Sonora, Sinaloa and Nayarit are 7 hours behind GMT. Baja California Norte observes Daylight Saving Time in the winter, making it 7 hours behind GMT in summer and 8 hours behind in the winter.

KEY HISTORICAL EVENTS

Pre-Columbian

The first of Mexico's ancient civilisations, the Olmecs (meaning 'people from the rubber country'), established itself around 1,000 BC in what are now the states of Veracruz and Tabasco. Before their civilisation mysteriously vanished around 400 BC they erected massive buildings, created an advanced calendar and left several massive carvings of human heads, some weighing up to 50 tons. They built 2 great cities: Teotihuacan, which had a population of 200,000, and Cholula, their religious centre. An advanced people religiously, architecturally and mathematically, they were a huge influence on the civilisations that succeeded them.

The Mayans originated around 1200 BC and are most noted for their complex systems of mathematics and astrology as well as their prolific city-building. By 1400 AD the Mayan State had splintered and virtually disappeared leaving only the remains of their ancient cities as testament to their achievements.

The Zapotecs were also great city builders and artisans. They were conquered by the Mixtecs who, in turn, became vassals of the Aztec Empire in the 1400s. Almost 2m. descendants of the Zapotecs and Mixtecs remain today, inhabiting areas in the State of Oaxaca.

The Toltecs originate from the northern reaches of the Valley of Mexico and are remembered for their reputation as great warriors. They built the city of Tula and were master craftsmen greatly influenced by the Mayan culture.

The largest and most famous of Mexico's pre-Columbian civilizations was the Aztecs. They dominated the region for nearly 200 years and controlled a flourishing empire stretching from the Yucatan peninsula to the Pacific, with over 370 individual nations under their authority, when the Spanish conquerors arrived in 1519. Their capital, Teochtitlan, was a picturesque city of pyramids, floating roads, aqueducts and market places set in a lake. It numbered some 100,000 residents making it the largest city in the then Americas.

Conquest and Colonial Domination

In 1519 Hernan Cortes landed in Veracruz, some 200 miles from the Aztec capital. It was here he heard about the magnificence of Tenochtitlan and, having burnt all but one of his ships to prevent any thought of turning back, began his march toward the interior of Mexico. That he was able to defeat an empire as powerful as the Aztecs with only a few hundred men and a handful of artillery pieces seems incredible but he was aided enormously by the Aztec's own superstition. Due to a myth concerning the eventual return of Quetzacuatyl (the white-faced god), the Aztecs offered hospitality to Cortes which he returned by taking the Aztec ruler, Moctezuma II, hostage. Having escaped in the night he returned a year later with 50,000 Indian allies to conquer the city which surrendered on 13 Aug. 1521—marking the end of the Aztec Empire.

Mexico became the jewel in Spain's imperial crown. It was heavily taxed, ruthlessly exploited, ruled directly from Spain and allowed no autonomy. Everything possible was done to try and suppress indigenous culture and supplant local tradition. New Spain, as the colony was known, was a rich source of mineral wealth, especially silver. The Spanish introduced a system of haciendas, large enclosures of land that produced a variety of crops and employed many workers who lived on the land. Missionaries were brought over from Spain to convert the Indians to Roman Catholicism. However, Spain's most effective exports to Mexico were the European diseases which decimated the already depleted Indian population. A caste system soon developed in the colony with Espanoles (Spaniards born in Spain), criollos (Mexican-born but of Spanish extraction), mestizos (Spanish and Indian) and the indigenes (the Indians).

Mexican Independence

Napoleon's conquest of Spain and replacement of the King with his own brother helped fan the flames of dissent which had already been stirring in Mexico. The simmering conflict between the criollos and Espanoles over what role Spain should actually have in the governing of Mexico's affairs became immediately relevant. On 16 Sept. 1810 in the town of Dolores a catholic priest, Father Miguel de Hidalgo y Costilla, urged his parishioners to fight for independence and led an armed rebellion of criollos and mestizos to fight for this aim. Although he was later captured and executed he had begun a war of independence which culminated on 27 Sept. 1821 when the rebel leader Vicente Guerrero and royalist Agustin de Iturbide signed the treaty of Cordoba finally establishing Mexico's independence. In 1824 a constitution was adopted and Mexico's first president, Guadelope Victoria, was inaugurated.

Independence led to a sustained period of internal and external fighting, the worst of which, the Mexican war of 1846–48 against the USA, resulted in the loss of nearly half the nation's territory. In 1858 a Zapotec Indian from Oaxaca, Benito Juárez, became President and instituted the liberalization of the constitution and land-reform. His initiatives included a total reform of the education system, granting free primary education to all, and the construction of a railway from Mexico City to Veracruz. These policies outraged Mexico's wealthy conservative classes leading to the War of Reform which lasted from 1858 to 1861. Despite the victory of Juárez's side Mexico was left bankrupt. Seeing Mexico weak, the French leader Napoleon III, who had been a major lender during the War of Reform, sent Archduke Maximilian of Austria to take control of the country. It was not until 1867 that Juárez was able to retake Mexico City and Maximilian was executed.

In 1871 Porfirio Diaz ran against Juárez for President and when defeated attempted to overthrow the government, an action he succeeded in five years later. He ruled as an unchallenged dictator for 40 years, overseeing, the building of new railways, the opening of new banks and the development of industry, mining and commerce as well as the sell-off of Mexico's industries to foreign interests and the suppression of any opposition. His period of rule became known as the Porfiriato and gave Mexico a degree of autocratic stability.

Revolution, Constitution and Corruption

The social revolution of 1910–21, lead by Francisco Madero, overthrew Diaz and left Madero as the elected President. His reign was short-lived as his own military commander, Victoriano Huerta, assassinated him leading to another civil war which finally ended in 1923 with General Alvero Obregon elected as President. Earlier, in 1917, under President Carranza's brief period of rule a new constitution had been created which established Mexico as a representative, democratic and federal republic, comprising 31 states and the federal district (Mexico City).

Despite democratic elections the Partido Revolucionario Institutional (PRI) has been in power for more than 70 years. In 1934 General Lazaro Cardenas became President and instituted widespread land reform, strengthened unions and nationalized the oil industry.

Post-war Mexico has been beset by economic crises and political corruption. Election fraud has been endemic and in 1968 the government brutally suppressed a student protest in Mexico City, killing hundreds. Lopez Portillo was elected as President in 1976 and brought the country to the brink of bankruptcy by negotiating a series of huge foreign loans borrowed against future oil revenues to finance a massive programme of economic and social development. The collapse of oil prices created major economic difficulties which, combined with corruption and mismanagement, created a serious political crisis in 1982.

Portillo's successor, Miguel de la Madrid, implemented economic reforms and anti-corruption measures but achieved only limited success. His successor, Carlos Salinas de Gortari, instigated a series of major economic reforms. He reduced public spending, devalued the Peso, introduced a programme of privatization, reformed the tax system, removed import controls and tariff reductions and attempted to renegotiate Mexico's US$100m. debt. Despite the widespread opposition and public sector strikes that greeted the reforms they were widely praised abroad and laid the groundwork for the implementation of the North American Free Trade Agreement (NAFTA) with the US and Canada.

NAFTA, Zapatista and Modern Mexico

The downside of Carlos Salinas' reforms have been the knock-on social effects. Living standards have fallen sharply for many poorer Mexicans and wealth inequality has widened. For the first time since they came to power the PRI has seen growing opposition in the form of parties representing the disaffected. On New Year's Day 1994, the day that the NAFTA was signed, an armed insurrection began in the southern state of Chiapas. Fighting under the name of the revolutionary hero Emiliano Zapata the rebels promote a series of land reform policies which have gained considerable sympathy among Mexican peasants. Despite the counter-insurgency war waged by the government the Zapatista problem has not gone away.

Although NAFTA has provided some recent economic hope, Mexico still suffers from major economic instability. In 1994, partly due to the Zapatista's undermining of the government, the currency virtually collapsed, sending the economy into chaos. In response to this crisis a new PRI government lead by Ernesto Zedillo won the 1994 presidential elections and sought a political solution to the Chiapas problem. At the same time changes were made to the electoral system which have given opposition parties representation in congress. In 1997, for the first time in its history, Mexico City elected a mayor who was not a PRI candidate, Cuauhtemoc Cardenas, who is now a front runner for the 2000 presidential election. Despite the emergence of a more representative political culture the Chiapas problem refuses to go away. In Dec. 1997 a massacre in a Chiapas village church killed 45 Indians, mainly women and children. Of those arrested in connection with the incident many appeared to have links with the anti-Zapatista para-military groups who have, in the past, received the tacit support of the authorities.

POLITICAL AND SOCIAL CHRONOLOGY FOR THE CENTURY

1900

Camilo Arriaga, a wealthy engineer, organizes a small party with the aim of restoring the liberalism of Juárez's rule.

1901

Arriaga calls a national meeting of liberal clubs. Most of his followers are later arrested and their newspaper, 'Regeneración', suppressed.

1906

The Regeneration group illicitly publishes a programme advocating sweeping reforms including a 1-term presidency, the expansion of public education and land reform. It is widely circulated throughout Mexico.

1908

Diaz states his intention of not seeking re-election. Francisco Madero publishes 'The Presidential Succession of 1910'.

1910

Francisco Madero stands against Diaz in the presidential election. Madero is imprisoned by Diaz, only to escape to Texas and incite a revolutionary uprising.

1911

President Porfirio Diaz's dictatorial period of rule comes to an end after 40 years. He is overthrown during the social revolution led by Francisco Madero who is elected President. Diaz flees into exile.

1912

Pascual Orozco rebels against Madero. Victoriano Huerta's troops crush the rebellion. Madero returns in triumph to Mexico City. Venustiano Carranza establishes constitutional government at Veracruz.

1913

Madero is assassinated and Victoriano Huerta, who is suspected of sanctioning the assassination, becomes President. Carranza, Villa and Alvaro Obregon lead a northern rebellion.

1914

The United States lands troops at Veracruz. Cut off from money and supplies, Huerta flees Mexico. Venustiano Carranza becomes President. Three years of fighting follow.

1915

Obregon turns against Villa who continues to fight and raids US border towns. The US recognizes Carranza as the chief of government forces.

1916

US General Pershing's pursuit of Villa provokes bitterness between the USA and Mexico.

1917

Carranza is formally elected as President and institutes a new constitution establishing Mexico as a democratic and federal republic.

1920

General Alvaro Obregon seizes power. Carranza is shot attempting to escape the country.

1923

Obregon is democratically elected as President. The USA recognises his government.

1924

Plutarco Elias Calles becomes President.

1926

Anticlerical policies spark Cristero Rebellion.

1928

The constitution of 1917 is amended to extend the presidential term from 4 to 6 years. The doctrine of 'no re-election' is changed to 'no successive re-election'. Obregon is re-elected but assassinated three weeks later. Emilio Portes Gil becomes President.

1929

The Cristero Rebellion is suppressed. The Partido Nacional Revolucionario (PNR) is founded.

1930

Pascual Ortiz Rubio becomes President.

1932

Abelardo Rodríguez becomes President after Rubio resigns.

1934

General Lazaro Cardenas becomes President. He establishes the Partido Revolucionario Institutional (PRI)—the broad-based party which still rules today—and instigates widespread land reforms.

1938

Cardenas nationalizes the oil companies.

1940

Manuel Avila Camacho becomes President.

1942

Mexico officially joins the Allied side in WWII.

1946

Miguel Aleman becomes President.

1952

Adolfo Ruiz Cortines becomes President.

1958

Adolfo Lopez Mateos becomes President.

1959

A national railway strike is suppressed and its leaders imprisoned.

1964

Gustavo Diaz Ordaz becomes President.

1968

The government brutally suppresses a student protest in Tlatelolco square, Mexico City, killing hundreds. Mexico City stages the Olympic Games, the first in the 'Third World'.

1970

Luis Echeverria Alvarez becomes President.

1976

José Lopez Portillo becomes President.

1982

Miguel de la Madrid becomes President and nationalizes the banks.

1985

Mexico City is hit by a huge earthquake which causes widespread destruction.

1988

Carlos Salinas de Gortari becomes President despite a strong showing from Cuauhtemoc Cardenas, son of Lazaro, as the leader of the National Democratic Front (FDN). For almost the first time since the PRI came to power opposition parties wins seats in the Senate.

1989

The leader of the main opposition party, Manuel Clouthier, dies in suspicious circumstances.

1993

The archbishop of Guadalajara, Juan Jesus Ocampo, is caught in the crossfire between warring drug gangs at Guadalajara airport, and shot dead.

1994

The Zapatista Army of National Liberation (EZLN), an armed guerrilla movement, takes control of 5 municipalities in the southernmost state of Chiapas. The army reacts to the uprising with brutal force. Negotiations are later instigated by President Salinas. Popular PRI candidate Luis Donaldo Colosio is assassinated. Ernesto Zedillo Ponce de Leon becomes President.

1995

President Zedillo launches an offensive against the EZLN.

1996

The San Andres Accords on Rights and Indigenous Cultures is signed.

1997

Congressional elections leave the PRI without an overall majority in the Chamber of Deputies for the first time. An attempted assassination is made on Bishop Samuel Ruiz by a paramilitary group financed by right-wingers. 45 displaced Tzotil Indians are massacred by paramilitary forces linked to PRI officials in Chiapas.

1999

In Sept. Diodoro Carrasco launches a new proposal to reinitiate peace dialogue in Chiapas. A week later the government agrees to release several Zapatistas and their sympathisers from state prisons. Major floods cause widespread damage and kill hundreds.

LEADING CULTURAL FIGURES

Diego Rivera (1886–1957)

Muralist and painter, Diego Rivera was the greatest Mexican painter of the 20th century and one of the world's finest artists. Born in Guanajuato, Mexico in 1892 he moved to Mexico City with his family. He studied in the San Carlos Academy and in the carving workshop of artist José Guadalupe Posada. In 1907 he left Mexico for Europe, arriving in Spain where he received a modest 4-year scholarship for European study from Governor Teodoro Dehesa. Having travelled through Spain, France and Belgium, and been exposed to the influence of post-modernism and cubism (the style he would first exhibit in), he met Pablo Picasso in 1914 who expressed admiration for Rivera's recent work. During the First World War Rivera became increasingly influenced by Cézanne and later Renoir. In 1920 he travelled through Italy to study renaissance art and a year later returned to Mexico.

It was in his native country that Rivera discovered the pre-conquest artistic sites and whose styles he developed as an important part of his own. By combining classicist, simplified and colourful painting he recaptured something of Mexico's pre-columbian past. His paintings were studies in Mexican history, full of moments in the lives of colourful characters, workers and costumes. In many ways he was a revolutionary painter trying to take art to the wider public through his murals, his vivid style and social awareness.

Octavio Paz (1914–98)

Writer and Nobel Prize winner Octavio Paz was born in Mexico City in 1914. His interest in literature developed through his grandfather's extensive library. His writing began from an early age so that by the age of 17 he had founded an avant-garde literary journal and had published his first collection of poetry, 'Forest Moon', by the age of

19. Having spent a year in Spain during the Spanish Civil War he returned to Mexico and joined the Mexican Foreign Service. He served in the Mexican embassies in Paris and Tokyo before becoming ambassador to India in 1962. When the Mexican government violently put down student protests in Mexico City in 1968 he resigned this position.

Primarily a poet, Paz has published numerous collections of poetry; however, he is perhaps better known for his meditation on Mexican culture, 'The Labyrinth of Solitude', published in 1959. His best known poem, 'Sun Stone', was inspired by the monumental stone Aztec calendar and Mexico's pre-columbian culture is a vivid presence in his work. Similarly Mexico's landscape is a constant source of imagery for his work.

Carlos Fuentes (1928–)

Novelist and short-story writer Carlos Fuentes was born in Panama in 1928. The son of a Mexican diplomat, Fuentes spent his early years away from his native country in the United States, Chile and Argentina. He attended college in Mexico City and studied law at both the School of Law at the National University of Mexico and at the Institut des Hautes Etudes Internationales in Geneva. It was in Geneva that he began his distinguished career in public service as a Mexican delegate, going on to serve in the UN, the Mexican government and as ambassador to France.

By far the best known Mexican writer outside Mexico, his novels synthesize fantasy and reality, placing him amongst the other proponents of the 'magic realism' genre. His novels include 'Where the Air is Clear' (1958), 'A Change of Skin' (1967), 'Terra Nostra' (1975), 'The Old Gringo' (1984) and 'The Campaign' (1991).

MAJOR CITIES

The country code is 52. The outgoing international code is 98.

MEXICO CITY

Estimated population 2000: 18,131,000 (Source: 1996 World Urbanization Prospects. United Nations Population Division.) Mexico City is located in the Valley of Mexico, a mountain-ringed basin 100 km long, 60 km wide and 2,500 km high. Long before Mexico existed as a nation the area of the present Mexico City was established as the region's centre. It was here that many of the great peoples of the pre-columbian Americas lived: the great metropolis of Teotihuacan, which numbered some 200,000 people, is 50 km to the northeast of the city, the Toltec's capital at modern day Tula is to the northwest of the city and the magnificent Aztec capital of Tenochtitlan was the foundation on top of which the Spanish conquerors built their capital, Mexico City.

It is difficult to imagine the impact the Aztec capital (Tenochtitlan) must have had on the first Spanish visitors. First settled by the Aztecs around 1345 it was, by the time of Cortes' arrival in 1519, a city of 300,000 people covering some 13 sq. km—the equal in size to anything in contemporary Europe. Built in the middle of a lake it was a rigidly organized city of causeways and stone buildings with the Great Temple (El Templo Mayor) towering over the surrounding buildings and houses.

Cortes was able to capture the city in 1521 after a three-month siege. His inferior number of troops was offset by his superior weaponry, his possession of horses (an animal the Aztecs had never seen before) and his utilization of suppressed tribes to fight against the Aztecs. Having captured the city the victorious Spanish proceeded to smash any remains of the old Aztec culture, using the stones of the Aztec temples and palaces to construct their own city in the colonial style. A new palace for Cortes was built on the site of the Aztec emperor's palace whilst a new cathedral was built on the ruins of the Great temple. Despite its fine new buildings the colonial city was a shadow of the glory of Tenochtitlan. Its population had been decimated by war and disease and took until the early years of the 20th century to attain the same population as the Aztec capital had had in 1519. Despite this it remained Mexico's dominant social and commercial urban area and when the country finally achieved independence in 1821 Mexico City became its capital. In 1917 President Carranza's new constitution established the city as the Republic's Federal Capital (the Distrito Federal), separate from the country's 31 states.

Modern Mexico is largely a result of massive 20th century industrialization. Its population is estimated at over 25m., the largest in the world. Many of the city's people live in appalling conditions in the city's shanty towns. In Sept. 1985 a major earthquake inflicted widespread damage on the city and many of its buildings are still recovering. Industrial and vehicular pollution is another major problem. The pollutants become trapped in the bowl of the city by the mountains leaving a permanent smog. In addition there are high levels of petty crime. However, none of this detracts millions of tourists from visiting one of the great world cities and making tourism one of Mexico's major industries.

Tourist Information

The **Mexico City Tourist Office** (Departamento de Turismo del Distrito Federal, or DDF) maintains information booths at both the international and domestic arrivals areas at the airport, at the Buenavista train station, and inside the Fonart handicraft store at Avenida Juárez 89. In town visit the lobby of its main office at Amberes 54 at the corner of Londres in the Zona Rosa. This office also provides information by phone with its **INFOTUR** service

(Tel: (0)5 525-9380) from 9·00–21·00 daily. Operators are multilingual and have access to an extensive data bank.

Financial and Currency

American Express Travel Services

Campos Eliseos 204 Local 5, Col. Polanco, 11560.

Tel: (0)5 281-1111 (Ext. 8940).

Open Monday to Friday from 9·00–18·00 and Saturday from 9·00–13·00.

Hotel Camino Real, Mariano Escobedo 700, 11590.

Tel: (0)5 203-2355.

Open Monday to Friday from 8·30–18·00.

Ave. Patriotismo 635 P.B., Col. Cd. De Los Deportes, 03710.

Tel: (0)5 326 2777.

Open Monday to Friday from 8·30–18·00 and Saturday from 8·30–13·00.

Centro Comercial Santa Fe, Ave. Vazco de Quiroga 3800, 05109.

Tel: (0)5 259-9555.

Open Monday to Saturday from 10·00–19·00.

Centro Comercial Perisur, Periferico Sur 4690 Local 231, 14000.

Tel: (0)5 606-9621.

Open Monday to Saturday from 10·00–19·00.

Paseo de la Reforma 234, Esq. Havre, Col. Juárez, 06600.

Tel: (0)5 207-6950.

Open Monday to Friday from 9·00–18·00 and Saturday from 9·00–13·00.

Taxis

Four different types of taxi operate in the city. The yellow and white taxis and the orange taxis are metered. Turismo taxis with English-speaking drivers are not metered and are available outside major hotels. Peseros taxis are green and white share taxis, which travel on fixed routes and charge fares according to the distance travelled.

Rail

Estación Central de Buenavista: Located just off Insurgentes Nte, at the junction of Alzate with Mosqueta (nearest metro is Revolución or Guerrero).

Postal Services

Main office located at Tacuba y Lazaro Cardenas, opposite the Palacio de Bellas Artes.

Open Monday to Friday from 8·00–24·00, Saturdays from 8·00–20·00 and Sundays from 9·00–16·00.

Internet Access

Coffee Net: Ave. Nuevo León 104–B, Col. Condesa, 06170 Mexico City.

Tel: (0)5 286-7104. E-mail: coffeenet@nova.net.mx

Open Monday to Saturday from 10.00–21.00.

Internet Café: Interlomas Mexico, Passeo de la Herradura No. 5, Colonia, San Fernando la Herradura, Mexico City.

E-mail: Intc@mail.www.teesa.com

Ciberpuerto: Alfonso Reyes 238, Condesa, 06100 Mexico City.

Tel: (0)5 286-4744.

Fax (0)5 286-0861. E-mail: ciberpuerto@ciberpuerto.com

Web site: www.ciberpuerto.com

Café with 8 computers.

Internet Station: Arquímedes 130 loc 20PB metro Polanco, D.F. 1600 Mexico City.
Tel: (0)5 280-6091. Fax: (0)5 280-6091. E-mail: isoff@altavista.net
Open Monday to Saturday from 11.00–20.00.
Purely an internet station with no access to refreshments.

Club Internet: Via Gustavo Baz No. 11–B, Col. Bosque de Echegaray, Naucalpan, Mexico City.
E-mail: ids@mail.internet.com.mx
Web site: members.tripod.com/~javachatcafe
Open Monday to Saturday from 9.00–21.00.

Javachat Café Internet: Genova 44–K Zona Rosa, 06600 Mexico City.
Tel: (0)5 525-6853. Fax: (0)5 514-6856. E-mail: javachat@yahoo.com
Open daily from 10.00–22·00.

Centro de Estudios Superiores Lafoel: Donceles 80, Colonia Centro, Mexico City.
Tel: (0)5 125-835. E-mail: aldo_27@hotmail.com
Web site: www.el-universal.com.mx
Located in the centre on the city's Centro Historico.

Bits Café y Canela: Hamburgo #165 Zona Rosa, 06600 Mexico City.
Tel: (0)5 525-0144. Fax: (0)5 525-0144.
E-mail: bits@bitscafeycanela.com
Web site: www.bitscafeycanela.com
Open Monday to Saturday from 10·00–22·00.
Café offering refreshment, art and music as well as net access.

Cybercafé and mail: b. de minas 55, 52783 Mexico City.
Tel: (0)5 789-1487.

Fax: (0)5 789-1487. E-mail: webmaster@korenfeld.zzn.com
Web site: akbmail.mainpage.net

Ciberpuerto: Alfonso Reyes 238, Hipodromo Condesa, 06140
Mexico City. Tel: (0)5 286-4744. Fax: (0)5 286-0861.
E-mail: cafe@ciberpuerto.com
Web site: www.ciberpuerto.com
Open Monday to Friday from 10.00–20.00.

Caffe 2000 INTER-NET: Mier y Pesado No.317–12, Colonia del Valle,
D.F. 03100 Mexico City. Tel: (0)5 687-9364. Fax: (0)5 687-9364.
E-mail: caffe_2000@email.com
Web site: www.angelfire.com/ca3/caffe2000
Open Monday to Friday from 10.00–20.00 and Saturday from
10·00–15·00.

Landmarks

El Zócalo and the Metropolitan Cathedral: Located in the centre of
Mexico City is El Zocalo, one of the largest public squares in the
world.

Dominating the Zocalo is the Metropolitan Cathedral, the biggest
and oldest in Latin America. Although the first church on the site was
started in 1525 it was rebuilt, to the designs of Herrara, the architect
of the Escorial in Spain, in 1573, consecrated in 1667 and finished in
1813. Built in a heavy, grey Baroque style the Cathedral was badly
damaged by fire in 1967 and by the earthquake of 1985. Also located
on El Zocalo is the Palacio Nacional (National Palace). Built on the
site of Moctezuma's palace from 1562 it became the official
residence of the Spanish Viceroy and later the Presidents of the
Republic. To this day it contains the official office of the President.
Rebuilt in 1692 in a colonial baroque style, the top floor was added
by President Calles in the 1920s.

Chapultepec Park, Castle and Zoo

Mexico City's largest park comprises some 1,000 acres. It is also the site of several historical and cultural attractions. Foremost among them are Chapultepec Castle and the **Museo Nacional de Antropología** (see the Museums and Galleries section). The Castillo itself was built in 1785 as a summer retreat for the Spanish Viceroy and is the former residence of Emperor Maximilian and later President Porfirio Diaz. The park is also home to the Museo Nacional de Historia and the city zoo.

El Templo Mayor: Located just off the Zocalo.
Next to the Cathedral lie the remains of the Aztec Templo Mayor or Teocalli, which were discovered in 1978. The Aztecs built a new temple every 52 years and 7 have been identified on top of each other. Although the ruins convey little of the magnificence of the original Temple a museum at the site gives detailed information as to its original status.

Museums and Galleries

Museo Nacional de Antropología: Located in Chapultepec Park, off Paseo de la Reforma, Mexico City, Distrito Federal.
Tel: (0)5 553-1902. Open every day except Mondays.

One of the world's great museums with arguably the finest collection of ancient American artefacts in the world. Opened in 1964 the museum is housed in an impressive and spacious building designed especially for the collection with exhibition halls surrounding a central patio. The wealth of the range of exhibits is staggering with some 5 km of exhibits.

Arguably the jewel in the museum's collection is the remarkable Piedra del Sol, the Aztec calendar stone. Rediscovered in 1790 in the Zocalo it was left against the walls of the city Cathedral before being exhibited.

Museo de Arte Moderno (Museum of Modern Art): Paseo de la
Reforma y Gandhi, Bosque de Chapultepec. Tel: 553-6233.
Fax: 553-6211.
Web site: www.arts-history.mx/museos/mam
Open Tuesday to Sunday from 10·00–18·00.
The Museum of Modern Art is located in the Chapultepec Woods
and is housed in a striking building finished in 1964. The collection
consists of works from nearly all the major Mexican artists of the last
century including Orozco, Rivera, Siqueiros, Kahlo, Dr. Atl,
Castellanos, Revueltas, Tamayo and Rodrigues Lozano.

Museo de Templo Mayor: Downtown, on Seminario, near the
Cathedral, Mexico City, Distrito Federal. Tel: (0)5 542-0606.
Housing the archaeological finds from the Templo Mayor (the former
great temple of the Aztecs) excavations the museum displays
numerous Aztec artefacts. The sculpture of Coyolxauhqui dominates
the collection, the finding of which prompted the rest of the
excavations.

Palacio de las Bellas Artes: Located at Lázaro Cárdenas between
Juárez and Hidalgo, Mexico City, Distrito Federal.
Mexico's premier cultural complex is home to important Mexican
paintings and murals as well as the National Symphony Orchestra,
the Ballet Folklorico, visiting orchestras and international exhibitions.
Housed in a magnificent white building with stunning art-deco
interiors it contains works by several major Mexican artists. The
centre was refurbished inside and out in 1994 to celebrate its
diamond jubilee. The theatre contains a glass curtain designed by
Tiffany. It is raised and lowered before each performance of the
Ballet Folklorico de Mexico.

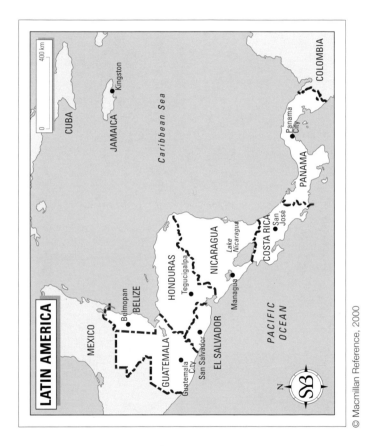

LATIN AMERICA

MEXICO

BELIZE
Belmopan

GUATEMALA
Guatemala
City

EL SALVADOR
San Salvador

HONDURAS
Tegucigalpa

NICARAGUA
Managua

Lake
Nicaragua

COSTA RICA
San
José

PANAMA
Panama
City

COLOMBIA

CUBA

JAMAICA
Kingston

Caribbean Sea

*PACIFIC
OCEAN*

N

SYB

0   400 km

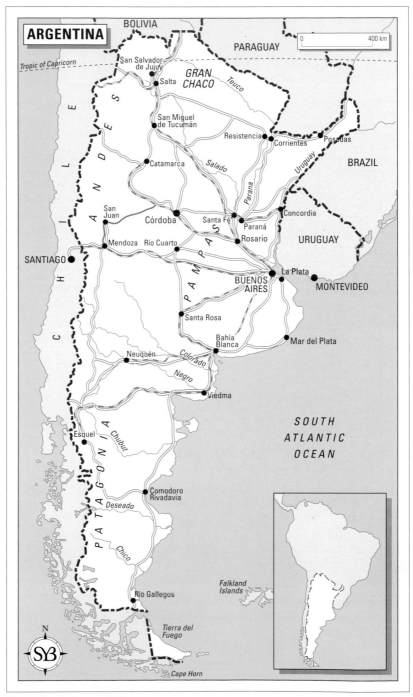

ARGENTINA

BOLIVIA

PARAGUAY

0 400 km

Tropic of Capricorn

San Salvador de Jujuy

GRAN CHACO

Teuco

Salta

San Miguel de Tucumán

Resistencia

Corrientes

Posadas

BRAZIL

Catamarca

Salado

Uruguay

A N D E S

Paraná

San Juan

Córdoba

Santa Fé

Concordia

Paraná

Mendoza

Río Cuarto

Rosario

URUGUAY

SANTIAGO

P A M P A S

La Plata

BUENOS AIRES

MONTEVIDEO

C H I L E

Santa Rosa

Bahía Blanca

Mar del Plata

Neuquén

Colorado

Negro

Viedma

SOUTH ATLANTIC OCEAN

Esquel

Chubut

P A T A G O N I A

Comodoro Rivadavia

Deseado

Chico

Falkland Islands

Río Gallegos

N

Tierra del Fuego

SYB

Cape Horn

© Macmillan Reference, 2000

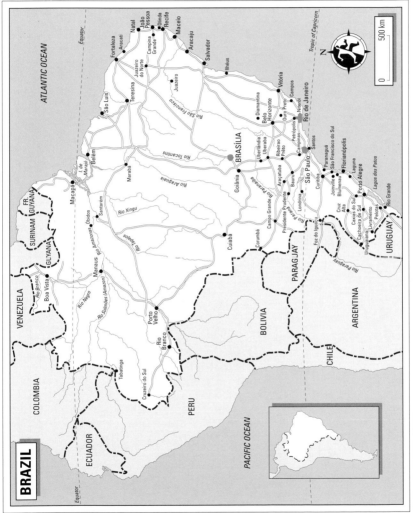

BRAZIL

ATLANTIC OCEAN

Equator

Natal
João Pessoa
Recife
Olinda
Maceió
Campina Grande
Aracaju
Salvador
Ilhéus
Fortaleza
Aracati
Juazeiro do Norte
Juazeiro
Teresina
São Luís
Belém
I. de Marajó
Macapá
Santarém
Óbidos
Rio Xingu
Cuiabá
Corumbá
Campo Grande
Presidente Prudente
Araçatuba
Bauru
Londrina
Foz do Iguaçu
Rio Tocantins
Rio Araguaia
Goiânia
Marabá
BRASÍLIA
Uberlândia
Uberaba
Ribeirão Preto
Campinas
Santos
São Paulo
Curitiba
Paranaguá
Joinville
Blumenau
São Francisco do Sul
Florianópolis
Laguna
Porto Alegre
Lagoa dos Patos
Rio Grande
Cruz Alta
Caxias do Sul
Cachoeira do Sul
Pelotas
Uruguaiana
Livramento
URUGUAY
Diamantina
Belo Horizonte
Ouro Preto
Vitória
Campos
Niterói
Rio de Janeiro
Petrópolis
Rio São Francisco
Rio Paranaíba
Rio Paraná

Rio Branco
Boa Vista
VENEZUELA
FR. GUYANA
SURINAM
GUYANA
COLOMBIA
ECUADOR
Tabatinga
Cruzeiro do Sul
Rio Branco
Porto Velho
Manaus
Rio Amazonas
Rio Negro
Rio Solimões (Amazon)
Rio Madeira
PERU
BOLIVIA
PARAGUAY
Rio Paraguay
ARGENTINA
CHILE

PACIFIC OCEAN

Equator
Tropic of Capricorn

N

0   500 km

© Rough Guides, 2000

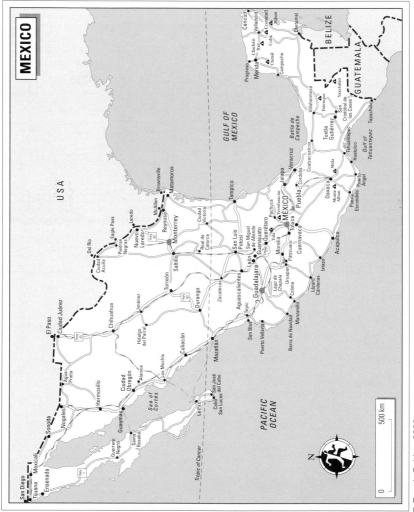

MEXICO

© Rough Guides, 2000

500 km

Theatre and Opera

Opera Nacional: Palacio de Bellas Artes, Av. Hidalgo 1, Mexico City, DF 06050. Tel: (0)5 521-3668.
Mexico's premier opera house can hold up to 1,750 spectators. Also the venue for the Ballet Folklorico (see section in Museums and Galleries).

Teatro de la Ciudad: Donceles 36. Tel: (0)5 510-2197.
Houses the Ballet Folklorico Nacional Aztlan.

Auditorio Nacional (National Auditorium): Reforma 50, Mexico City.
Tel: (0)5 280-9243. Fax: (0)5 280-9979.
One of the largest concert halls in the city.

Teatro de la Danza, Unidad Artistica y Cultural del Bosque: Paseo de la Reforma and Campo Marte, next to Auditorio Nacional.
Tel: (0)5 280-8771.
Offers contemporary dance programmes.

SOCIAL STATISTICS

Statistics for calendar years:

	Births	Deaths	Marriages	Divorces
1995	2,750,444	430,278	658,114	37,455
1996	2,707,718	436,321	670,523	38,545
1997	2,698,425	440,437	707,456	40,792

Rates per 1,000 population, 1997: births, 28·1; deaths, 4·6. In 1996 the most popular age range for marrying was 20–24 for both males and females. Infant mortality was 29 per 1,000 live births in 1997. Life expectancy at birth in 1997 was 69·5 years for males and 75·5 years for females. Annual growth rate, 1990–95, 1·8%. Fertility rate, 1997, 2·8 births per woman.

Statistics Offices

INEGI National Headquarters: Av. Heroe de Nacozari Sur núm. 2301, Edif. de Atencion a Usarios, Fracc. Jardines del Parque, CP 20270, Aguascalientes, Ags., Mexico.

Tel: (0)4 918-1948. Fax: (0)4 918-0739. Web site: www.inegi.gob.mx

Instituto Nacional de Estadistica, Geografia e Informatica (National Institute of Statistics, Geography and Information).

CLIMATE

Latitude and relief produce a variety of climates. Arid and semi-arid conditions are found in the north, with extreme temperatures, whereas in the south there is a humid tropical climate, with temperatures varying with altitude. Conditions on the shores of the Gulf of Mexico are very warm and humid. In general, the rainy season lasts from May to Nov. Mexico City, Jan. 55°F (12·6°C), July 61°F (16·1°C). Annual rainfall 30" (747 mm). Guadalajara, Jan. 59°F (15·2°C), July 69°F (20·5°C). Annual rainfall 36" (902 mm). La Paz, Jan. 64°F (17·8°C), July 85°F (29·4°C). Annual rainfall 6" (145 mm). Mazatlán, Jan. 66°F (18·9°C), July 82°F (27·8°C). Annual rainfall 33" (828 mm). Mérida, Jan. 72°F (22·2°C), July 83°F (28·3°C). Annual rainfall 38" (957 mm). Monterrey, Jan. 58°F (14·4°C), July 81°F (27·2°C). Annual rainfall 23" (588 mm). Puebla de Zaragoza, Jan. 54°F (12·2°C), July 63°F (17·2°C). Annual rainfall 34" (850 mm).

CONSTITUTION AND GOVERNMENT

A new Constitution was promulgated on 5 Feb. 1917 and has been amended from time to time. Mexico is a representative, democratic and federal republic, comprising 31 states and a federal district, each state being free and sovereign in all internal affairs, but united in a federation established according to the principles of the Fundamental Law. The head of state and supreme executive authority is the *President*, directly elected for a non-renewable 6-year term.

There is complete separation of legislative, executive and judicial powers (Art. 49). Legislative power is vested in a General Congress of 2 chambers, a *Chamber of Deputies* and a *Senate*. The Chamber of Deputies consists of 500 members directly elected for 3 years, 300 of them from single-member constituencies and 200 chosen under a system of proportional representation. In 1990 Congress voted a new Electoral Code. This establishes a body to organize elections (IFE), an electoral court (TFE) to resolve disputes, new electoral rolls and introduce a voter's registration card. Priests were enfranchised in 1991.

The Senate comprises 128 members, 4 from each state and 4 from the federal district, directly elected for 6 years. Members of both chambers are not immediately re-eligible for election. Congress sits from 1 Sept. to 31 Dec. each year; during the recess there is a permanent committee of 15 deputies and 14 senators appointed by the respective chambers.

National Anthem

'Mexicanos, al grito de guerra' ('Mexicans, at the war-cry'); words by F. González Bocanegra, tune by Jaime Nunó.

RECENT ELECTIONS

At the presidential and parliamentary elections of Aug. 1994 the electorate was 45·7m. Ernesto Zedillo was elected President by 48·77% of votes cast against 2 opponents. In the Chamber of Deputies 277 of the single-member seats were won by the Institutional Revolutionary Party (PRI) and 27 by proportional representation (PR); 18 by the Party of National Action (PAN) and 101 by PR; 5 by the Revolutionary Democratic Party (PRD) and 66 by PR; and 10 by the Workers' Party (PT), all by PR.

Elections were held on 6 July 1997 for the Chamber of Deputies, 32 members of the Senate, 6 State Governors and the Mayor of Mexico City. In the Chamber of Deputies PRI gained 239 seats, PRD 125, PAN 122, the Ecology Party 8 and the Labour Party 6. Following the election the composition of the Senate was: PRI, 77 seats; PAN, 33; PRD, 13. The PRI gained 4 State Governorships and the PAN 2. This was the first time the PRI had lost its overall majority in the lower house, but the PRI continues to govern Mexico, as it has for over 70 years, making it the current ruling party to have been the longest time in power continuously anywhere in the world.

After the elections of Aug. 1994, the party composition of the Senate was: PRI, 95; PAN, 25; PRD, 8. The PRI won 60 seats and the FDN 4 seats.

The next presidential and parliamentary elections are to take place on 2 July 2000.

CURRENT ADMINISTRATION

President: Ernesto Zedillo Ponce de León, b. 1952 (PRI; sworn in 1 Dec. 1994).

In Jan. 2000 the government comprised:
Minister of Government, Secretary of the Interior: Diódoro
Carrasco Altamirano. *Foreign Relations:* Rosario Green. *Defence:*
Gen. Enrique Cervantes Aguirre. *Naval Affairs:* Adm. José Ramón
Lorenzo Franco. *Finance and Public Credit:* José Angel Gurría
Treviño. *Social Development:* Carlos Jarque Uribe. *Comptroller-
General:* Arsenio Farell Cubillas. *Energy:* Luis Téllez Kuenzler.
Trade and Industry: Herminio Blanco Mendoza. *Agriculture, Rural
Development and Livestock:* Romarico Arroyo Marroquin.
Communication and Transport: Carlos Ruiz Sacristán. *Education:*
Miguel Limón Rojas. *Health:* José Antonio Gonzalez Fernandez.
Labour and Social Welfare: Mariano Palacios Alcocer. *Agrarian
Reform:* Eduardo Robledo Rincon. *Tourism:* Oscar Espinosa
Villarreal. *Fishing, Environment and Natural Resources:* Julia
Carabias Lillo. *Attorney-General:* Jorge Luis Madrazo Cuéllar.

POLITICAL PROFILES

Ernesto Zedillo (1951–)

Ernesto Zedillo has been the President of the United States of Mexico
since 1 Dec 1994. The candidate of the PRI party, he was elected
President as an unprecedented 78% of registered voters
participated in the election.

   He was born in Mexico City on 27 Dec. 1951 but grew up in
Mexicali, Baja California. A graduate of Mexico's public school
system, Mr Zedillo returned to Mexico City aged 14 and enrolled at
age 18 at the Advanced School of Economics at the Instituto
Politécnico Nacional, where he received his bachelor's degree in
economics in 1972. Mr Zedillo studied at Bradford, England and
earned Master's and Ph.D. degrees in economics from Yale

University, where he studied the issue of public indebtedness in Mexico and its link to future growth of petroleum exports.

From 1978 Mr Zedillo engaged in economic research and analysis at the Banco de Mexico. He became widely recognized as one of the main proponents of economic modernization policies. It was at the Banco de Mexico that Mr Zedillo established the Exchange Risk Coverage Trust Fund (FICORCA), the agency that made it possible to restructure the debt of many Mexican companies in the early 1980s.

From 1988 to 1992, Mr Zedillo served as Secretary of Programming and Budget. In this post, he formulated the National Development Plan and prepared the federal expenditure budgets for the fiscal years 1989 to 1992. He became Secretary of Public Education in 1992 and began a thorough reform of pre-school, primary and secondary education in Mexico. He initiated the decentralization of the nation's educational system and developed special education programmes for Mexico's less-developed areas.

Mr Zedillo is married to Mrs Nilda Patricia Velasco. They have 5 children.

Diódoro Carrasco (1954–)

Diódoro Carrasco is the Mexican Secretary of the Interior.

Mr Carrasco was born in Oaxaca on 30 Jan. 1954. He received a degree in economics from the Instituto Tecnologico Autonomo de Mexico (ITAM), and has held various positions within Mexico's Public Administration. These include those of assistant Director of Programming at the General Department of Agro-Industrial Development at the Department of Agriculture and Water Resources (SARH), General Assistant Director of Agro-Industrial Planning at SARH, Private Secretary to the Assistant Secretary of Industrial and Commercial Planning at SECOFI (the Department of Commerce and Industrial Development), Secretary of Planning at the state government of Oaxaca, and Assistant Government Secretary at the Department of the Interior.

Mr Carrasco has also been President of the Asociación Nacional de Economistas at the Department of Agriculture and Water Resources (ANESARH), a board member of the ANESARH Advisory Council, Foreign Secretary at the Board of Directors of the Colegio Nacional de Economistas and Vice President of the Colegio Nacional de Economistas. Mr Carrasco is married to Clara Scherer Castillo, with whom he has 3 children.

Rosario Green

Professor Rosario Green became Mexico's Secretary for Foreign Relations on 7 Jan. 1998.

She obtained a bachelor's Degree in International Relations from the Political and Social Sciences Department of the Universidad Nacional AutoNumber de Mexico. Having received a Master's in Economics from the Centro de Estudios Economicos of the Colegio de Mexico she continued her graduate studies at Columbia University in New York, specialising in International Economics and Latin American Problems.

Upon finishing at Columbus University she took a course to specialize in Latin American Integration at the Instituto para la Integración de Latinoamerica (INTAL) in Buenos Aires. Since 1968 she has been a professor and researcher at the Colegio de Mexico and has published 9 books, 3 of which have been translated into English, and more than 50 articles.

Professor Green has held the positions of First Secretary of the Mexican Foreign Service to the United Nations agencies in Geneva from 1972–74, consultant to the Department of Foreign Relations from 1976–77, Advisor to the Centre for Third World Economic and Social Studies from 1979–89 and Associate Director of the magazine "Foro Internacional", published by the Colegio de Mexico. She is a founding member of the Mexican Academy of Human Rights and, since 1983, also heads the Matias Romero Institute of Diplomatic Studies. During 1989 she served as Director of the International Affairs Commission of the National Executive Committee of the Partido Revolucionario Institucional (PRI). She was appointed Mexican Ambassador to Germany in Oct. 1989 and Executive Secretary for Latin America, Cultural Affairs and International Cupertino for the Department of Foreign Relations in Mexico in June 1990.

Enrique Cervantes Aguirre (1935–)

Enrique Cervantes Aguirre is Mexico's Secretary for National Defence.

He was born in Puebla in 1935 and obtained first place in his age group at the Ecuela Superior de Guerra (Higher School of War) in Command and Joint Chiefs of Staff.

He obtained first place during the promotional selections from Lieutenant to Lieutenant Colonel and was later made Colonel due to professional merit, aptitude and ability. He was given the rank of Brigadier General in 1978, Brigade General in 1980 and Division General in 1982.

In addition to his military career he has been Private Secretary to the Secretary for National Defence, Director of the Heroico Colegio Militar (Heroic Military School), commander of various military zones and regions and, until Nov. 1994, General Director of National Defence Factories.

Abroad he has been Military and Air Attaché to the Mexican Embassy in Washington, D.C. and was decorated for military merit in 1976 for his campaign against the planting, cultivation and trafficking of narcotics in the State of Guerrero.

José Angel Gurría Treviño (1950–)

José Angel Gurría Treviño became the Secretary of the Department of the Treasury and Public Credit in Mexico on 5 Jan. 1998.

He was born on 8 May 1950 in Tampico, Tamaulipas. Having graduated in Economics from the Universidad Nacional Autonoma de Mexico he studied for a Masters Degree in Public Finances from the University of Leeds in the UK. He took a course in Financial Administration at Harvard University and another in International Relations at the University of Southern California.

His career in public service began in 1968, as an analyst in the international department of the Comision Federal de Electricidad (Federal Electricity Commission). In addition he has been Private Secretary to the General Director of National Financiera, Permanent Mexican Delegate to the International Coffee Organisation, General Director of Public Credit and member of the negotiating team for the external debt, Under-secretary at the Department of the Treasury and Public Credit, one of the major negotiators for the financial chapter of NAFTA, General Director of the Banco Nacional de Comercio Exterior and General Director of Nacional Financiera. He was appointed Secretary of Foreign Relations in 1994.

He is the author of several books and essays on external debt and was awarded the Legion of Honour by the French Government.

LOCAL GOVERNMENT

Mexico is divided into 31 states and a Federal District. The latter is co-extensive with Mexico City and is administered by a Governor directly elected for a 6 year term. Each state has its own constitution, with the right to legislate and to levy taxes (but not inter-state customs duties); its Governor is directly elected for 6 years and its unicameral legislature for 3 years; judicial officers are appointed by the state governments. Mexico City is sub-divided into 16 districts and the 31 states into 2,428 municipalities.

DEFENCE

In 1997 defence expenditure totalled US$3,755m. (US$39 per capita).

Army

Enlistment into the regular army is voluntary, but there is also one year of conscription (4 hours per week) by lottery. Strength of the regular army (1999) 130,000 (60,000 conscripts). There are combined reserve forces of 300,000. In addition there is a rural defence militia of 14,000.

Navy

The Navy is primarily equipped and organized for offshore and coastal patrol duties. It includes 3 destroyers and 6 frigates. The naval air force, 1,100 strong, operates 9 combat aircraft.

Naval personnel in 1999 totalled 37,000, including the naval air force and 10,000 marines.

Air Force

The Air Force had (1999) a strength of about 11,770 with over 125 combat aircraft, including F-5Es, and 95 armed helicopters.

INTERNATIONAL RELATIONS

Mexico is a member of the UN (and most UN System organizations), OAS, Inter-American Development Bank, LAIA, ACS, APEC, WTO, NAFTA and OECD.

ECONOMY

The Mexican economy has changed markedly in the last 20 years. The number of state-owned enterprises has fallen from more than 1,000 in 1982 to fewer than 200 in 1998. Privatization and competition has been encouraged and has seen success in the oil, electricity and telecommunications fields. Trade with the USA and Canada has nearly doubled since the introduction of NAFTA (the North American Free Trade Agreement) in 1994. Recently, however, the economy has been set back by a series of international economic shocks. Economic uncertainty mounts considerably during election periods and the 1994 campaign resulted in the depreciation of the peso by 76% between Dec 1994 and May 1995. A strong export sector, however, has helped to cushion the economy's decline in 1995 and was the major force behind its recovery in 1996 and 1997. In the last 3 years real GDP growth has averaged more than 5% a year and has helped job creation. In 1998 the international financial crisis and the fall in oil prices, which account for 30% of government revenues, caused the peso to depreciate and required successive tightenings of macro-economic policies to preserve confidence and curb the deterioration of the external balance. This approach proved broadly successful in preserving confidence and protecting the real economy.

The Brazilian crisis unsettled the financial markets again in Jan. 1999. Although the impact on Mexico was much less severe than after the Russian crisis and was quickly reversed, the external environment remains uncertain. The outlook for 2000 is somewhat more hopeful. Barring new major shocks growth could pick up again. However, unless international financial markets settle down durably and the peso strengthens, monetary policy will have to remain tight to put the country back on a deflationary path. Inflation control holds the promise of a reasonably rapid return to economic growth and rising living standards.

Income distribution is still very unequal with the top 20% of income earners accounting for 55% of income. Despite this the government's recent handling of the economy has drawn IMF praise. Stanley Fischer, First Deputy Managing Director of the IMF, stated that the 'Directors commended the authorities for their pursuit of sound economic policies and structural reforms, which have restored confidence and set the stage for sustainable growth' as a result of which 'the resilience of the Mexican economy has increased'. However, he also cautioned that 'the Mexican economy remains vulnerable to shocks. The continued fragility of the banking system is a major weakness'. Perhaps the most positive sign is that the Zedillo government's economic caution and spending stringency has lent them new credibility and public confidence, which can only aid the development of the Mexican economy.

Agriculture accounted for 5% of GDP in 1997, industry 26% and services 69%.

Policy

An economic programme for 1995 aimed to reduce inflation and provided tax concessions to stimulate investment. After the peso was devalued in Dec. 1994 an emergency economic plan was introduced to include an agreement between labour and employers to contain inflation, a fiscal adjustment to reduce the current account deficit, further privatization of infrastructural enterprises and the establishment of an international assistance fund. In 1997 the economy grew by 7% and 800,000 new jobs were created. An economic programme to attack 'the roots of poverty' was announced.

Performance

Real GDP grew by 5·1% in 1996 (in 1995 it had contracted by 6·2%), by 6·9% in 1997 and by 4·7% in 1998. For 1999 growth of 2·9% has been forecast.

Budget

In 1996 revenue was 392,566m. new pesos; expenditure, 372,874m. new pesos.

Currency

The unit of currency is the *Mexican peso* (MXP) of 100 *centavos*. A new peso was introduced on 1 Jan. 1993: 1 new peso = 1,000 old pesos. The peso was devalued by 13·94% in Dec. 1994. Foreign exchange reserves were US$28,469m. in Feb. 1998 and gold reserves were 170,000 troy oz. The annual inflation rate, which in 1995 was over 50%, was 18·6% in 1998. For 1999 a rate of 13% has been forecast. Total money supply in Jan. 1998 was 261,132m. new pesos.

Banking and Finance

The Bank of Mexico, established 1 Sept. 1925, is the central bank of issue (*Governor*, Guillermo Ortíz Martínez). It gained autonomy over monetary policy in 1993. Exchange rate policy is determined jointly by the bank and the Finance Ministry. Banks were nationalized in 1982, but in May 1990 the government approved their reprivatization. The state continues to have a majority holding in foreign trade and rural development banks. Foreign holdings are limited to 30%. There were 23 banks in 1993; deposits were 4,500,000m. old pesos in 1992.

There is a stock exchange in Mexico City.

Major Banks

Banco Santander Mexicano: Boulevard Manuel Avila Camacho Num. 170, Colonia Lomas de San Isidro, 11620 Mexico, D.F.

A financial holding company whose main holding is Banco Mexicano, a Mexican Bank with assets of over 70bn. pesos.

Banamex Accival (BANACCI): Juárez, Mexico F.D. 06600.

Tel: (0)5 225-3000. Fax: (0)5 225-6140. Web site: www.banamex.com

BANACCI is a holding company which owns over 99% of the share capital of Banco Nacional de Mexico (BANAMEX), the former federal bank of Mexico.

BANCOMER: Av. Universidad 1200, Delegación Benito Juárez, Mexico D.F.

Tel: (0)5 621-3434. Fax: (0)5 621-5054.

Web site: www.bancomer.com.mx

Offers commercial, corporate, mortgage, consumer and private banking services.

BANORTE: Edificio-Sur Gran Plaza, Zaragoza, 920, 64000 Monterray N.L. Tel: (0)8 319-7200. Fax: (0)8 319-5235.

Web site: www.gfnorte.com.mx

Operates over 425 branches throughout Mexico and several representative offices abroad.

Multibanco Mercantil Probursa: Bvld. Adolfo Lopez Mateos 2448, Altavista, 01060 Mexico, D.F. Tel: (0)5 723-7999.

Bank, owned by the holding company Probursa, which accounts for 4% of the Mexican market with 37 branches in 23 cities.

Multibanco Comermex: Bosque de Ciruelos 120, Piso 4, 11700 Mexico D.F.

Tel: (0)5 229-2271. Fax: (0)5 229-2036.

Banca Serfin: Prolongación Paseo de la Reforma No 500, Colonia Lomas de Santa Fe, 01219 Mexico D.F. Tel: (0)5 662-0200.

Web site: www.serfin.com.mx

Stock Exchange

The Mexican Stock Exchange (**Bolsa Mexicana de Valores**) is a private institution governed by the Mexican Securities Market Act. Any foreign individual can invest in Mexican securities listed on the Bolsa Mexicana de Valores directly through authorized Mexican brokerage firms or through the acquisition of American Depository Receipts (ADRs) in the USA. ADRs are negotiable receipts for the securities of a foreign company which allow Americans to trade the foreign securities in the United States while accruing any dividends and capital gains.

The Mexican Stock Exchange has approximately 250 issuers of paper with an index of only 40 companies that are actively traded. There is also an intermediate market of issuers which tends to be narrow and not actively traded.

Chambers of Commerce

British Chamber of Commerce: Rio de la Plata No.30, 06500 Mexico City-D.F. Tel: (0)5 256-0901. Fax: (0)5 211-5451.

Canadian Chamber of Commerce: Tel: (0)5 525-0741.

German Chamber of Commerce: Tel: (0)5 251-4022.

US Chamber of Commerce: Tel: (0)5 377-0628 or 377-4464.

US-Mexico Chamber of Commerce: United States Trade Center, Ron Brown 100, Liverpool 31, Col. Juárez, 06600 Mexico, D.F. Tel: (0)5 140-2670. Fax: (0)5 535-2545.
Web site: www.usmcoc.org

Weights and Measures

The metric system is legal.

ENERGY AND NATURAL RESOURCES

Environment

Mexico is currently facing several environmental challenges. Large areas of the tropical forests in the south and southeast of the country have been denuded for cattle and agriculture. For instance, the tropical forests that once covered nearly half of the state of Tabasco now cover less than 10%. This deforestation has led to large-scale soil erosion. In 1985 the government classified 17% of all land as having been totally eroded with even greater amounts partially eroded or showing signs of eroding. More than 60% of land in the north and northwest is partially or totally eroded, leading to a major desertification problem throughout the region.

Mexico's oil industry has also caused serious environmental problems. The waters and fisheries of Rio Coatzacoalcos have been badly damaged by badly regulated local petroleum exploitation. In 1992, 190 people were killed and another 1,500 injured by an oil industry related explosion in an area of Guadalajara.

The problem of urban pollution is arguably Mexico's most pressing environmental issue. Due to Mexico City's location, in a valley surrounded by mountains, contaminates produced by the city's industry, transport and domestic needs, become easily trapped. It is estimated that carbons and hydrocarbons from the regions 3m. vehicles account for around 80% of all contaminants. A study of 12 international urban areas found that Mexico City's residents had the highest levels of lead and cadmium in their blood.

Government environmental policy has mainly centred on limiting vehicle pollutants. Some initiatives, such as emission inspections and the introduction of unleaded petrol and catalytic converters have helped to reduce toxic emissions. The government's No Driving Day programme has proved less successful. The scheme, whereby residents are prohibited from driving one day a week depending on the last number on their licence plate, was undermined by wealthier residents purchasing second cars with appropriate licence plates thus increasing the overall number of vehicles in the region.

Electricity

Installed capacity, 1995, 32,737 MW. Output in 1996 was 145·7bn. kWh. Consumption per capita in 1996 was 1,754 kWh.

Oil and Gas

Crude petroleum production was 1·13bn. bbls. in 1998 (3·1m. bbls. a day). Mexico produced 4·9% of the world total oil output in 1996, and had reserves amounting to 50bn. bbls. in 1998. Natural gas output, 1996, 118·8m. cu. metres.

Minerals

Output, (in 1,000 tonnes) 1996: lead, 167·1; copper, 328·0; zinc, 348·3; gypsum, 3,758·9; silica, 1,424·8; fluorite, 524·66; iron, 6,109·5; sulphur, 921·3; manganese, 173·4; barite, 470·0; graphite, 40·4; silver, 2·54; gold, 24,083 kg; coal, 8,779·5; feldspar, 140·0. Mexico is the biggest producer of silver in the world.

Agriculture

In 1997 Mexico had 25·2m. ha of arable land and 2·10m. ha of permanent cropland. There were 6·5m. ha of irrigated land. There were 172,000 tractors and 19,500 harvester-threshers in 1997. In 1997 agriculture contributed 5% of GDP. Some 60% of agricultural land belongs to about 30,000 *ejidos* (with 15m. members), communal lands with each member farming his plot independently. *Ejidos* can now be inherited, sold or rented. A land-titling programme (PROCEDE) is establishing the boundaries of 4·6m. plots of land totalling 102m. ha. Other private farmers may not own more than 100 ha of irrigated land or an equivalent in unirrigated land. There is a theoretical legal minimum of 10 ha for holdings, but some 60% of private farms were less than 5 ha in 1990. Laws abolishing the *ejido* system were passed in 1992.

Sown areas, 1995 (in 1,000 ha) included: maize, 9,082; beans, 2,367; sorghum, 1,592; wheat, 964; cotton-seed, 297; barley, 272; soya, 151; safflower, 107; rice, 90.

Production in 1995 (in 1,000 tonnes): wheat, 3,468; rice (washed), 367; beans, 1,271; soya, 190; barley, 487; maize, 18,353; sorghum, 4,170; cotton-seed, 369; grapes, 550; apples, 427; oranges, 3,922; lemons, 961; mangoes, 1,088; pineapples, 229 (1994); bananas, 2,069; melons, 404; watermelons, 402; avocado pears, 787.

Livestock (1996): cattle, 28·14m.; sheep, 5·9m.; pigs, 18m.; goats, 9·0m.; horses, 6·25m.; mules, 3·28m.; assess, 3·25m.; chickens, 386m. Meat production, 1994 (in 1,000 tonnes): beef, 1,364·7; pork, 807·5; goat meat, 40·1; sheep meat, 31·4. Dairy production, 1995 (in tonnes): milk, 7,537,647; eggs, 1,241,987; honey, 49,228; wool, 4,045.

Forestry

Forests extended over 55·39m. ha in 1995, representing 29% of the land area (down from 57·93m. ha in 1990), containing pine, spruce, cedar, mahogany, logwood and rosewood. There are 14 forest reserves (nearly 0·8m. ha) and 47 national park forests of 0·75m. ha. Timber production was 23·21m. cu. metres in 1997.

Fisheries

Total catch, 1997, 1,489,020 tonnes (approximately 92% sea fish).

INDUSTRY

In 1996 the manufacturing industry provided 18·7% of GDP. Output in 1996 (in 1,000 tonnes): petrol, 16,975; cement, 28,168; crude iron,

6,109; crude steel, 5,867; aluminium, 95·8; copper, 328; lead, 167·1; zinc, 348·3; wheat flour, 1,835; butter, 34; passenger cars (units), 782,743; lorries, 429,843. Car production in particular has benefited from membership of NAFTA. Production has increased from 600,000 in 1993 to approaching 1·5bn. in 1999.

Top 20 Companies

Rank	Company	Market Capital ($1m.)
1	Telefonos de México	17,653·5
2	Cifra	5,962·2
3	Televisa	4355·0
4	Kimberly Clark Mexico	3,274·4
5	Cemex	3,264·8
6	Empresas La Moderna	2,683·6
7	Grupo Ind Bimbo	2,651·0
8	Grupo Carso	2,536·0
9	Femsa	2,521·8
10	Carso Global Telecom	2,176·8
11	Grupo Fin Inbursa	2,029·3
12	El Puerto de Liverpool	1,677·7
13	Grupo Mexico	1,650·9
14	Grupo Fin Banamex-Accl	1,598·9
15	Grupo Ind Alfa	1,506·7
16	Soriana	1,433·3
17	Grupo Modelo	1,432·8
18	Desc	1,228·5
19	Penoles	1,223·1
20	Seguros Comercial-America	1,195·5

Labour

In 1996 the workforce was 24,063,283 (5,644,588 female). The daily minimum wage at the end of 1998 was 40 new pesos. Registered unemployment rate, 1998, 3·2% (1997, 4·3%).

Trade Unions

The Mexican Labour Congress (CTM) is incorporated into the Institutional Revolutionary Party, and is an umbrella organization numbering some 5m. An agreement, 'Alliance for Economic Recovery', was reached in Nov. 1995 between the government, trade unions and business, providing for an increase in the minimum wage of 10·1%, increased unemployment benefits, tax incentives, the staggering of price increases, and a commitment to reduce public spending. A breakaway from CTM took place in 1997 when rebel labour leaders set up the National Union of Workers (UNT) to combat what they saw as a sharp drop in real wages.

Other major union federations include the **Confederación Regional de Obreros Mexicanos** (Regional Confederation of Mexican Workers), the **Confederación Revolucionaria de Obreros y Campesinos** (the Revolutionary Confederation of Mexican Workers and Peasants), the **Federación Nacional de Sindicatos Independientes** (the National Federation of Independent Unions) and the **Federación de Sindicatos de Trabajadores al Servicio del Estado** (the Federation of Unions of Workers in the Service of the State). 90% of all industrial employers that employ more than 25 workers belong to trade unions.

Confederación de Trabajadores de México: Vallarta No.8, Piso 3, México D.F. 06030.
Tel: (0)5 350-658. Fax: (0)5 705-0966.
The body to which most Mexican unions are affiliated.

INTERNATIONAL TRADE

In Sept. 1991 Mexico signed the free trade Treaty of Santiago with Chile, envisaging an annual 10% tariffs reduction from Jan. 1992. The North American Free Trade Agreement (NAFTA), between Canada, Mexico and the USA, was signed on 7 Oct. 1992. A free trade agreement was signed with Costa Rica in March 1994. Some 8,300 products were freed from tariffs, with others to follow over 10 years. The Group of Three (G3) free trade pact with Colombia and Venezuela, came into effect 1 Jan. 1995. Total foreign debt was US$149,690m. in 1997, a figure exceeded only by Brazil.

Imports and Exports

Trade for calendar years in US$1m.:

	1994	1995	1996	1997	1998
Imports	79,346	72,453	89,469	78,814	91,852
Exports	60,882	79,542	96,030	80,716	86,671

Of total imports in 1996, 75·4% came from USA, 4·4% from Japan, 3·5% from Germany and 0·8% from UK.

Of total exports in 1997, 85% went to USA, 4·8% to Latin America, 2% to Canada, 1·1% to Japan, 1·0% to Spain, 0·6% to UK. In 1998 exports to the USA accounted for 21% of GDP.

The in-bond (*maquiladora*) assembly plants along the US border generate the largest flow of foreign exchange. Manufactured goods account for 90% of trade revenues.

COMMUNICATIONS

Roads

Total length, 1996, was estimated at 252,000 km, of which
6,740 km were motorways, 45,600 km were main roads, 63,500 km
were secondary roads and 136,000 km other roads. In 1996 there
were 8,607,000 passenger cars, 4,287,000 trucks and vans,
139,000 buses and coaches and 270,000 motorcycles and
mopeds.

Rules of the Road

Driving is on the right in Mexico. Mileage and speed limits are given
in km with 100 kph (62 mph) and 80 kph (50 mph) most common—
although some of the newer toll roads allow 110 kph (68·4 mph). In
urban areas the speed limit can be as low as 20 kph (12 mph). The
best-kept roads in Mexico are the toll roads (Cuota) which mostly
cover the last stretches of major highways (carreteras) leading to
Mexico City.

To reduce smog and traffic congestion the strictly enforced 'Un
Dia Sin Auto' law has been introduced. The law prohibits any
privately-owned vehicle to be used on one designated weekday.
During emergency smog-alert months (usually Dec. and Jan.) the
prohibition rises to two days a week. The rule is applied to all private
vehicles and is specified by the last number of the licence plate (look
for 'Hoy no Circula' notices to find out which).

A circle with a diagonal line across the letter E means no parking
and any illegally parked cars are either towed or their licence plates
removed.

Rail

International rail connections can be made with Mexico from any city
in the USA or Canada. Domestically Mexico has a good and
extensive rail network linking all the main towns and cities.

The National Railway, *Ferrocarriles Nacionales de Mexico*, was split into 5 companies in 1996 as a preliminary to privatization. It comprises 20,445 km of 1,435 mm gauge (246 km electrified). In 1996 it carried 59·1m. tonnes of freight and 6m. passengers. There is a 178 km metro in Mexico City. There are light rail lines in Guadalajara (48 km) and Monterrey (35 km).

Civil Aviation

There are 4 main international airports in Mexico:

Mexico City (MEX) is located 13 km south of the city. There is a regular bus service to and from the city centre.

Guadalajara (GDL) is located 20 km southeast of the city. There are regular buses and taxis to and from the city centre.

Acapulco (ACA) is located 26 km southeast of the city. There are coaches and taxis to the city centre.

Monterrey (MTY) is located 24 km northeast of the city. There are regular coaches and taxis to and from the city centre.

The national carriers are Aeromexico, Mexicana, Taesa, Aerocalifornia and Aerolíneas Internacionales, with Aeromexico and Mexicana, both privatized in the late 1980s, being the main ones. In 1996 Aeromexico carried 6,852,800 passengers and Mexicana 6,367,200 passengers. In 1998 services were also provided by Aeroejecutivo, Aeroflot, Aerolíneas Argentinas, Aeroperú, Air France, Alitalia, America West Airlines, American Airlines, Austrian Airlines, Aviacsa, Avianca, Aviateca, British Airways, Canadian Airlines International, City Bird, Condor Flugdienst, Continental Airlines, COPA, Cubana, Delta Air Lines, Ecuatoriana, Iberia, JAL, KLM, LACSA, Lan-Chile, Lloyd Aéreo Boliviano, LTU International Airways,

Lufthansa, Northwest Airlines, SAS, Servivensa, Swissair, Taca International Airlines, TAESA, Transportes Aeromar, United Airlines and Varig. In 1996 Mexico City handled 16,265,384 passengers (10,955,196 on domestic flights) and 114,080 tonnes of freight. Cancun was the second busiest airport for passengers in 1996, with 5,095,589 (3,718,318 on international flights) and Guadalajara the second busiest for freight, with 18,210 tonnes.

Shipping

Mexico has 49 ocean ports, of which, on the Gulf coast, the most important include Coatzacoalcos, Ciudad del Carmen (Campeche), Tampico, Veracruz and Tuxpan. On the Pacific Coast are Salina Cruz, Isla de Cedros, Guaymas, Santa Rosalia, Manzanillo, Lázaro Cárdenas and Mazatlán. It was announced in 1992 that ports would be privatized.

Merchant shipping loaded 139·5m. tonnes and unloaded 62m. tonnes of cargo in 1996. In 1995 the merchant marine had a total tonnage of 1·55m. GRT, including oil tankers, 0·71m. GRT, and container ships, 0·14m. GRT.

Telecommunications

Telmex, previously a state-controlled company, was privatized in 1991. It controls about 98% of all the telephone service. In 1993 Telmex inaugurated a US$30bn. modernization programme. In 1994 the US company Microwave Communications announced plans to collaborate with the financial group Banamex-Accival in constructing a new long-distance telephone network in Mexico valued at US$1bn. This high level of growth in the telecommunications industry stems from the increase in US-Mexican telephone communications resulting from NAFTA.

There were 9,253,700 telephone main lines in 1997, or 96 for every 1,000 persons. Mobile phone subscribers numbered 1,747,000 in

1997, and there were 3,600,000 PCs (37 per 1,000 population) and 285,000 fax machines. In Nov. 1997 there were approximately 370,000 Internet users.

IDD is extensively available although long distance calls are expensive. Most major hotels have fax facilities.

Postal Services

Airmail to Europe takes on average 6 days. Surface mail is slow. There is an immediate delivery service within Mexico City that takes 2 or 3 days.

There were 7,382 post offices in 1995, equivalent to 1 for every 12,300 persons.

SOCIAL INSTITUTIONS

Justice

Magistrates of the Supreme Court are appointed for 6 years by the President and confirmed by the Senate; they can be removed only on impeachment. The courts include the Supreme Court with 21 magistrates, 12 collegiate circuit courts with 3 judges each and 9 unitary circuit courts with 1 judge each, and 68 district courts with 1 judge each.

The penal code of 1 Jan. 1930 abolished the death penalty, except for the armed forces.

There were 15,596 murders in 1995 (a rate of 17·2 per 100,000 population).

Religion

In 1998 an estimated 89·6% of the population was Roman Catholic. The Church is separated from the State, and the constitution of 1917

provided strict regulation of this and all other religions. In Nov. 1991
Congress approved an amendment to the 1917 constitution
permitting the recognition of churches by the state, the possession of
property by churches and the enfranchisement of priests. Church
buildings remain state property. Diplomatic relations with the Vatican
were established in Sept. 1992. In 1998 there were estimated to be
3·67m. Protestants, plus followers of various other religions.

In recent years evangelical Protestant churches have seen a rapid
expansion in their membership, growing from 1·8% of the population
in 1970 to 4·9% in 1990. This expansion has been led by congrega-
tions affiliated with churches such as the Assemblies of God, the
Seventh Day Adventists, the Church of Jesus Christ of Latter Day
Saints (Mormons) and Jehovah's Witnesses. Mormon membership
has risen from 248,000 in 1980 to 811,000 in 1998. Evangelical
growth was especially strong in southeastern Mexico. In addition
there are smaller numbers of followers of various other religions.

Education

Adult literacy was 90·1% in 1997 (male, 92·3%; female, 87·9%).
Primary and secondary education is free and compulsory, and
secular, although religious instruction is permitted in private schools.
In 1996–97 there were:

	Establishments	Teachers	Students (in 1,000)
Pre-school	63,319	146,247	3,238·3
Primary	95,855	524,922	14,650·5
Secondary	24,402	275,331	4,809·3
Vocational training	4,710	27,543	498·8
Professional	1,900	36,131	383·8
Higher education	1,786	142,952	1,329·7
Postgraduate education	860	12,674	94·3

In 1994–95 in the public sector there were 36 universities, 1
technical institute and 3 specialized universities (1 agricultural;
2 pedagogical). In the private sector there were 48 universities,
1 institute of technical and higher educational studies, 1 women's
university and 1 technical university.

In 1994 total expenditure on education came to 5·8% of GNP.

Health

In 1993 there were 1,539 hospitals, with a provision of 10 beds per
10,000 population. In 1994 there were 146,021 doctors, 5,612
government-employed dentists and 166,644 government-employed
nurses.

Health Requirements

There are no required inoculations for Mexico but it is worth checking
in advance of travel that you are up to date with polio, tetanus,
typhoid and hepatitis A jabs. The most likely medical problem visitors
will encounter is diarrhoea (or Montezuma's Revenge as it is known
amongst travellers in Mexico) against which there are no reliable
preventative measures. Most cases should pass within 24–48 hours;
any longer and it is advisable to visit a doctor. The main advice is to
consume considerable amounts of water with rehydration salts in
order to replace lost fluid and body salts.

Malaria is endemic in much of Mexico. Any area over 1,000 metres
above sea level is malaria free; this includes Mexico City, Cancun,
Cozumel, Isla Mujeres and the beach resorts of the Baja and Pacific
coasts. The most dangerous places are low-lying, inland areas. The
risk of infection comes from mosquito bites and can be avoided
through careful use of repellents and protective clothing at night.

Unprotected sex in Mexico carries the risk of AIDS, although it is
no more prevalent than in most other countries. Reported cases are,
unsurprisingly, mostly located in Mexico City.

Welfare

In 1997 there were 11·28m. workers insured as permanent benefi-
ciaries with the Social Security Institute.

CULTURE

Broadcasting

There are over 1,500 stations licensed by the Dirección General de
Concesiones y Permisos de Telecomunicaciones. Most carry the
'National Hour' programme. Television services are provided by the
recently privatized Televisión Azteca and Azteca Televisa. There
were 30m. radio receivers in 1996 and 24·2m. TV sets (colour by
NTSC) in 1997.

Radio

Mexico has a large number of commercial radio networks, which
dominate the private commercial sector. Half of all stations are
controlled by the 5 largest networks: the **Grupo Acir**, which controls
140 stations, **Organización Impulsora de Radio (OCR)**, **Agentes de
Radio y Televisión (ARTSA)**, and **Mexico Radio Programs**. In all in 1993
there were over 700 commercial medium-wave and a further
22 short-wave stations. There are several state-run networks
including the **Instituto Mexicano de la Radio (IMER)**, **Radio México**
and **Exact Time Radio**.

Television

The majority of the 326 television stations in Mexico in 1995 were
owned by or affiliated with the Telesistema Mexicano (**Televisa**) or the
state-run Instituto Mexicano de Televisión (**Imevisión**). Televisa was
considered to be the largest communications conglomerate in the
developing world and although a private company is linked to the

ruling PRI. As well as its 3 Mexican television networks it also owns 4 stations in the USA.

Imevisión runs 2 national television networks and several regional and specialised channels. In addition the government runs **Televisión de la Republica Mexicana** which broadcasts news and educational programmes to rural areas. The main competition to Televisa is **Televisión Azteca**, an extensive communications operation that is responsible for 179 stations in 2 national networks. The television network **Televisión Independiente** operates 7 stations. In 1996 there were 800 television transmitters in Mexico with an average of 1 television set per 8·9 viewers.

Cinema

In 1995 there were 1,495 cinemas and 63m. admissions.

Press

In 1995 there were 310 daily newspapers with a circulation of 10,500,000, equivalent to 115 per 1,000 inhabitants.

Major titles include:

La Cronica de Hoy: Rio Hudson 25, colonia Cuauhtemoc, CP 06500, Mexico City. Tel: (0)5 286-1378.

Web site: www.cronica.com.mx

El Economista: Av. Coyoacan 515, Col. Del Valle 03100, Mexico City. Tel: (0)5 326-5454. Fax: (0)5 687-3821.

Web site: www.economista.com.mx

Weekday economic tabloid specializing in financial news. Daily circulation of 28,000.

Excelsior: E-mail: buzon@excelsior.com.mx

Web site: www.excelsior.com.mx

El Financiero: Lago Bolsena 176, Col. Anahuac, C.P.11320.
Tel: (0)5 227-7600/01.
Web site: www.elfinanciero.com.mx

El Heraldo: Dr Carmona y Valle 150, C.P.06720, Mexico City.
Tel: (0)5 578-7022.
Fax: (0)5 578-9824.
E-mail: heraldo@iwm.com.mx Web site: www.heraldo.com.mx

La Jornada: Francisco Petrarca 118, Chapultepec Morales,
delegación Miguel Hidalgo, Mexico City 11570. Tel: (0)5 262-4300.
Fax: (0)5 262-4356.
Web site: www.unam.netgate.mx/jornanda
  National paper, often critical of government policy.

El Norte: Web site: www.elnorte.infosel.com
  Monterrey based newspaper with a daily circulation of 130,000
and a Sunday circulation of 160,000.

El Sol de México: Guillermo Prieto 7, 2o. Piso, Col. San Rafael,
C.P.06470, Mexico City.
Tel: (0)5 566-1511. Fax: (0)5 566-1511. E-Mail: solmex@oem.com.mx
Web site: www.oem.com.mx/solmex

El Universal: E-mail: comenta@aguila.el-universal.co.mx
Web site: www.aguila.el-universal.com.mx

Tourism

There were 19.3m. tourists in 1997, putting Mexico 8th in the world
list; gross revenue, including border visitors, amounted to
US$7,593m.

Tourist Organizations

Fondo Nacional de Fomento al Turismo (FONATUR): 22nd Floor, Insurgentes Sur 800, Colonia del Valle, 03100 Mexico City. Tel: (0)5 687-2697. Fax: (0)5 687-5052.

The official government tourist board is **SECTUR:** Web site: www.mexico-travel.com

Visas

All EU, Australian, Canadian, American and Japanese visitors require a passport valid up to 6 months from the date of entry and a tourist card to visit Mexico for tourist purposes for up to 180 days. Tourist cards can be issued by any Mexican consulate, on board the plane or at any point of entry in Mexico free of charge. For business visitors a Business Visitors Card is required from a Mexican consulate or Embassy.

Festivals

Jan: **Feast of the Epiphany:** Nationwide celebration when children are traditionally given presents.

Feb–March: **Carnival:** Celebrated throughout Mexico. Traditionally the last week for taking one's pleasures before the 40 day abstinence of Lent.

March–April: **Holy Week:** (Semana Santa): Observed throughout the country. Still a deeply religious festival in Mexico, most shops and services close for the week.

July 24–31: **Guelaguetza Dance Festival:** An Oaxacan affair that dates from pre-Columbian times.

Oct: **October Festivals:** A month of cultural and sporting events in Guadalajara.

Oct–Nov: **International Cervantes Festival:** A major cultural event in Guanajuato that attracts dancers, singers and actors from a number of different countries.

Nov 2: **Day of the Dead:** When Mexicans remember the departed with skulls made of sweets sold on street corners and picnics eaten in cemeteries.

Nov–Dec: **National Silver Fair:** An annual Taxco event in which silver is exhibited and sold.

Dec: **Festival of the Radishes:** Local farmers compete to produce the best or biggest radish; others make radish carvings and exhibit them.

Dec 12: **Feast Day of the Virgin of Guadeloupe:** The day on which Mexico's patron saint is feted with processions and native folk dances, particularly at her shrine in Mexico City.

Dec 25: **Christmas:** Still a deeply religious festival in Mexico. Presents are usually not given until Jan 6 (Epiphany).

Public Holidays 2000

1 Jan.	New Year's Day.
5 Feb.	Constitution Day.
21 March	Birthday of Benito Juárez.
21–24 April	Easter.
1 May	Labour Day.
5 May	Anniversary of the Battle of Puebla.
15–16 Sept.	Independence Day.
12 Oct.	Discovery of America (Columbus Day).
1 Nov.	All Saints' Day.
2 Nov.	All Souls' Day—Day of the Dead.
20 Nov.	Anniversary of the Mexican Revolution of 1910.
12 Dec.	Day of our Lady of Guadeloupe.
25 Dec.	Christmas Day.

Social Etiquette

Most European courtesies are current in Mexico. Handshaking is the usual form for greeting and departing. Personal relationships are very important to Mexicans and invade all aspects of their lives from religion to work. Friendship should be established in most dealings with Mexicans and it should be remembered that they are not afraid to display their emotions. Time is a relative thing in Mexico. The present drives out the future and, perhaps because of the instability of their history, most Mexicans live for the moment. Although punctuality is respected it is by no means strictly adhered to. Showing impatience is seen as childish and looked down upon.

Attempts at Spanish from non-native speakers are always appreciated by the Mexicans. Mistakes are tolerated and the attempt will earn their respect. Normal clothing is casual throughout the country unless in unusually formal circumstances. It is advisable, however, not to wear T-shirts and shorts in big cities as this only advertises your status as a tourist. Service is rarely included in restaurant or hotel bills and a tip of 15–20% is expected.

Doing Business in Mexico

To conduct successful business in Mexico the expert management of cultural differences is vital. Although the business culture is not dissimilar to that of the USA and western Europe there are important differences in the way that Mexicans conduct their business relationships which need to be understood.

Mexican businessmen and women, like Mexicans in general, feel a need to establish a warm relationship with those that they wish to do business with. The person must be considered to be simpatico, as having a warm and likeable personality, if negotiations are to succeed. To conduct any negotiations in a cold, businesslike manner will label you as antipatico, as being impersonal and aloof. Because of this it is vital not to assume negotiations and discussing business are one and the same thing. It is important to establish good relations during the warm-up period before the main substance of the business is discussed.

There is a strong cultural and historical emphasis on single, strong personalities in Mexican life. This is illustrated by the dominance of strong political leaders in Mexico who are followed for their personal nature rather than any ideology they adhere to. Similarly in Mexican business it is likely that there will be a single decision-maker involved in negotiations rather than a committee of various businessmen with different specialities. It is important to identify this figure so as to appeal to his way of thinking as early as possible.

Trust is a key feature of the way Mexicans do business and it should be remembered that Mexicans are all too wary of being taken advantage of by more powerful foreign influences. This can be traced to a national history of European domination and North American intervention. When conducting business it is a good idea to demonstrate your recognition that you are negotiating on a level playing field.

It is important not to end negotiations that appear to be failing in an abrupt manner. Mexicans prefer discussions to fade out rather than end suddenly as a gradual end within a simpatico relationship gives them a chance to come back at some point if circumstances change. The feeling that business has ended sharply and coldly would remove any willingness to do this. Because of this presenting a 'this is the final offer' attitude is likely to jeopardise any future business opportunities. Similarly most Mexicans are suspicious of definite agreements and documents at the end of negotiations which offer them no flexibility. This is due to the greater change and uncertainty that exists in their economy. For them the real substance of the negotiations lies in the quality of the business relationship that has been established. If the relationship is good a sense of trust will be considered to have been created which will go a long way to guaranteeing fair and successful future business.

DIPLOMATIC REPRESENTATIVES

Of Mexico in Great Britain (42 Hertford Street, London W1Y 7TF)
  Ambassador: Santiago Oñate Laborde.
Of Great Britain in Mexico (Rio Lerma 71, Col. Cuauhtémoc, 06500
Mexico City, D.F.)
  Ambassador: A. C. Thorpe, CMG.
Of Mexico in the USA (1911 Pennsylvania Ave., NW, Washington,
D.C., 20006)
  Ambassador: Jesús Reyes Heroles.
Of the USA in Mexico (Paseo de la Reforma 305, México City 5, D.F.)
  Ambassador: Jeffrey Davidow.
Of Mexico to the United Nations
  Ambassador: Manuel Tello.
Of Mexico to the European Union
  Ambassador: Armendariz Etchegaray.

FURTHER READING

Instituto Nacional de Estadística, Geografía e Informática. *Anuario
  Estadístico de los Estados Unidos Mexicanos. Mexican Bulletin of
  Statistical Information.* Quarterly.
Aspe, P., *Economic Transformation: the Mexican Way.* Cambridge
  (MA), 1993
Bailey, J. J., *Governing Mexico: The Statecraft of Crisis Management.*
  London and New York, 1988
Bartra, R., *Agrarian Structure and Political Power in Mexico.* Johns
  Hopkins Univ. Press, 1993
Bazant, J., *A Concise History of Mexico.* CUP, 1977
Bethell, L. (ed.) *Mexico since Independence.* CUP, 1992

Camp, R. A., *Politics in Mexico.* 2nd ed. OUP, 1996

Grayson, G. W., *Oil and Mexican Foreign Policy.* Univ. of Pittsburgh Press, 1988

Hamilton, N. and Harding, T. F., (eds.) *Mexico: State, Economy and Social Conflict.* London, 1986

Krauze, E., *Mexico, Biography of Power: A History of Modern Mexico, 1810–1996.* London, 1997

Philip, G., (ed.) *Politics in Mexico.* London, 1985.—*The Presidency in Mexican Politics.* London, 1991.—*Mexico.* [Bibliography] 2nd ed. ABC-Clio, Oxford and Santa Barbara (CA), 1993

Riding, A., *Distant Neighbours.* London, 1985.—*Mexico: Inside the Volcano.* London, 1987

Robbins, N. C., *Mexico.* [Bibliography] ABC-Clio, Oxford and Santa Barbara (CA), 1984

Rodríguez, J. E., *The Evolution of the Mexican Political System.* New York, 1993

Ruíz, R. E., *Triumphs and Tragedy: a History of the Mexican People.* New York, 1992

Whiting, V. R., *The Political Economy of Foreign Investment in Mexico: Nationalism, Liberalism, Constraints on Choice.* Johns Hopkins Univ. Press, 1992

National statistical office: Instituto Nacional de Estadística, Geografía e Informática (INEGI), Aguascalientes.

Website: http://www.inegi.gob.mx/

BELIZE

Capital: Belmopan
Population estimate, 2000: 242,000

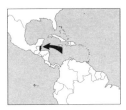

KEY HISTORICAL EVENTS

From the 17th century, British settlers, later joined by British soldiers
and sailors disbanded after the capture of Jamaica from Spain in
1655, governed themselves under a form of democracy by public
meeting. A constitution was granted in 1765 and, with some
modification, continued until 1840 when an executive council was
created. In 1862 what was then known as British Honduras was
declared a British colony with a legislative assembly and a Lieut.-
Governor under the Governor of Jamaica. The administrative
connection with Jamaica was severed in 1884. Universal suffrage
was introduced in 1964 and thereafter the majority of the legislature
were elected rather than appointed. In June 1974 British Honduras
became Belize. Independence was achieved on 21 Sept. 1981 and a
new constitution introduced.

TERRITORY AND POPULATION

Belize is bounded in the north by Mexico, west and south by
Guatemala and east by the Caribbean. Fringing the coast there are 3
atolls and some 400 islets (cays) in the world's second longest
barrier reef (140 miles) which was declared a world heritage site in
1997. Area, 22,963 sq. km.

There are 6 districts as follows, with area, population estimates and chief city:

District	Area (in sq. km)	Population 1994	Chief City	Population 1996
Corozal	1,860	31,412	Corozal	8,020
Belize	4,307	62,939	Belize City	52,670
Orange Walk	4,636	33,855	Orange Walk	14,960
Cayo	5,196	41,594	San Ignacio	11,315
Stann Creek	2,554	19,957	Dangriga	6,435[1]
Toledo	4,413	19,243	Punta Gorda	3,458[1]

[1]1991 figure.

Population (1996 census, est.), 219,296; density, 10 per sq. km.

The UN gives a projected population for 2000 of 242,000.

In 1997 an estimated 53·6% of the population were rural. The proportion of the population considered as rural had been 52·5% in 1990. No other country saw such a considerable percentage swing away from urbanization over the same period. In 1995 some 45,000 Belizeans were working abroad.

The capital is Belmopan (1996 population, 6,490).

English is the official language. Spanish is widely spoken. At the 1996 census (est.) the main ethnic groups were Mestizo (Spanish-Maya), 44%; Creole (African descent), 30%; Mayans, 11%; and Garifuna (Caribs), 7%.

SOCIAL STATISTICS

1996 births, 7,200; deaths, 1,250. In 1996 (est.) the birth rate per 1,000 was 32·8 and the death rate 5·7; infant mortality in 1997 was

35 per 1,000 births and there were 1,138 marriages. Life expectancy in 1997 was 73·4 years for males and 76·1 for females. Fertility rate, 1997, 3·7 children per woman.

CONSTITUTION AND GOVERNMENT

The Constitution, which came into force on 21 Sept. 1981, provided for a National Assembly, with a 5-year term, comprising a 29-member *House of Representatives* elected by universal suffrage, and a *Senate* consisting of 8 members, 5 appointed by the Governor-General on the advice of the Prime Minister, 2 on the advice of the Leader of the Opposition and 1 on the advice of the Belize Advisory Council.

RECENT ELECTIONS

At the general election of 27 Aug. 1998 the opposition People's United Party (PUP) won 26 seats with 59·4% of the votes cast against just 3 for the ruling United Democratic Party (UDP). Turn-out was 78·1%.

CURRENT ADMINISTRATION

Governor-General: Sir Colville Young, GCMG, b. 1932 (sworn in 17 Nov. 1993).

The cabinet in Jan. 2000 comprised as follows:

Prime Minister and Minister of Finance and Foreign Affairs: Said Musa (PUP), b. 1944 (sworn in 28 Aug. 1998).
Senior Minister: George Price.
Deputy Prime Minister, Minister of Natural Resources, Environment and Industry: John Briceno. *Budget Planning, Economic Development, Investment and Trade:* Ralph Fonseca. *Health, Civil Society, Labour and Public Services:* José Coye. *Agriculture, Fisheries and Co-operatives:* Daniel Silva. *Public Utilities, Energy and Communications:* Maxwell Samuels. *Education and Sports:* Cordel Hyde. *Housing, Urban Renewal and Home Affairs:* Richard "Dickie" Bradley. *Rural Development and Culture:* Marcial Mes. *Women's Affairs and Human Development:* García Balderamose Oolores. *National Co-ordination and Mobilization:* Ruben Campos. *National Security and Immigration:* Jorge Espat. *Information:* Godfrey Smith.

The *Speaker* is B. Q. Pitts.

DEFENCE

The Belize Defence Force numbers 1,050 (1999) with a reserve militia of 700. There is an Air Wing and a Maritime Wing.

In 1998 defence expenditure totalled US$16m. (US$70 per capita).

ECONOMY

Performance

Real GDP growth was 3·4% in 1998 (4·4% in 1997).

Budget

The 1997 budget (forecast) had revenues of $B283·36m. and
expenditure of $B362·26m.

Currency

The unit of currency is the *Belize dollar* (BZD) of 100 *cents*. Since
1976 $B2 has been fixed at US$1. Total money supply was $B170m.
in Feb. 1998. There was deflation of 0·7% in 1998 following inflation of
1·0% in 1997. Foreign exchange reserves in Feb. 1998 were US$54m.

Banking and Finance

A Central Bank was established in 1981 (*Governor*, Keith Arnold). There
were (1993) 4 commercial banks of which 2 were locally owned, and a
Government Savings Bank. The Development Finance Corporation
provides long-term credit for development of agriculture and industry.
Amendments to the Banking Ordinance permit offshore banking.

INDUSTRY

Manufacturing is mainly confined to processing agricultural products
and timber. There is also a clothing industry. Sugar production was
110,500 tonnes in 1996; molasses, 46,500 (1995).

Labour

The labour market alternates between full employment, often accom-
panied by local shortages in the citrus and sugarcane harvesting
(Jan.–July), and under-employment during the wet season
(Aug.–Dec.), aggravated by the seasonal nature of the major industries. In 1996 the labour force totalled 73,000 (78% males), of whom
13% were unemployed.

INTERNATIONAL TRADE

Imports and Exports

In 1996 imports amounted to US$256m., exports US$168m. Main exports are sugar and molasses, citrus products, clothes, fish products and bananas. Main imports are machinery and transport equipment, basic manufactures, and food and live animals.

Main export markets in 1995: UK (42·4%), USA (36·6%), Germany (5·2%) and Canada (4·3%). Main import suppliers in 1995 were USA (54·1%), Mexico (11·0%), UK (6·3%), Netherlands (5·8%).

BOLIVIA

República de Bolivia
Capital: Sucre
Seat of government: La Paz
Population estimate, 2000: 8·33m.

KEY HISTORICAL EVENTS

Bolivia was part of the Inca Empire until conquered by the Spanish in
the 16th century. Independence was won and the Republic of Bolivia
was proclaimed on 6 Aug. 1825. During the first 154 years of its
independence, Bolivia had 189 governments, many of them installed
by *coups*. In the 1960s the Argentinian revolutionary and former
minister of the Cuban government, Ernesto 'Che' Guevara, was killed
in Bolivia while fighting with a left-wing guerrilla group. In 1971,
Bolivian instability reached a peak with the brief establishment of a
revolutionary Popular Assembly during the regime of Gen. Torres.
Later repression under Gen. Hugo Banzer took a heavy toll on the
left-wing parties. Banzer was followed by a succession of military-led
governments until civilian rule was restored in Oct. 1982 when Dr
Siles Zuazo became president. He introduced a period of economic
reform embracing free markets and open trade.

TERRITORY AND POPULATION

Bolivia is a landlocked state bounded in the north and east by Brazil,
south by Paraguay and Argentina, and west by Chile and Peru, with
an area of some 424,165 sq. miles (1,098,581 sq. km). A coastal strip
of land on the Pacific passed to Chile after a war in 1884. In 1953
Chile declared Arica a free port and Bolivia has certain privileges
there.

Population estimate, 1998: 7,949,933 (60·3% urban); density, 6·9 per sq. km.

The UN gives a projected population for 2000 of 8·33m.

Area and population of the departments (capitals in brackets) at the 1992 census and as estimated in 1998:

Departments	Area (sq. km)	Census 1992	Estimate 1998
La Paz (La Paz)	133,98	1,900,786	2,313,877
Cochabamba (Cochabamba)	55,631	1,110,205	1,445,990
Potosí (Potosí)	118,218	645,889	755,895
Santa Cruz (Santa Cruz)	370,621	1,364,389	1,703,901
Chuquisaca (Sucre)	51,524	453,756	562,917
Tarija (Tarija)	37,623	291,407	379,704
Oruro (Oruro)	53,588	340,114	386,980
Beni (Trinidad)	213,564	276,174	346,180
Pando (Cobija)	63,827	38,072	54,489
Total	1,098,581	6,420,792	7,949,933

Population (1993 estimates, in 1,000) of the principal towns: La Paz, 785; Santa Cruz, 767; Cochabamba, 449; El Alto, 446; Oruro, 202; Sucre, 145; Potosí, 123.

Spanish is the official and commercial language. The Amerindian languages Aymará and Quechua are spoken exclusively by 22% and 5·2% of the population respectively; Tupi Guaraní is also spoken.

SOCIAL STATISTICS

The population growth rate has been estimated at 2·3% for the years 1995–2000; in 1996 births totalled an estimated 258,000 (birth rate of

34·0 per 1,000 population); deaths totalled an estimated 71,000 (rate, 9·4 per 1,000); infant mortality (1997), 69 per 1,000 live births, the highest in South America. Expectation of life was 61·65 years in 1998. Fertility rate, 1997, 4·4 children per woman, also the highest in South America.

CONSTITUTION AND GOVERNMENT

Bolivia's first constitution was adopted on 19 Nov. 1826. The *President* is elected by universal suffrage for a 5-year term. If 50% of the vote is not obtained, the result is determined by a secret ballot in Congress amongst the leading 2 candidates. The President appoints the members of his Cabinet. There is a bicameral legislature; the *Senate* comprises 27 members, 3 from each department, and the *Chamber of Deputies* 130 members, all serving terms of 5 years. A constitutional amendment of 1996 introduced direct elections for 65 deputies; the remainder are nominated by party leaders. Voting is compulsory.

RECENT ELECTIONS

Presidential and parliamentary elections were held on 1 June 1997. The electorate was 3·2m. Gen. Hugo Banzer Suárez (ADN) gained 22·3% of the votes cast, and Juan Carlos Durán Saucedo (MNR) 17·7%. As no candidate gained an absolute majority, Congress elected Gen. Hugo Banzer Suárez President on 4 Aug. 1997.

In elections to the 130 seat National Congress, the Nationalist Democratic Alliance (ADN) won 33 seats (22·3% of the vote), the Nationalist Revolutionary Movement (MNR) 26 seats (17·7%), the Movement of the Revolutionary Left (MIR) 25 (16·7%), the Citizens'

Solidarity Union (UCS) 21 (15·9%), Conscience of the Fatherland (Condepa) 17 (15·9%), the United Left (IU) 4 (3·7%) and Movement Free Bolivia (MBL) 4 (2·5%). ADN won 13 of the 27 available seats in the Chamber of Deputies, MNR 3, MIR 6, UCS 2 and Condepa 3. Presidential and parliamentary elections are scheduled for June 2002.

CURRENT ADMINISTRATION

President: Gen. Hugo Banzer Suárez, b. 1926 (ADN; sworn in 6 Aug. 1997).

Vice-President: Jorge Quiroga (ADN).

The Cabinet was composed as follows in Jan. 2000:

Foreign Affairs and Worship: Dr Javier Murillo de la Rocha. *Finance:* Herbert Muller Costas. *Economic Development:* José Luis Lupo Flores. *Sustainable Development and Planning:* Erick Alberto Reyes Villa. *Presidency:* Franz Ondarza Lineres. *Health:* Guillermo Cuentas. *Defence:* Jorge Crespo Velasco. *Government:* Walter Guiteras Dennis. *Labour and Microbusiness:* Luis Vasquez Villamor. *Justice and Human Rights:* Carlos Alberto Subirana. *Education, Culture and Sports:* Tito Hoz de Vila. *Housing and Basic Services:* Ruben Poma Rojas. *International Trade and Investment:* Carlos Saavedra Bruno. *Agriculture:* Oswaldo Antezana Vaca Diez. *Information:* Jorge Landivar Roca.

Parties represented: Acción Democrática Nacionalista/National Democratic Alliance (ADN), Movimiento de Izquierda Revolucionaria/Movement of Revolutionary Left (MIR), Unidad Cívica Solidaridad/Citizens' Solidarity Union (UCS), Conciencia de Patria/Conscience of the Fatherland (CONDEPA), Nueva Fuerza Republicana/New Republican Force (NFR).

DEFENCE

There is selective conscription for 12 months at the age of 18 years. There has been optional pre-military training for high school pupils since 1998.

In 1998 defence expenditure totalled US$147m. (US$17 per capita).

ECONOMY

Performance

Real GDP growth was 4·5% in 1998.

Budget

In 1m. bolivianos:

	1993	1994	1995	1996	1997
Revenue	3,993	4,446	5,256	6,565	7,467
Expenditure	5,876	6,400	6,802	8,720	9,490

Currency

The unit of currency is the *boliviano* (BOB) of 100 *centavos*, which replaced the *peso* on 1 Jan. 1987 at a rate of 1 boliviano = 1m. pesos. Inflation was an annualized 4·4% in 1998. Foreign exchange reserves were US$903m. in Feb. 1998 and gold reserves 940,000 troy oz. Total money supply was 5,692,000 bolivianos in Dec. 1997.

Banking and Finance

The Central Bank (*Governor*, Juan Antonio Morales) is the bank of issue. In 1998 there were 14 commercial banks operating, including

5 foreign and 8 specialized development banks.
There are stock exchanges in La Paz and Santa Cruz.

INDUSTRY

At the 1992 census there were 14,389 factories employing a total of
76,718 persons. The principal manufactures are foodstuffs and
tobacco, and textiles.

Labour

Out of 1,256,000 people in employment in 1995, 348,000 were in
wholesale and retail, 231,000 in manufacturing, 106,000 in
construction and 95,000 in transport, storage and communications.
The unemployment rate in 1995 was 3·6%. In 1998 the minimum
wage was 300 bolivianos a month.

INTERNATIONAL TRADE

Imports and Exports

The value of imports and exports in US$1m.

	1992	1993	1994	1995	1996	1997
Imports	1,130·50	1,176·95	1,196·35	1,433·59	1,656·61	1,909·36
Exports	742·07	786·71	1,091·00	1,139·07	1,216·19	1,255·64

Main exports, 1996 (in US$1m.): soya beans, 201; zinc, 151; gold,
119; natural gas, 94; jewellery, 88; timber, 83; tin, 83. Main import
commodities are road vehicles and parts, machinery for specific

industries, cereals and cereal preparations, general industrial machinery, and iron and steel.

Main export markets, 1996: USA, 26·1%; EU (especially UK, Germany and Belgium), 22·3%; Argentina, Peru and Colombia, 39·3%. Main import suppliers: Brazil, Argentina and Chile, 36·8%; EU (Germany, Belgium and Italy), 36·8%; Japan, 12%.

CHILE

República de Chile
Capital: Santiago
Population estimate, 2000: 15·21m.

KEY HISTORICAL EVENTS

Magellan sighted what is now Chile in 1520. Subsequently Spaniards colonized the land in the 1530s and 1540s, defeating the Incas in the north and subjugating the Araucanian Indians in the South. In 1810 the Republic of Chile threw off allegiance to the Spanish crown. However, there were seven years of fighting before Chile was recognized as an independent republic. A constitution was adopted in 1883, and the country enjoyed stable government. In 1925 the constitution was amended to strengthen the executive at the expense of the legislature. In 1970 Dr Salvador Allende Gossens was elected president as the Marxist leader of a left-wing coalition. This government was overthrown in 1973 by a military junta headed by Gen. Augusto Pinochet Ugarte. President Allende died in the course of the *coup* and tens of thousands of his supporters were murdered. A new constitution came into force on 11 March 1981 providing for a return to democracy. Gen. Pinochet continued as head of state until 1989 and army commander until March 1998 when he claimed his constitutional right to become a senator for life (and hence immune from prosecution). While clearing the way for much-needed economic reforms, the Pinochet regime was responsible for wholesale human rights abuses, a legacy which had its consequences in 1999 when Pinochet, in Britain for medical treatment, was held on human rights charges instigated by Spain.

TERRITORY AND POPULATION

Chile is bounded in the north by Peru, east by Bolivia and Argentina, and south and west by the Pacific Ocean. The area is 736,905 sq. km (284,520 sq. miles) excluding the claimed Antarctic territory. Many islands to the west and south belong to Chile: the Islas Juan Fernández (179 sq. km with 516 inhabitants in 1982) lie about 600 km west of Valparaíso, and the volcanic Isla de Pascua (Easter Island or Rapa Nui, 118 sq. km with 1,867 inhabitants in 1982), lies about 3,000 km west-northwest of Valparaíso. Small uninhabited dependencies include Sala y Goméz (400 km east of Easter Is.), San Ambrosio and San Félix (1,000 km northwest of Valparaíso, and 20 km apart) and Islas Diego Ramírez (100 km southwest of Cape Horn).

In 1940 Chile declared, and in each subsequent year has reaffirmed, its ownership of the sector of the Antarctic lying between 53° and 90° W. long., and asserted that the British claim to the sector between the meridians 20° and 80° W. long. overlapped the Chilean by 27°. Seven Chilean bases exist in Antarctica. A law of 1955 put the governor of Magallanes in charge of the 'Chilean Antarctic Territory' which has an area of 1,269,723 sq. km. and a population (1982) of 1,368.

The population at the census of 1992 was 13,231,803 (6,730,478 females). Estimate, 1997, 14,656,200 (84·2% urban in 1997; 7,416,500 females in 1997); density, 20 per sq. km.

The UN gives a projected population for 2000 of 15·21m.

Area, population and capitals of the 13 regions:

Region	Sq. km	Population (1992 census)	Capital	Population (1992 census)
Tarapacá	58,786	341,112	Iquique	152,654
Antofagasta	125,253	407,409	Antofagasta	226,749
Atacama	74,705	230,786	Copiapó	100,946
Coquimbo	40,656	502,460	La Serena	120,336

Valparaíso	16,396	1,373,967	Valparaíso	276,736
Metropolitan	15,549	5,170,293	Santiago	5,180,757[1]
Libertador	16,456	688,385	Rancagua	187,134
Maule	30,518	834,053	Talca	171,467
Bíobío	36,939	1,729,920	Concepción	330,448
Araucanía	31,946	774,959	Temuco	240,880
Los Lagos	67,247	953,330	Puerto Montt	130,737
Aysén	108,997	82,071	Coihaique	31,167[2]
Magallanes	132,034	143,058	Punta Arenas	113,661

[1]Metropolitan area; city proper, 4,385,481. [2]1982 census.

Other large towns (1992 census population) are: Viña del Mar (302,765), Puente Alto (254,534), Talcahuano (246,566), San Bernardo (188,850), Arica (169,217), Chillán (158,731), Los Angeles (142,136), Osorno (128,709), Coquimbo (122,872), Valdívia (122,436), Calama (120,602), Curicó (103,919) and Quilpué (102,824). 79% of the population is mixed or mestizo, 20% are of European descent and 1% are indigenous Amerindians of the Araucanian, Fuegian and Chango groups. Language and culture remain of European origin, with the 675,000 Araucanian-speaking (mainly Mapuche) Indians the only sizeable minority.

The official language is Spanish.

SOCIAL STATISTICS

1996 births, 253,000; deaths, 80,000; 1995 marriages, 87,205. Rates, 1996 (per 1,000 population): birth, 18·1; death, 5·7; growth rate, 1996, 1·24%. Infant mortality, 1997 (per 1,000 live births), 11. In 1995 the most popular age range for marrying was 20–24 for both males and females. Expectation of life at birth (1997): males 72·3 years, females 78·3 years. Chile has the highest life expectancy in South America. Fertility rate, 1997, 2·4 children per woman.

CONSTITUTION AND GOVERNMENT

A new Constitution was approved by 67·5% of the voters on 11 Sept. 1980 and came into force on 11 March 1981. It provided for a return to democracy after a minimum period of 8 years. Gen. Pinochet would remain in office during this period after which the government would nominate a single candidate for President. At a plebiscite on 5 Oct. 1988 President Pinochet was rejected as a presidential candidate by 54·6% of votes cast.

The *President* is directly elected for a non-renewable 6-year term. Parliament consists of a 120-member *Chamber of Deputies* and a *Senate* of 48 members.

RECENT ELECTIONS

In the presidential run-off held on 16 Jan. 2000 the Socialist candidate Ricardo Lagos polled 51·3%, thus defeating Joaquín Lavin. 4 other candidates had participated in the first round of voting.

In elections to the Chamber of Deputies on 11 Dec. 1997 the Christian Democratic Party (PDC) won 39 seats, National Renewal 23 (RN), the Independent Democratic Union (UDI) 17, Party for Democracy 16 (PPD), the Socialist Party (PS) 11, the Radical Social Democratic Party (PRSD) 4 and ind 8. 2 other parties won 1 seat each. Member parties of the Concertación alliance (PDC, PPD, PS and PRSD) won 70 of the 120 seats.

CURRENT ADMINISTRATION

In Jan. 2000 the government comprised:

President: Ricardo Lagos (PPD; elected 16 Jan. 2000).

Minister of Agriculture: Angel Sartori. *Defence:* Edmundo Pérez Yoma. *Economy, Development and Reconstruction:* Jorge Leiva. *Public Education:* José Pablo Arellano Marín. *National Energy Commission:* Oscar Landerretche. *Finance:* Manuel Marfan. *Foreign Affairs:* Juan Gabriel Valdes. *Health:* Alex Figueroa. *Housing and Urbanization:* Sergio Henriquez Diaz. *Interior:* Raúl Troncoso. *Justice:* José Antonio Gómez. *Labour:* German Molina. *Mining:* Sergio Jimenez Moraga. *National Resources:* Jorge Heine. *Planning and Co-operation:* Roberto Pizarro Hofer. *Public Works:* Jaime Toha. *Transportation and Telecommunications:* Claudio Hohmann Barrientos. *General Secretary of the Government:* Carlos Mladinic. *General Secretary of the Presidency:* José Miguel Insulza.

DEFENCE

Military service is for 1 year in the Army and 2 in the Navy and Air Force. Plans for weapons' modernization amounting to nearly US$2bn., which would benefit both the army and the air force, were announced in April 1998.

In 1998 defence expenditure totalled US$2,952m. (US$200 per capita, the highest percentage in Latin America).

ECONOMY

Performance

Real GDP growth averaged 7·7% between 1991 and 1997, leading to Chile being labelled the 'tiger of South America'. In 1998 GDP growth was 3·3%.

Budget

The fiscal year is the calendar year. Revenues in 1997 (1996 in brackets) were 7,366·764bn. pesos (6,633·84bn. pesos) and expenditure 6,695·35bn. pesos (5,982·77bn. pesos). VAT is 16–18%.

Currency

The unit of currency is the *Chilean peso* (CLP) of 100 *centavos*. The peso was revalued 3·5% against the US dollar in Nov. 1994. Inflation, which was 7·4% in 1996, was forecast to be 5% in 1999 and 4·5% in 2000. Total money supply in Feb. 1998 was 2,608m. pesos. In Jan. 1998 gold reserves were 1·86m. troy oz. Foreign exchange reserves were US$381m. in Feb. 1998.

Banking and Finance

Banking is regulated by legislation of 1995. There is a Central Bank and a State Bank. The Central Bank was made independent of government control in March 1990. The *Governor* is Carlos Massad Abud. There were 12 domestic and 23 foreign banks in 1996. In May 1995 deposits in domestic banks totalled 8,623,323m. pesos; in foreign banks, 1,771,057m. pesos, and in other finance companies, 347,415m. pesos.

There are stock exchanges in Santiago and Valparaíso.

INDUSTRY

Output of major products in 1995 (in 1,000 tonnes): fishmeal, 877; cellulose, 1,219·8; newsprint, 201·5; paper and cardboard, 198·7; motor tyres, 2,329,900 items; cement, 2,885·2; iron or steel plates, 294·1; copper wire, 5·6; beer, 331·7m. litres; motor vehicles, 21,574 items.

Labour

In 1996 the workforce numbered 5,294,100, of whom 240,100 were unemployed. In June 1996, 1,338,500 persons were employed in social or personal services, 770,900 in agriculture, forestry and fisheries, 907,900 in trade, 847,200 in manufacturing, 389,400 in transport and communications, and 401,600 in building. In 1992 there was a monthly minimum wage of 38,600 pesos. In 1999 an estimated 9·0% of the workforce was unemployed, up from 6·5% in 1991.

INTERNATIONAL TRADE

Imports and Exports

Trade in US$1m.:

	1991	1992	1993	1994	1995	1996
Imports	8,094	10,129	11,125	11,825	15,914	17,828
Exports	8,942	10,007	9,199	11,604	16,137	15,353

In 1995 the principal exports were (in US$1m.): agricultural products, 1,562; minerals, 7,984 (of which copper, 6,487); manufactures, 6,847. Major export markets (in US$1m.), 1995: Japan, 2,906; USA, 2,375; UK, 1,076; Brazil, 1,056; South Korea, 896; Germany, 837. Major import suppliers: USA, 3,793; Argentina, 1,385; Brazil, 1,195; Japan, 1,013; Germany, 790.

COLOMBIA

República de Colombia
Capital: Bogotá
Population estimate, 2000: 42·3m.

KEY HISTORICAL EVENTS

In 1564 the Spanish Crown appointed a President of New Granada, which included the territories of Colombia, Panama and Venezuela. In 1718 a viceroyalty of New Granada was created. This viceroyalty gained its independence from Spain in 1819, and together with the present territories of Panama, Venezuela and Ecuador was officially constituted as the state of 'Greater Colombia'. This new state lasted only until 1830 when it split up into Venezuela, Ecuador and the republic of New Granada, later renamed *Estados Unidos de Colombia.* The constitution of 5 Aug. 1886, forming the Republic of Colombia, abolished the sovereignty of the states, converting them into departments with governors appointed by the President of the Republic. The department of Panama, however, became an independent country in 1903. Conservatives and Liberals fought a civil war from 1948 to 1957 (*La Violencia*) during which some 300,000 people were killed. Subsequently, powerful drugs lords have made violence endemic. Two Marxist guerrilla forces are active, the Colombian Revolutionary Armed Forces (FARC), and the smaller National Liberation Army (ELN). They are opposed by a well-armed paramilitary organization which emerged after the setting up of rural self-defence groups. Killings and other abuses by paramilitary squads, guerrillas and the military in 1996 made it the most infamous year in the nation's history for human rights violations. On average, 10 Colombians were killed every day for political or ideological reasons, while one person disappeared every two days.

There were hopes of a fresh start in 1998 when Andrés Pastrana was elected president. Offers to talk peace were taken up by the rebels and by their paramilitary enemies. But political differences are wide, with FARC demanding sweeping agrarian reform and a redistribution of wealth. FARC controls around 40% of the country including areas which produce the bulk of illegal drugs. Approximately 80% of the cocaine and 60% of the heroin sold in the USA originates in Colombia. In Jan. 1999 Colombia suffered its worst earthquake this century.

TERRITORY AND POPULATION

Colombia is bounded in the north by the Caribbean Sea, northwest by Panama, west by the Pacific Ocean, southwest by Ecuador and Peru, northeast by Venezuela and southeast by Brazil. The estimated area is 1,141,815 sq. km (440,855 sq. miles). Population census (1993), 37,127,293; density, 40·2 per sq. km.

The projected population for 2000 is 42·3m.

In 1997, 73·6% lived in urban areas. Bogotá, the capital (estimate 1999): 6,276,000.

The following table gives population estimates for departments and their capitals for 1999:

Departments	Area (sq. km)	Population	Capital	Population
Amazonas	109,665	69,000	Leticia	30,000[2]
Antioquia	63,612	5,300,000	Medellín	1,958,000
Arauca	23,818	232,000	Arauca	69,000[2]
Atlántico	3,388	2,081,000	Barranquilla	1,226,000
Bogotá[1]	–	6,276,000	–	–
Bolívar	25,978	1,951,000	Cartagena	877,000

Boyacá	23,189	1,355,000	Tunja	118,000[2]
Caldas	7,888	1,094,000	Manizales	362,000
Caquetá	88,965	410,000	Florencia	115,000[2]
Casanare	44,640	278,000	Yopal	69,000[2]
Cauca	29,308	1,234,000	Popayán	218,000[2]
César	22,905	944,000	Valledupar	297,000[2]
Chocó	46,530	406,000	Quibdó	123,000[2]
Córdoba	25,020	1,308,000	Montería	321,000
Cundinamarca	24,275	2,099,000	Bogotá[1]	–
Guainía	72,238	36,000	Puerto Inírida	20,000[2]
Guaviare	53,460	114,000	San José del	54,000[2]
			Guaviare	
Huila	19,890	911,000	Neiva	322,000
La Guajira	20,848	475,000	Riohacha	115,000[2]
Magdalena	23,188	1,260,000	Santa Marta	343,000[2]
Meta	85,635	686,000	Villavicencio	314,000
Nariño	33,268	1,603,000	Pasto	379,000
Norte de Santander	21,659	1,316,000	Cúcuta	624,000
Putumayo	24,885	324,000	Mocoa	30,000[2]
Quindío	1,845	552,000	Armenia	284,000[2]
Risaralda	4,140	928,000	Pereira	457,000
San Andrés y				
Providencia	44	71,000	San Andrés	61,000[2]
Santander	30,537	1,939,000	Bucaramanga	521,000
Sucre	10,917	779,000	Sincelejo	214,000[2]
Tolima	23,562	1,293,000	Ibagué	420,000[2]
Valle del Cauca	22,140	4,104,000	Cali	2,111,000
Vaupés	54,135	29,000	Mitú	14,000[2]
Vichada	100,242	80,000	Puerto Carreño	12,000[2]

[1]Capital District. [2]1997.

Ethnic divisions (1996): mestizo 58%, white 20%, mulatto 14%, black 4%, mixed black-Indian 3%, Indian 1%. The official language is Spanish.

SOCIAL STATISTICS

1997 births, 988,000; deaths, 191,000. 1997 birth rate (per 1,000 population) 26·4; death rate, 5·1. Annual growth rate, 1990–95, 1·7%. Life expectancy at birth, 1997, was 67·3 years for men and 74·3 years for women. Infant mortality, 1997, 25 per 1,000 live births; fertility rate, 1997, 2·8 children per woman.

CONSTITUTION AND GOVERNMENT

Simultaneously with the presidential elections of May 1990, a referendum was held in which 7m. votes were cast for the establishment of a special assembly to draft a new constitution. Elections were held on 9 Dec. 1990 for this 74-member 'Constitutional Assembly' which operated from Feb. to July 1991. The electorate was 14·2m.; turn-out was 3·7m. The Liberals gained 24 seats, M19 (a former guerrilla organization), 19. The Assembly produced a new constitution which came into force on 5 July 1991. It stresses the state's obligation to protect human rights, and establishes constitutional rights to healthcare, social security and leisure. Indians are allotted 2 Senate seats. Congress may dismiss ministers, and representatives may be recalled by their electors.

The *President* is elected by direct vote for a term of 4 years, and is not eligible for re-election until 4 years afterwards. A vice-presidency was instituted in July 1991.

The legislative power rests with a *Congress* of 2 houses, the *Senate*, of 102 members, and the *House of Representatives*, of 165 members, both elected for 4 years by proportional representation. Congress meets annually at Bogotá on 20 July.

RECENT ELECTIONS

In the first round of the presidential election on 31 May 1998, the Liberal Party candidate, Horacio Serpa, won by a mere 25,000 votes from a total of 10·8m, but in the second round on 21 June the Conservative Party candidate, Andrés Pastrana, received approximately 50·5% against 46·5% for Serpa.

Congressional elections were held on 8 March 1998, the ruling Liberal Party beating the Social Conservatives into second place amidst indications of large-scale vote buying. Hundreds of people were arrested with forged identity cards or other evidence of attempted fraud. Voting was cancelled in more than 50 towns and in other incidents, election officials were kidnapped, transport disrupted and electricity supplies sabotaged. The Liberal Party claimed 98 of the 161 available seats, against the Social Conservatives 52. Other parties shared the remaining 11 seats.

CURRENT ADMINISTRATION

President: Andrés Pastrana (b. 1954; sworn in 7 Aug. 1998).

Vice President: Lemas Gustavo Bell.

In Jan. 2000 the government comprised:

Minister of Interior: Nestor Humberto Martínez. *Defence:* Luis Fernando Ramírez Acuña. *Finance:* Juan Camilo Restrepo.

Agriculture and Livestock: Rodrigo Villalba. *Economic Development:* Fernando Araujo Perdomo. *Labour:* Gina Magnolia Riano. *Public Health:* Virgilio Galvez. *Development:* Jaime Alberto Cabal. *Mines and Energy:* Luis Carlos Valenzuela Delgado. *Education:* German Bula. *Communications:* Claudia de Francisco de Pardo. *Foreign Trade:* Marta Lucia Ramírez. *Foreign Relations:* Guillermo de Soto Fernandez. *Justice:* Romulo Gonzalez. *Environment:* Juan Mayr Maldonaldo. *Transport:* Gustavo Canal. *Culture:* Juan Luis Mejia. *Planning:* Jaime Ruiz. *Sustainable Development:* Erick Reyes Villa.

DEFENCE

Selective conscription at 18 years varies from 1 to 2 years of service. In 1998 defence expenditure totalled US$2,474m. (US$68 per capita). In 1985 expenditure had been US$604m.

ECONOMY

Performance

In 1998 the economy shrank by 5·0%, and for 1999 it was forecast to shrink again, by 3·5%. 1998 current account deficit, 7·5% of GDP. Government policy is to reduce this to 2% by 2000. GDP (1996): 88,827,760m. pesos.

Budget

Revenue (1996), US$26bn.; expenditure, US$30bn.

Currency

The unit of currency is the *Colombian peso* (COP) of 100 *centavos*. Inflation was 18% in 1998. In Dec. 1997 gold reserves were 360,000 troy oz and foreign exchange reserves were US$8,979m. Total money supply was 10,014bn. pesos. in Jan. 1998.

Banking and Finance

In 1923 the Bank of the Republic (*Governor*, Miguel Urrutia Montoya) was inaugurated as a semi-official central bank, with the exclusive privilege of issuing banknotes. Its note issues must be covered by a reserve in gold of foreign exchange of 25% of their value. Its international reserves in May 1992 were US$7,315·2m. Interest rates of 40% plus are imposed.

There are 24 commercial banks, of which 18 are private or mixed, and 6 official. There is also an Agricultural, Industrial and Mining Credit Institute, a Central Mortgage Bank and a Social Savings Bank. Bank deposits totalled 1,446,686 pesos in May 1991.

There are stock exchanges in Bogotá, Medellín and Cali.

INDUSTRY

Production (1998): steel ingots, 264,466 tonnes; cement, 8,463,995 tonnes; motor cars, 49,807; industrial vehicles, 14,162; sugar, 2,125,575 tonnes.

Labour

The economically active workforce (1998 estimate) was 7,828,397, of which 6,586,668 were employed and 1,241,729 unemployed; the rate of unemployment was estimated to be 15·8%.

INTERNATIONAL TRADE

Imports and Exports

In US$1,000:

	1996	1997	1998
Imports	11,754·7	14,410·3	13,726·4
Exports	9,708·5	10,823·8	10,823·8

Main export markets, 1998: USA (37%), Venezuela (11%), Germany (6%), Ecuador (5%). Main import suppliers (1998): USA (34%), Venezuela (10%), Japan (6%), Germany (5%).

COSTA RICA

República de Costa Rica
Capital: San José
Population estimate, 2000: 3·8m.

KEY HISTORICAL EVENTS

Discovered by Columbus in 1502 on his last voyage, Costa Rica
(Rich Coast) was part of the Spanish viceroyalty of New Spain from
1540 to 1821. It was part of the Central American Federation until
1838 when it achieved full independence. Coffee was introduced in
1808 and became a mainstay of the economy, helping to create a
peasant land-owning class. In 1948 accusations of election fraud led
to a 6-week civil war, at the conclusion of which José Figueres Ferrer
won power at the head of a revolutionary junta. A new constitution
was promulgated with, amongst other changes, the abolition of the
army. In 1986 Oscar Arias Sánchez was elected president. He
promised to prevent Nicaraguan anti-Sandinista (*contra*) forces
using Costa Rica as a base. In 1987 he received the Nobel Peace
Prize as recognition of his Central American peace plan, agreed to
by the other Central American states. Costa Rica was beset with
economic problems in the early 1990s when several politicians,
including President Calderón, were accused of profiting from drug
trafficking.

TERRITORY AND POPULATION

Costa Rica is bounded in the north by Nicaragua, east by the
Caribbean, southeast by Panama, and south and west by the Pacific.
The area is estimated at 51,100 sq. km (19,730 sq. miles). The

population at the census of 1 June 1984 was 2,416,809. Estimate (1995) 3,367,400; density, 66·2 per sq. km. In 1997, 50·3% of the population were urban.

The UN gives a projected population for 2000 of 3·8m.

There are 7 provinces (with 1995 population): Alajuela (607,674); Cartago (378,188); Guanacaste (266,198); Heredia (270,096); Limón (255,248); Puntarenas (375,639); San José (1,220,412).

The population is mainly of Spanish (85%) and mixed (8%) descent. About 3% are Afro-Caribbean (including some 70,000 speakers of an English Creole along the Caribbean coast). There is a residual Amerindian population of about 10,000.

Spanish is the official language.

SOCIAL STATISTICS

Statistics for calendar years:

	Marriages	Births	Deaths
1994	21,520	80,391	13,313
1995	24,274	80,306	14,061
1996	23,574	78,203	13,993
1997	24,300	78,018	14,260

1995 rates per 1,000 population: births, 23·8; deaths, 4·2. Annual growth rate, 1990–95, 3·5%. Life expectancy at birth, 1997, was 74·3 years for men and 78·9 years for women. Infant mortality, 1997, 12 per 1,000 live births; fertility rate, 1997, 2·8 children per woman.

CONSTITUTION AND GOVERNMENT

The Constitution was promulgated in Nov. 1949. The legislative power is vested in a single-chamber *Legislative Assembly* of 57 deputies elected for 4 years. The Presidentand 2 Vice-Presidents are elected for 4 years; the candidate receiving the largest vote, provided it is over 40% of the total, is declared elected, but a second ballot is required if no candidate gets 40% of the total. Elections are normally held on the first Sunday in February.

The President may appoint and remove members of the cabinet.

RECENT ELECTIONS

Presidential elections took place on 1 Feb. 1998. Miguel Angel Rodríguez of the Social Christian Unity Party (PUSC) was elected by 46·9% of votes cast, defeating José Miguel Corrales, of the National Liberation Party (PLN), who obtained 44·4% of the votes, and 4 other candidates.

At the simultaneous parliamentary elections the Social Christian Unity Party won 29 seats (with 41·3% of the votes), the National Liberation Party 22 (with 34·9%) and others 6.

CURRENT ADMINISTRATION

President: Miguel Angel Rodríguez (b. 1940; sworn in 8 May 1998).

In Jan. 2000 the govenment comprised:

First Vice President: Astrid Fischel Volio. *Second Vice President and Minister of Environment and Energy:* Elizabeth Odio Benito.

Agriculture and Livestock: Esteban Brenes Castro. *Economy and Foreign Trade:* Samuel Guzowski Rose. *Education:* Guillermo Vargas. *Finance:* Leonel Baruch Goldberg. *Foreign Relations and Religion:* Roberto Rojas Lopez. *Health:* Rogelio Pardo Evans. *Housing:* Donald Monroe. *Justice:* Monica Nagel Berger. *Labour and Social Security:* Victor Morales Mora. *Presidency:* Danilo Chaverri. *Public Education:* Claudio Gutierrez Carranza. *Public Security, Government and Police:* Juan Rafael Lizano Saenz. *Public Works and Transportation:* Rodolfo Mendez Maia. *Women's Situation:* Yolanda Ingianna.

DEFENCE

In 1997 defence expenditure totalled US$59m. (US$17 per capita).

ECONOMY

Performance

Costa Rica, the most stable country in Central America, experienced GDP growth of 6·2% in 1998, with a forecast of 5·0% growth in both 1999 and 2000.

Budget

In 1996 revenue was 500·96bn. colones (427·41bn. in 1995) and expenditure 572·97bn. colones (472·25bn. in 1995).

Currency

The unit of currency is the *Costa Rican colón* (CRC) of 100 *céntimos.* The official rate is used for all imports on an essential list and by the government and autonomous institutions, and a free rate is used for all other transactions. Total money supply was 274m. colones in Dec. 1997. Inflation was 13·0% in Dec. 1998. Foreign exchange reserves were US$1,129m. in Feb. 1998.

Banking and Finance

The bank of issue is the Central Bank (founded 1950) which supervises the national monetary system, foreign exchange dealings and banking operations. The bank has a board of 7 directors appointed by the government, including *ex officio* the Minister of Finance and the Planning Office Director. The *Governor* is Eduardo Lizano Fait.

There is a stock exchange, which in 1998 was the most successful market in the world, gaining in value by 88% in the course of the year.

INDUSTRY

The main manufactured goods are foodstuffs, textiles, fertilizers, pharmaceuticals, furniture, cement, tyres, canning, clothing, plastic goods, plywood and electrical equipment.

Labour

Out of 1,168,000 people in employment in 1995, 287,000 were in community, social and personal services, 263,000 in agriculture and 226,000 in trade, restaurants and hotels. There were 63,500 unemployed persons, or 5·2% of the workforce.

INTERNATIONAL TRADE

Imports and Exports

The value of imports and exports in US$1m. was:

	1995	1996	1997
Imports	3,274	3,886	3,503
Exports	2,624	2,881	2,995

Chief exports: manufactured goods and other products, coffee, bananas, sugar, cocoa. Main export markets, 1996: USA, 39·0%; Germany, 7·2%; Italy, 5·2%; Belgium-Luxembourg, 4·4%. Main import suppliers, 1996: USA, 49·9%; Mexico, 6·5%; Venezuela, 6·5%; Guatemala, 3·0%.

ECUADOR

República del Ecuador
Capital: Quito
Population estimate, 2000: 12·65m.

KEY HISTORICAL EVENTS

In 1532 the Spaniards founded a colony in Ecuador, then called
Quito. In 1821 a revolt led to the defeat of the Spaniards at Pichincha
and thus independence from Spain. On 13 March 1830, Quito
became the Republic of Ecuador. Political instability was endemic.
From the mid-1930s, President José Maria Velasco Ibarra gave more
continuity to the presidential régimes, although he was deposed by
military *coups* from four of his five presidencies.

From 1963 to 1966 and from 1976 to 1979 military juntas ruled the
country. The second of these juntas produced a new constitution
which came into force on 10 Aug. 1979. Since then presidencies
have been more stable but civil unrest continued in the wake of
economic reforms and attempts to combat political corruption.

In Jan. 2000 President Mahaud declared a state of emergency as
protesters demanded his resignation over his handling of the
country's economic crisis. There was a coup on 21 Jan., but after 5
hours in control the military junta handed power to the former vice
president, Gustavo Noboa.

TERRITORY AND POPULATION

Ecuador is bounded in the north by Colombia, in the east and south
by Peru and in the west by the Pacific ocean. The frontier with Peru
has long been a source of dispute. The latest delimitation of it was in

the Treaty of Rio, 29 Jan. 1942, when, after being invaded by Peru, Ecuador lost over half her Amazonian territories. Ecuador unilaterally denounced this treaty in Sept. 1961. Fighting between Peru and Ecuador began again in Jan. 1981 over this border issue but a ceasefire was agreed in early Feb. Following a confrontation of soldiers in Aug. 1991 the foreign ministers of both countries signed a pact creating a security zone, and took their cases to the UN in Oct. 1991. On 26 Jan. 1995 further armed clashes broke out with Peruvian forces in the undemarcated mutual border area ('Cordillera del Cóndor'). On 2 Feb. talks were held under the auspices of the guarantor nations of the 1942 Protocol of Rio de Janeiro (Argentina, Brazil, Chile and the USA), but fighting continued. Ceasefires were agreed on 17 Feb. which were broken, and on 28 Feb. On 25 July 1995 an agreement between Ecuador and Peru established a demilitarized zone along their joint frontier. The frontier was re-opened on 4 Sept. 1995. Since 23 Feb. 1996 Ecuador and Peru have signed 3 further agreements to regulate the dispute. The dispute was settled in Oct. 1998. Confirming the Peruvian claim that the border lies along the high peaks of the Cóndor, Ecuador gained navigation rights on the Amazon within Peru.

No definite figure of the area of the country can yet be given. One estimate of the area of Ecuador is 275,830·0 sq. km, excluding the litigation zone between Peru and Ecuador, which is 190,807 sq. km, but including the **Galápagos** Archipelago (8,010 sq. km), situated in the Pacific ocean about 960 km west of Ecuador, and comprising 13 islands and 19 islets. These were discovered in 1535 by Fray Tomás de Berlanga and had a population of 10,207 in 1996. They constitute a national park, and had about 80,000 visitors in 1995.

The population is an amalgam of European, Amerindian and African origins. Some 40% of the population is Amerindian: Quechua, Swiwiar, Achuar and Zaparo. In May 1992 they were granted title to the 1m. ha of land they occupy in Pastaza.

The official language is Spanish. Quechua and other languages
are also spoken.
Census population in 1990, 9,648,189. Estimate, 1996,
11,698,400; density, 42 per sq. km.
The UN gives a projected population for 2000 of 12·65m.
In 1997, 60·4% lived in urban areas.
The population was distributed by provinces as follows in 1996:

Province	Sq. km	Population	Capital	Population[1]
Azuay	8,124·7	529,177	Cuenca	194,981
Bolívar	3,939·9	166,957	Guaranda	15,730
Cañar	3,122·1	194,529	Azogues	21,060
Carchi	3,605·1	146,343	Tulcán	37,069
Chimborazo	6,569·3	378,111	Riobamba	94,505
Cotopaxi	6,071·9	289,774	Latacunga	39,882
El Oro	5,850 1	441,025	Machala	144,197
Esmeraldas	15,239·1	327,931	Esmeraldas	98,558
Guayas	20,502·5	2,689,745	Guayaquil	1,508,444
Imbabura	4,559·3	286,155	Ibarra	80,991
Loja	11,026·5	392,877	Loja	94,305
Los Ríos	7,175·0	553,479	Babahoyo	50,285
Manabi	18,878·8	1,076,966	Portoviejo	132,937
Pichincha	12,914·7	1,893,744	Quito	1,100,847
Sucumbíos	18,327·5	90,222	Nueva Loja	13,165
Tungurahua	3,334·8	383,460	Ambato	124,166
Napo	33,930·9	114,380	Tena	7,873
Pastaza	29,773·7	46,095	Puyo	14,438
Morona-Santiago	25,690·0	104,737	Macas	8,246
Zamora-Chinchipe	23,110·8	73,383	Zamora	8,048
Galápagos	8,010·0	10,207	Puerto Baquerizo Moreno	3,023
Non-delimited zones	2,288·8	74,842		

[1]1990 census population.

SOCIAL STATISTICS

1995: births, 408,983; deaths, 50,867; marriages, 70,480. Rates, 1995 (per 1,000 population): birth, 35·7; death, 4·4; marriage, 6·2. Life expectancy at birth, 1997, was 67·3 years for males and 72·5 years for females. Annual growth rate, 1990–95, 2·2%. Infant mortality, 1997, 30 per 1,000 live births; fertility rate, 1997, 3·1 children per woman.

CONSTITUTION AND GOVERNMENT

A new Constitution came into force on 10 Aug. 1979. It provides for an executive President and a Vice-President to be directly elected for a non-renewable 4-year term by universal suffrage, with a further 'run-off' ballot being held between the two leading candidates where no-one has secured an absolute majority of the votes cast. The President appoints and leads a Council of Ministers. A referendum on constitutional reform was held in Nov. 1995. and in the election of Nov. 1997 Ecuador voted in favour of constitutional reform to strengthen the presidency and to limit the participation of the state in the economy.

Legislative power is vested in a 125-member *National Congress*, 105 members in 2- or multi-seat constituencies and 20 members elected at large by proportional representation. Voting is obligatory for all literate citizens of 18–65 years.

RECENT ELECTIONS

Dissatisfaction with President Fabián Alarcón led to presidential elections in 1998. Jamil Mahuad, candidate of the centre-right

Popular Democracy party (DP), won in the second round of the presidential election on 12 July 1998, with 51·3% of the votes, against 48·7% for Alvaro Noboa, a populist businessman. In the first round on 31 May he had defeated 5 other candidates to win 35·3% of the vote.

In *National Congress* elections on 31 May 1998 the People's Democracy-Christian Democrat Union (DP-UDC) won 35 seats, the Social Christian Party (PSC) 26, Ecuadorian Roldosist Party (PRE) 25, the Party of the Democratic Left (ID) 17 and Pluri-National Pachakutik Movement-New Country (MUPP-NP) 6. No other party won more than 3 seats.

Elections to the 70-member *Constitutional Assembly* (members of the *National Congress*) were held on 30 Nov. 1997. The Social Christian Party won 20 seats and the People's Democracy-Christian Democrat Union 10 seats, with the remaining 40 seats going to 15 other parties.

CURRENT ADMINISTRATION

President: Gustavo Noboa (b. 1937; installed 22 Jan. 2000).

In Jan. 2000 the government comprised:

Prime Minister: Eduardo Huerta. *Minister of Agriculture and Livestock:* Salomon Larrea Rodríguez. *Education and Culture:* Rosangela Adoum. *Energy and Mines:* Teodoro Abdo. *Environment:* Yolanda Cacabasse. *Finance and Credit:* Alfredo Arizaga. *Foreign Relations:* Benjamin Ortiz Brennan. *Government, Police and Municipality:* Vladimiro Alvarez Grau. *Industrialization, Foreign Trade, Tourism and Fisheries:* José Luis Icaza. *National Defence:* José Gallardo. *Public Health:* Edgar Rodas. *Public Works:* José Antenor Macchiavello. *Urban Development and Housing:* Teodoro Pena. *Labour and Social Action:* Angel Chavez.

DEFENCE

Military service is selective, with a 1-year period of conscription. The country is divided into 4 military zones, with headquarters at Quito, Guayaquil, Cuenca and Pastaza.

Defence expenditure totalled US$522m. in 1998 (US$42 per capita).

ECONOMY

Performance

Real GDP growth was 1·8% in 1998, but is forecast to be negative in 1999, at −5·1%, partly owing to years of mismanagemnet and partly to El Niño. The economy is forecast to recover in 2000, however, with a growth rate of 4·7%.

Budget

Total revenue and total expenditure from 1991 to 1995 (in 1bn. sucres) was as follows:

	1991	1992	1993	1994	1995
Revenue	1,907	3,096	4,371	5,374	8,030
Expenditure	1,739	3,145	4,166	5,717	8,451

The budget deficit in 1998 was nearly 6% of GDP.

Currency

The monetary unit is the *sucre* (ECS), of 100 *centavos*. The sucre was devalued by 8% in Aug. 1996. Inflation was 24% in 1996 and had risen to 43% by Dec. 1998. Economic reforms of Nov. 1996 envisaged the convertibility of the currency as from 1 July 1997, with the sucre pegged to the US dollar at US$1 = 4 sucres. Under the reform programme foreign exchange reserves must at least match currency in circulation. In Feb. 1998 foreign exchange reserves were US$1,957m. and gold reserves were 410,000 troy oz. Total money supply was 6,956m. sucres in Dec. 1997.

Banking and Finance

The Central Bank of Ecuador (*Governor*, Dr Pablo Better), the bank of issue, with a capital and reserves of US$1,557m. at 31 Dec. 1995, is modelled after the Federal Reserve Banks of the USA; through branches opened in 16 towns, it now deals in mortgage bonds. All commercial banks must be affiliated to the Central Bank. Legislation of May 1994 liberalized the financial sector.

There are stock exchanges in Quito and Guayaquil.

INDUSTRY

Production in 1994 included: residual fuel oils, 3·0m. tonnes; cement, 2·1m. tonnes.

Labour

Out of 2,697,000 people in employment in 1994, 815,000 were in trade, restaurants and hotels, 811,000 in community, social and personal services, and 415,000 in manufacturing industries. In 1999 an estimated 17% of the workforce was unemployed, up from 8·6% in 1991.

INTERNATIONAL TRADE

Imports and Exports

Imports and exports for calendar years, in US$1m.:

	1993	1994	1995	1996	1997
Imports	2,562	3,690	4,193	3,935	4,944
Exports	2,904	3,820	4,307	4,900	5,190

Ecuador is a major exporter of shrimps (US$673m. in 1995). Other major exports (1995, in US$1m.): bananas, 845; coffee beans, 244; cocoa beans and products, 133; cut flowers, 79. Main export markets, 1995 (in US$1m.): USA, 1,847 (42%); Colombia, 246; Chile, 193; Germany, 166; Spain, 149. Main import suppliers: USA, 1,290 (32%); Colombia, 396; Japan, 328; Germany, 192; Brazil, 187.

EL SALVADOR

República de El Salvador
Capital: San Salvador
Population estimate, 2000: 6·32m.

KEY HISTORICAL EVENTS

Conquered by Spain in 1526, El Salvador remained under Spanish rule until 1821. Thereafter, El Salvador was a member of the Central American Federation comprising the states of El Salvador, Guatemala, Honduras, Nicaragua and Costa Rica until this federation was dissolved in 1839. In 1841 El Salvador declared itself an independent republic.

The country's history has been marked by political violence. The repressive dictatorship of President Maximiliano Hernandez Martínez lasted from 1931 to 1944 when he was deposed as were his successors in 1948 and 1960. The military junta that followed gave way to more secure presidential succession although left-wing guerrilla groups were fighting government troops in the late 1970s. As the guerrillas grew stronger and gained control over a part of the country, the USA sent economic aid and assisted in the training of Salvadorean troops. A new constitution was enacted in Dec. 1983 but the presidential election was boycotted by the main left-wing organization, the Favabundo Marti National Liberation Front (FMLN). Talks between the government and the FMLN in April 1991 led to constitutional reforms in May, envisaging the establishment of civilian control over the armed forces and a reduction in their size. On 16 Jan. 1992 the government and the FMLN signed a peace agreement.

TERRITORY AND POPULATION

El Salvador is bounded in the northeast by Guatemala, northeast and east by Honduras and south by the Pacific Ocean. The area (including 247 sq. km of inland lakes) is 21,041 sq. km. Population (1992 census), 5,047,925 (female 52%); 1996 est., 5·79m., giving a population density of 275 per sq. km.

The UN gives a projected population for 2000 of 6·32m.

In 1997, 54·4% of the population were rural. In 1995, 1m. Salvadoreans were living abroad, mainly in the USA.

The republic is divided into 14 departments. Areas (in sq. km) and 1992 census populations:

Department	Area	Population	Chief town	Population
Ahuachapán	1,240	260,563	Ahuachapán	83,885
Cabañas	1,140	136,293	Sensuntepeque	38,073
Chalatenango	2,017	180,627	Chalatenango	27,600
Cuscatlán	756	167,290	Cojutepeque	43,564
La Libertad	1,653	522,071	Nueva San Salvador	116,575
La Paz	1,224	246,147	Zacatecoluca	57,032
La Unión	2,074	251,143	La Unión	36,927
Morazán	1,447	166,772	San Francisco	20,497
San Miguel	2,077	380,442	San Miguel	182,817
San Salvador	886	1,477,766	San Salvador	422,570[1]
San Vicente	1,184	135,471	San Vicente	45,842
Santa Ana	2,023	451,620	Santa Ana	202,337
Sonsonate	1,226	354,641	Sonsonate	76,200
Usulatán	2,130	317,079	Usulután	62,967

[1]Greater San Salvador conurbation, 1,522,126.

The official language is Spanish.

SOCIAL STATISTICS

1995 births, 164,000; deaths, 35,000. Rates (1995, per 1,000 population): births, 28·9; deaths, 6·1. Life expectancy at birth in 1997 was 66·5 years for males and 72·5 years for females. Annual growth rate, 1990–95, 2·2%. Infant mortality, 1997, 31 per 1,000 live births; fertility rate, 1997, 3·2 births per woman.

CONSTITUTION AND GOVERNMENT

A new Constitution was enacted in Dec. 1983. Executive power is vested in a *President* and *Vice-President* elected for a non-renewable term of 5 years. There is a *Legislative Assembly* of 84 members elected by universal suffrage and proportional represen-tation: 64 locally and 20 nationally, for a term of 3 years.

RECENT ELECTIONS

Presidential elections were held on 7 March 1999. Francisco Guillermo Flores Pérez (Alianza Republicana Nacionalista, ARENA) won with 51·4% against 6 other candidates. Turn-out was 35% (compared to 55% at the previous presidential election in 1994). In parliamentary elections on 16 March 1997, ARENA gained 28 seats in the Legislative Assembly, the FMLN 27, and 6 other parties 29 seats between them.

The next parliamentary elections were scheduled to take place on 12 March 2000.

CURRENT ADMINISTRATION

President: Francisco Guillermo Flores Pérez, b. 1959 (ARENA; sworn in 1 June 1999).

In Jan. 2000 the Cabinet comprised:

Vice-President: Carlos Quintãnilla.

Minister of the Presidency: Enrique Borgo Bustamante.

Agriculture and Livestock: Salvador Urrutia. *Economy:* Miguel Ernesto Lacayo. *Defence:* Gen. Juan Antonio Martínez Valera. *Environment and Natural Resources:* Miguel Eduardo Araujo. *Finance:* José Luis Trigueros. *Foreign Affairs:* Maria Eugenia Brizuela De Avila. *Health:* José Francisco Lopez Beltran. *Interior:* Mario Acosta Oertel. *Public Security:* Francisco Bertrand Galindo. *Justice:* Nelson Segovia. *Labour and Social Security:* Jorge Nieto. *Public Works:* José Angel Quiróz. *Public Health and Social Assistance:* Dr Eduardo Interiano. *Education:* Evelyn Jacir de Lovo. *Chief of Cabinet:* Juan José Daboub.

DEFENCE

There is selective conscription for 2 years. In 1998 defence expenditure totalled US$157m. (US$26 per capita).

ECONOMY

Performance

Real GDP growth in 1998 was 3·5%, with a forecast of 1·1% growth in 1999 and 2·9% in 2000.

Budget

Central government budgetary revenue and expenditure in ₡1m. for calendar years:

	1993	1994	1995	1996	1997
Revenue	6,550·4	8,654·4	10,534·7	10,527·9	11,228·0
Expenditure	7,753·0	10,264·3	11,376·3	12,305·6	12,027·3

Currency

The monetary unit is the *colón* (SVC) of 100 *centavos*. Inflation was 2·5% in 1998. Foreign exchange reserves were US$1,631m. in Feb. 1998 and gold reserves were 470,000 troy oz. Total money supply was ₡9,084m. in Feb. 1998.

Banking and Finance

The bank of issue is the Central Reserve Bank (*Governor*, Rafael Barraza Dominguez), formed in 1934 and nationalized in 1961. There are 15 commercial banks (2 foreign). Individual private holdings may not exceed 5% of the total equity.

There is a stock exchange in San Salvador, founded in 1992.

INDUSTRY

Production (1988, in 1,000 tonnes): petroleum, 136; fuel oil, 208; paper and products, 16. Traditional industries include food processing and textiles.

Labour

Out of 1,973,000 people in employment in 1995, 532,000 were in agriculture, forestry and fishing, 414,000 in community, social and personal services, and 399,000 in trade, restaurants and hotels. There were 163,400 unemployed persons, or 7·7% of the workforce.

INTERNATIONAL TRADE

Imports and Exports

Imports (including parcels' post) and exports in calendar years (in US$1m.):

	1993	1994	1995	1996	1997
Imports	1,912	2,574	2,853	2,671	2,973
Exports	732	844	998	1,024	1,359

In 1991, 139,000 quintals of coffee were exported. Main import suppliers, 1996: USA, 40·0%; Guatemala, 10·5%; Panama, 6·6%; Mexico, 6·5%. Main export markets, 1996: Guatemala, 20·6%; USA, 19·3%; Germany, 15·5%; Honduras, 9·5%.

GUATEMALA

República de Guatemala
Capital: Guatemala City
Population estimate, 2000: 12·22m.

KEY HISTORICAL EVENTS

From 1524 Guatemala was part of a Spanish captaincy-general,
comprising the whole of Central America. It became independent in
1821 and formed part of the Confederation of Central America from
1823 to 1839. The overthrow of the right-wing dictator Jorge Ubico in
1944 opened a decade of left-wing activity which alarmed the USA.
In 1954 the leftist régime of Jacob Arbenz Guzmán was overthrown
by a CIA-supported *coup.* A series of right-wing governments failed
to produce stability while the toll on human life and the violation of
human rights was such as to cause thousands of refugees to flee to
Mexico. Elections to a National Constituent Assembly were held on
1 July 1984, and a new constitution was promulgated in May 1985.
Amidst violence and assassinations, the presidential election was
won by Marco Vinicio Cerezo Arévalo. On 14 Jan. 1986 Cerezo's
civilian government was installed – the first for 16 years and only the
second since 1954. Violence continued, however, and there were
frequent reports of torture and killings by right-wing 'death squads'.
The presidential and legislative elections of Nov. 1995 saw the return
of open politics for the first time in over 40 years. Meanwhile the
Guatemalan Revolutionary Unit (URNG) declared a ceasefire. On 6
May and 19 Sept. 1996 the government agreed reforms to military,
internal security, judicial and agrarian institutions. A ceasefire was
concluded in Oslo on 4 Dec. 1996 and a final peace treaty was
signed on 29 Dec. 1996.

In Nov. 1999 the country's first presidential elections took place
since the end of the 36-year-long civil year in 1996.

TERRITORY AND POPULATION

Guatemala is bounded on the north and west by Mexico, south by the Pacific ocean and east by El Salvador, Honduras and Belize, and the area is 108,889 sq. km (42,042 sq. miles). In March 1936 Guatemala, El Salvador and Honduras agreed to accept the peak of Mount Montecristo as the common boundary point.

The population was 11,277,600 in July 1996. Estimate (1997) 11,685,700; density, 107 per sq. km.

The UN gives a projected population for 2000 of 12·22m.

In 1997 the percentage of the population considered rural was 60·6%. In 1996, 44% were Amerindian, of 21 different groups descended from the Maya; 56% Mestizo (mixed Amerindian and Spanish). 60% speak Spanish, with the remainder speaking one or a combination of the 23 Indian dialects.

Guatemala is administratively divided into 22 departments, each with a governor appointed by the President. Population, 1994:

Departments	Area (sq. km)	Population	Departments	Area (sq. km)	Population
Alta Verapaz	8,686	650,120	Petén	35,854	295,169
Baja Verapaz	3,124	200,019	Quezaltenango	1,951	606,556
Chimaltenango	1,979	374,898	Quiché	8,378	631,785
Chiquimula	2,376	268,379	Retalhuleu	1,858	261,136
El Progreso	1,922	115,469	Sacatepéquez	465	196,537
Escuintla	4,384	592,647	San Marcos	3,791	766,950
Guatemala City	2,126	2,188,652	Santa Rosa	2,955	285,456
Huehuetenango	7,403	790,183	Sololá	1,061	265,902
Izabal	9,038	359,056	Suchitepéquez	2,510	392,703
Jalapa	2,063	206,355	Totonicapán	1,061	324,225
Jutiapa	3,219	378,601	Zacapa	2,690	171,146

In 1995 Guatemala City, the capital, had a population of 2,205,000. Populations of other major towns, 1993 estimates (in 1,000): Quezaltenango, 98; Escuintla, 66; Mazatenango, 41; Puerto Barrios, 39; Retalhuleu, 38.

SOCIAL STATISTICS

Births, 1996, 382,000; deaths, 62,000. 1996 rates per 1,000 population: birth, 36·4; death rate, 5·9. Life expectancy, 1997: male 61·4 years, female 67·2. Annual growth rate, 1990–95, 2·9%. Infant mortality, 1997, 43 per 1,000 live births; fertility rate, 1997, 4·9 births per woman.

CONSTITUTION AND GOVERNMENT

A new Constitution, drawn up by the Constituent Assembly elected on 1 July 1984, was promulgated in June 1985 and came into force on 14 Jan. 1986. In 1993, 43 amendments were adopted, reducing *inter alia* the President's term of office from 5 to 4 years. The President and Vice-President are elected by direct election (with a second round of voting if no candidate secures 50% of the first-round votes) for a non-renewable 4-year term. The unicameral *Congress* comprises 80 members, 64 elected locally and 16 from a national list, for 4-year terms.

A referendum on constitutional reform was held on 30 Jan. 1994. The electorate was 3·4m.; turn-out was 17·5%. The reforms were approved by 83% of votes cast.

RECENT ELECTIONS

In a run-off for the presidency on 26 Dec. 1999 Alfonso Portillo Cabrera (FRG) won with 68·3% of the vote against Óscar Berger Perdomo (PAN). A further 6 candidates had participated in the first round of voting on 7 Nov. 1999.

Congressional elections were held on 7 Nov. 1999. The Guatemalan Republic Front (FRG) won 63 of a possible 113 seats, the National Progress Party (PAN) won 37 seats, the Guatemalan National Revolutionary Alliance 9, the Guatemalan Christian Democracy 2, the Progressive Liberator Party 1 and an alliance of the Green Organization and the Democratic Union 1.

CURRENT ADMINISTRATION

President: Alfonso Portillo Cabrera b. 1951 (FRG; sworn in 14 Jan. 2000). Alfonso Portillo has admitted to murdering 2 rival law professors in 1982.

In Jan. 2000 the government comprised:

Minister of Agriculture: Roger Valenzuela. *Communications:* Luis Rabbé. *Defence:* Col. Juan de Dios Estrada Velásquez. *Education:* Mario Torres. *Energy and Mining:* Raúl Archila. *Culture:* Otilia Lux de Cotí. *Finance:* Manuel Hiram Maza Castellanos. *Foreign Affairs:* Gabriel Orellana. *Health:* Mario Bolaños. *Government:* Guillermo Ruiz Wong. *Labour:* Juan Francisco Alfaro. *Economy:* Eduardo Weymann.

DEFENCE

There is selective conscription for 30 months. In 1998 defence expenditure totalled US$153m. (US$13 per capita).

ECONOMY

Performance

Real GDP growth was 4·9% in 1998. Growth was forecast to be 3·9% in 1999 and 3·8% in 2000.

Budget

Government revenue and expenditure (in Q.1m.):

	1994	1995	1996	1997
Revenue	5,697·35	7,124·20	8,445·10	9,627·66
Expenditure	6,648·98	7,562·12	8,612·70	10,418·73

VAT is 10%.

Currency

The unit of currency is the *quetzal* (CTQ) of 100 *centavos*, established on 7 May 1925. Foreign exchange reserves were US$1,012m. in Feb. 1998; gold reserves were 210,000 troy oz. Inflation was 7·0% in 1998. In Jan. 1998 total money supply was Q.11,737m.

Banking and Finance

The Banco de Guatemala is the central bank and bank of issue (*Governor*, Edin H. Velázquez). Constitutional amendments of 1993 placed limits on its financing of government spending. In 1996 there were 21 private banks, 3 state banks, 4 international banks and 18 foreign banks, of which latter 2 are authorized to operate as commercial banks.

There are 2 stock exchanges.

INDUSTRY

Manufacturing contributed 14·1% of GDP in 1995. The principal industries are food and beverages, tobacco, chemicals, hides and skins, textiles, garments and non-metallic minerals. Raw sugar production in 1992 was 943,000 tonnes. New industries include electrical goods, plastic sheet and metal furniture.

Labour

In 1995 the workforce totalled 3,316,723 including: agriculture, 1,513,600; commerce, 572,011; services, 439,719; manufacturing, 439,121; building, 214,102; transport and communications, 77,476; finance, 40,474.

The working week is 44 hours, with a 12-day paid holiday annually.

INTERNATIONAL TRADE

Imports and Exports

Values in US$1m. were:

	1992	1993	1994	1995	1996
Imports	2,532	2,599	2,604	3,293	3,146
Exports	1,295	1,340	1,522	2,156	2,031

In 1995 the principal exports were (in US$1m.): coffee, 550; sugar, 237; bananas, 138; cardamom, 41. Main export markets, 1995: USA, 31%; El Salvador, 13·8%; Honduras, 6·4%; Germany, 5·8%; Costa Rica, 5·2%. Main import suppliers: USA, 43%; Mexico, 9·3%; El Salvador, 5%; Venezuela, 4·6%; Japan, 3·7%.

GUYANA

Co-operative Republic of Guyana
Capital: Georgetown
Population estimate, 2000: 874,000

KEY HISTORICAL EVENTS

First settled by the Dutch West Indian Company about 1620, the
territory was captured by Britain to whom it was ceded in 1814 and
named British Guiana. To work the sugar plantations African slaves
were transported here in the 18th century and East Indian and
Chinese labourers indentured in the 19th century. From 1950 the anti-
colonial struggle was spearheaded by the Peoples Progressive Party
(PPP) led by Cheddi Jagan and Forbes Burnham. By the time internal
autonomy was granted in 1961 Burnham had split with Jagan to form
the more moderate People's National Congress (PNC). Guyana
became an independent member of the Commonwealth in 1966 with
Burnham as the first prime minister, later president. By the 1980s,
desperate economic straits had forced Guyana to seek outside help
which came on condition of restoring free elections. Dr Jagan
returned to power in 1992. Following his death in March 1997 his
wife, Janet Jagan, was sworn in as President.

TERRITORY AND POPULATION

Guyana is situated on the northeast coast of Latin America on the
Atlantic Ocean, with Suriname on the east, Venezuela on the west
and Brazil on the south and west. Area, 83,000 sq. miles (214,969 sq.
km). Estimated population (1997), 847,000.

The UN gives a projected population for 2000 of 874,000.

Guyana has the highest proportion of rural population in South America, with only 36·4% living in urban areas in 1997. Ethnic groups by origin: 49% Indian, 36% African, 7% mixed race, 7% Amerindian and 1% others. The capital is Georgetown (1995 population, 254,000); other towns are New Amsterdam, Linden, Rose Hall and Corriverton.

Venezuela demanded the return of the Essequibo region in 1963. It was finally agreed in March 1983 that the UN Secretary-General should mediate. There was also an unresolved claim (1984) by Suriname for the return of an area between the New River and the Corentyne River.

The official language is English.

SOCIAL STATISTICS

Births, 1997, 29,000; deaths, 7,000. 1997 birth rate per 1,000 population, 34·7; death rate, 8·6; life expectancy, male 61·1 years and female 67·9 years). Annual growth rate, 1990–95, 1·0%. Infant mortality, 1997, 59 per 1,000 live births; fertility rate, 1997, 2·3 births per woman.

CONSTITUTION AND GOVERNMENT

A new Constitution was promulgated in Oct. 1980. There is an *Executive Presidency*, and a *National Assembly* which consists of 53 elected members and 12 members appointed by the regional authorities. Elections for 5-year terms are held under the single-list system of proportional representation, with the whole of the country forming one electoral area and each voter casting a vote for a party list of candidates.

RECENT ELECTIONS

Janet Jagan and the PPP won the presidential, parliamentary and regional elections of 15 Dec. 1997. The PPP won 220,667 or 55·3% of the national vote (29 seats in the National Assembly), compared to the 161,901 or 40·6% cast for the PNC (22 seats in the National Assembly). In the regional elections the PPP received 219,651 votes, the PNC 160,019 votes. The chief justice rejected the PNC's claims of election rigging. PNC supporters retaliated with looting and rioting in Georgetown.

CURRENT ADMINISTRATION

President: Bharrat Jagdeo (b. 1964; sworn in 11 Aug. 1999).

In Jan. 2000 the government comprised:

Prime Minister and Minister of Public Works: Samuel Hinds. *Vice-President, Minister of Agriculture and Parliamentary Affairs:* Reepu Daman Persaud.

Attorney-General and Minister of Legal Affairs: Charles Rishiram Ramson. *Cabinet Secretary:* Roger Luncheon. *Minister ofFinance:* Saisnarine Kowlessar. *Foreign Affairs:* Clement Rohee. *Health and Labour:* Henry Benfield Jeffrey. *Education:* Dale Bisnauth. *Home Affairs:* Ronald Gajraj. *Trade, Industry and Tourism:* Geoff Da Silva. *Amerindian Affairs:* Vibert D'Souza. *Housing:* Shaik Baksh. *Culture, Youth and Sports:* Gail Teixeira. *Information:* Moses Nagamootoo. *Local Government:* Harripersaud Nokta. *Human Services and Social*

Security: Indra Chandrapal. *Marine Resources:* Satyadeow Sawah. *Public Service and Office of the President:* George Fung-On. *Transport and Hydraulics:* Carl Anthony Xavier.

DEFENCE

Military expenditure totalled US$7m. in 1998 (US$9 per capita).

ECONOMY

Performance

GDP growth in 1998 was negative, at −3·0%.

Budget

Current revenue and expenditure for calendar years (in G$1m.):

	1991	1992	1993	1994	1995
Revenue	11,823·5	17,769·5	21,778·0	23,809·1	28,961·4
Expenditure	15,273·4	23,070·7	17,716·8	19,360·8	22,422·3

In 1995 capital account receipts totalled G$3,151·2m.; expenditure, G$12,090·4m. Components of current revenue, 1995 (in G$1m.): income taxes, 10,865·9; property taxes, 427·8; taxes on production and consumption, 7,351; taxes on international trade, 4,117·4; other taxes, 2,562·5; non-tax revenue, 1,479·5.

Currency

The unit of currency is the *Guyana dollar* (GYD) of 100 *cents*. Inflation was 5·0% in 1998. Foreign exchange reserves were US$291m. in Feb. 1998. Total money supply in Feb. 1998 was G$16,786.

Banking and Finance

The bank of issue is the Bank of Guyana (*Governor*, Archibald Meredith). Of the 6 commercial banks operating 2 are foreign-owned. At March 1996, the total assets of commercial banks were G$62,587,892,000. Savings deposits were G$26,564·2m.

INDUSTRY

The main industries are agro-processing (sugar, rice, timber and coconut) and mining (gold and diamonds). There is a light manufacturing sector, and textiles and pharmaceuticals are produced by state and private companies. Production, 1995: sugar, 253,870 tonnes; rum, 17,926 litres; beer, 8,470 litres; soft drinks, 3,032,130 cases; textiles, 322m. metres; footwear, 54,132 pairs; margarine, 1,262,420 kg; edible oil, 2,388,120 litres; refrigerators, 2,763; paint, 923,847 litres.

Labour

In 1996 the labour force was 353,000 (67% males).

INTERNATIONAL TRADE

Imports and Exports

In 1996 exports were valued at US$574·8m. and imports at US$595·0m. In the budgeted figures for 1998, exports were valued at US$616·0m. and imports at US$652·0m. Principal commodities exported, 1996 (in US$1m.): sugar, 150·7; gold, 105·9; rice, 93·7; bauxite, 86·0. Other important export commodities included shrimps, timber and rum. Exports by volume, 1995: bauxite, 1,971,063 tonnes; sugar, 225,421 tonnes; rice, 200,544 tonnes; gold, 275,305 oz; shrimps, 827 tonnes; timber, 35,873 cu. metres.

HONDURAS

República de Honduras
Capital: Tegucigalpa
Population estimate, 2000: 6·48m.

KEY HISTORICAL EVENTS

Discovered by Columbus in 1502, Honduras was ruled by Spain until independence in 1821. Political instability was endemic throughout the 19th and most of the 20th century. The end of military rule seemed to come in 1981 when a general election gave victory to the more liberal and non-military party, PLH (Partido Liberal de Honduras). Considerable power, however, remained with the armed forces. Internal unrest continued into the 1990s with politicians and military leaders at loggerheads, particularly over attempts to investigate violations of human rights. In Oct. 1998 Honduras was devastated by Hurricane Mitch, the worst natural disaster to hit the area in modern times.

TERRITORY AND POPULATION

Honduras is bounded in the north by the Caribbean, east and southeast by Nicaragua, west by Guatemala, southwest by El Salvador and south by the Pacific Ocean. The area is 112,088 sq. km (43,277 sq. miles). The estimated population in 1997 was 5,751,400 (2,870,700 female), giving a density of 51 per sq. km. In 1997, 55·0% of the population were rural.

The UN gives a projected population for 2000 of 6·48m.

The chief cities (populations in 1,000, 1994) were Tegucigalpa, the capital (775·3), San Pedro Sula (368·5), El Progreso (81·2),

Choluteca (72·8), Danlí (43·3) and the Atlantic coast ports of La Ceiba (86·0), Puerto Cortés (33·5) and Tela (24·8); other towns include Olanchito (17·9), Juticalpa (25·6), Comayagua (52·3), Siguatepeque (37·5) and Santa Rosa de Copán (23·4). Areas and 1988 census populations of the 18 departments and the Central District (Tegucigalpa):

Department	Area (in sq. km)	Popu-lation	Department	Area (in sq. km)	Popu-lation
Atlántida	4,251	238,742	Islas de la Bahía	261	22,062
Choluteca	4,211	295,484	La Paz	2,331	105,927
Colón	8,875	149,677	Lempira	4,290	177,055
Comayagua	5,196	239,859	Ocotepeque	1,680	74,276
Copán	3,203	219,455	Olancho	24,350	283,852
Cortés	3,954	662,772	Santa Bárbara	5,115	278,868
El Paraíso	7,218	254,295	Valle	1,565	119,645
Francisco Morazán	6,298	251,613	Yoro	7,939	333,508
Gracias a Dios	16,630	34,970	Central District	1,648	576,661
Intibucá	3,072	124,681			

The official language is Spanish. The Spanish-speaking population is of mixed Spanish and Amerindian descent (90%), with 7% Amerindians.

SOCIAL STATISTICS

Births, 1997 estimates, 187,000; deaths, 32,000. 1997 birth rate, 32·6 per 1,000 population; death rate 5·6. 1997 life expectancy, 67·5 years for men and 72·3 for women; population growth rate, 2·55%. Infant mortality, 1997, 36 per 1,000 live births; fertility rate, 1997, 4·3 births per woman.

CONSTITUTION AND GOVERNMENT

The present Constitution came into force in 1982. The *President* is elected for a 4-year term. Members of the *National Congress* (total 128 seats) and municipal mayors are elected simultaneously on a proportional basis, according to combined votes cast for the Presidential candidate of their party.

RECENT ELECTIONS

Elections were held on 30 Nov. 1997. The PLH gained 67 seats in Congress (49·7% of votes cast), with the remaining seats apportioned to the following parties: Nacional 54 seats (41·3%), Inovación y Unidad 5 seats (4·2%), Unificación Democrática 1 seat (2·6%) and Demócrata Cristiano 1 seat (2·2%). The presidential election on the same day was won by Carlos Roberto Flores Facussé (PLH), with 52·8% of the votes cast against 4 other candidates.

CURRENT ADMINISTRATION

President: Carlos Roberto Flores Facussé, b. 1950 (PLH; sworn in 27 Jan. 1998).

First *Vice President:* William Handal. *Second Vice President:* Gladys Caballero de Arevalo. *Third Vice President:* Hector Vidal Cerrato Hernandez.

In Jan. 2000 the government consisted of:

Minister of Agriculture and Livestock: Guillermo Alvarado Downing. *Culture, Arts and Sports:* Herman Allan Padgett.

Defence: Edgardo Dumas Rodríguez. *Education:* Ramón Calix
Figueroa. *Finance:* Gabriela Nuñez. *Foreign Relations:* Roberto
Flores Bermúdez. *Government and Justice:* Enrique Flores Valeriano.
Industry and Commerce: Oscar Kafati. *Labour:* Rosa America
Miranda de Galo. *Natural Resources and Environment:* Silvia
Xiomara Gómez de Caballero. *Presidency:* Gustavo Adolfo Alfaro
Zelaya. *Public Health:* Plutarco Castellanos. *Public Works,
Transportation and Housing:* Tomás Lozano Reyes. *Security:*
Elizabeth Chiuz Sierra. *Tourism:* Ana Abarca Uclés. *Ministers
without Portfolio:* Jorge Arturo Reina, Nahun Valladares, Roberto
Leiva.

DEFENCE

Conscription was abolished in 1995. In 1998 defence expenditure
totalled US$95m. (US$15 per capita).

ECONOMY

Performance
Real GDP growth was 2·9% in 1998. Hurricane Mitch, which struck in
Oct. 1998, is thought to have set back the economy by 15 to 20
years. As a result the economy was forecast to shrink in 1999 by
12·2%, before recovering in 2000 with a growth rate of 3·0%.

Budget
1997 estimate: Expenditure was US$850m. (including capital expen-
ditures of US$150m.); revenues totalled US$655m.

Currency

The unit of currency is the *lempira* (HNL) of 100 *centavos*. Foreign exchange reserves were US$672m. in Feb. 1998 and gold reserves were 20,000 troy oz. Inflation was 13·7% in 1998 (20·2% in 1997). Total money supply in Dec. 1997 was 8,677m. lempiras.

Banking and Finance

The central bank of issue is the Banco Central de Honduras (*President:* Victoria Asfura de Diaz). There is an agricultural development bank, Banadesa, for small grain producers, a state land bank and a network of rural credit agencies managed by peasant organizations. The Central American Bank for Economic Integration (BCIE) has its head office in Tegucigalpa. In 1999 there were 40 private banks, including 4 foreign.

There are stock exchanges in Tegucigalpa and San Pedro Sula.

INDUSTRY

Industry is small-scale and local. 1994 output: cement, 999·6 tonnes; fabrics, 11,286 yards. 217,835 bottles of beer and 5,300 litres of rum were produced in 1994.

Labour

The workforce was 1·3m. in 1996. In 1995, 37·2% of those in employment were in agriculture, forestry and fishing, 18·0% were in manufacturing industries and 17·0% in community, social and personal services. Unemployment rate (1996 estimate): 15%.

INTERNATIONAL TRADE

Imports and Exports

Imports in 1996 were valued at US$1,840m. and exports at US$1,317m.

Main exports are bananas, coffee, shrimps and lobsters, fruit, lead and zinc, timber, and refrigerated meats. Main imports are machinery and electrical equipment, industrial chemicals and mineral products and lubricants. Principal export markets, 1995: USA, 42·7%; Germany, 19·3%; Japan, 6·7%; Spain, 3·9%. Principal import suppliers, 1995: USA, 46·6%; Netherlands, 7·5%; Guatemala, 6·8%; Mexico, 4·2%.

NICARAGUA

República de Nicaragua
Capital: Managua
Population estimate, 2000: 4·69m.

KEY HISTORICAL EVENTS

Colonization of the Nicaraguan Pacific coast was undertaken by
Spaniards from Panama, beginning in 1523. France and Britain,
however, and later the USA, all tried to play a colonial or semi-
colonial role in Nicaragua. Nicaragua became an independent
republic in 1838 but its independence was often threatened by US
intervention. Between 1910 and 1930 the country was under almost
continuous US military occupation.

In 1914 the Bryan-Chamarro Treaty entitled the USA to a
permanent option for a canal route through Nicaragua, a 99-year
option for a naval base in the Bay of Fonseca on the Pacific coast
and occupation of the Corn Islands on the Atlantic coast. The Bryan-
Chamarro Treaty was not abrogated until 14 July 1970 when the Corn
Islands returned to Nicaragua.

The Samoza family dominated Nicaragua from 1933 to 1979.
Through a brutal dictatorship imposed through the National Guard,
they secured for themselves a large share of the national wealth. In
1962 the radical Sandanista National Liberation Front was formed
with the object of overthrowing the Samozas. After 17 years of civil
war the Sandanistas triumphed. On 17 July 1979 President Samoza
fled into exile. The USA made efforts to unseat the revolutionary
government by supporting the Contras (counter-revolutionary
forces). It was not until 1988 that the state of emergency was lifted as
part of the Central American peace process. Rebel anti-Sandinista
activities had ceased by 1990; the last organized insurgent group
negotiated an agreement with the government in April 1994.

In Oct. 1998 Hurricane Mitch devastated the country causing 3,800 deaths.

TERRITORY AND POPULATION

Nicaragua is bounded in the north by Honduras, east by the Caribbean, south by Costa Rica and west by the Pacific. Area, 130,671 sq. km (121,428 sq. km dry land). The coastline runs 450 km on the Atlantic and 305 km on the Pacific. Population: July 1996, 4,272,400 (1997 estimate, 4,386,400; density, 34 per sq. km). In 1997, 32·2% of the population were urban.

The UN gives a projected population for 2000 of 4·69m.

16 administrative departments are grouped in 3 zones. Areas (in sq. km), populations (in 1,000) and chief towns in 1993:

	Area	Population	Chief town
Pacific Zone	18,429	2,622·5	
Chinandega	4,926	357·7	Chinandega
León	5,107	373·4	León
Managua	3,672	1,188·1	Managua
Masaya	590	225·1	Masaya
Granada	929	165·2	Granada
Carazo	1,050	165·2	Jinotepe
Rivas	2,155	147·8	Rivas
Central-North Zone	35,960	1,417·0	
Chontales	6,378	276·6	Juigalpa
Boaco	4,244	129·0	Boaco
Matagalpa	8,523	403·7	Matagalpa
Jinotega	9,755	190·1	Jinotega
Estelí	2,335	181·2	Estelí
Madriz	1,602	104·4	Somoto

Nueva Segovia	3,123	132·0	Ocotal
Atlantic Zone	67,039	225·3	
Río San Juan	7,473	37·6	San Carlos
Zelaya	59,566	187·7	Bluefields

The capital is Managua with (1995 estimate) 1,200,000 inhabitants. Other cities: León, 100,982; Granada, 88,636; Masaya, 74,946; Chinandega, 67,792; Matagalpa, 36,983; Estelí, 30,635; Tipitapa, 30,078; Chichigalpa, 28,889; Juigalpa, 25,625; Corinto, 24,250; Jinotepe, 23,538.

The population is of Spanish and Amerindian origins with an admixture of Afro-Americans on the Caribbean coast. Ethnic groups in 1997: Mestizo (mixed Amerindian and white), 69%; white, 17%; black, 9%; Amerindian, 5%. The official language is Spanish.

SOCIAL STATISTICS

1996 births, estimate, 150,000; deaths, 26,000. Birth rate 35 (per 1,000 population), death rate 6. Annual growth rate, 1990–95, 3·2%. 1997 life expectancy: male 65·8 years, female 70·6. Infant mortality, 1997, 42 per 1,000 live births; fertility rate, 1997, 4·4 births per woman.

CONSTITUTION AND GOVERNMENT

A new Constitution was promulgated on 9 Jan. 1987. It provides for a unicameral *National Assembly* comprising 90 members directly elected by proportional representation, together with unsuccessful presidential election candidates obtaining a minimum level of votes. The *President* and *Vice-President* are directly elected for a 5-year term commencing on the 10 Jan. following their date of election. The President may stand for a second term, but not consecutively.

RECENT ELECTIONS

Presidential and parliamentary elections were held on 20 Oct. 1996. The electorate was 2·4m. Turn-out was 76%. There were 23 presidential candidates. Arnoldo Alemán was elected by 51·0% of votes cast. At the parliamentary elections the Liberal Alliance gained 42 seats; the Sandinista National Liberation Front, 36; the Christian Way Party, 4; 8 minor parties, 11.

CURRENT ADMINISTRATION

President: Arnoldo Alemán Lacayo, b. 1946 (Liberal Alliance; sworn in on 10 Jan. 1997).

Vice President: Enrique Bolanos Geyer.

In Jan. 2000 the government included:

Minister of Agriculture and Livestock: Jaime Cuadra Sommarriba. *Infrastructure and Transportation:* David Robleto. *Education, Sports and Culture:* Fernando Robleto. *Defence:* José Antonio Alvarado. *Development, Industry and Commerce:* Noel Sacasa. *Environment and Natural Resources:* Roberto Stadhagen. *Finance:* Esteban Duque Estrada. *Foreign Affairs:* Eduardo Montealegre. *Foreign Co-operation:* David Robleto Lang. *Health:* Cabezas Lombardo

Martínez. *Labour:* Mario Montenegro. *Government:* Rene Herrera.
Family: Humberto Belli.

DEFENCE

In 1998 defence expenditure totalled US$29m. (US$6 per capita).

ECONOMY

Performance

Nicaragua's economy is experiencing a boom, with GDP growth of
4·0% in 1998 and forecasts of 4·5% for 1999 and 6·0% for 2000.

Budget

(in 1m. córdobas)

	1992	1993	1994	1995
Revenue	1,893·92	2,162·38	2,476·72	3,136·35
Expenditure	2,497·27	2,982·56	3,514·57	4,176·86

Expenditure by function (1994): defence 231·56, public order
316·29, education 615·86, health 531·36, social security 584·43.

Currency

The monetary unit is the *córdoba* (NIO), of 100 *centavos*, which
replaced the córdoba oro in 1991 at par. Inflation was 17·0% in 1998.
In Feb. 1998 total money supply was 2,205m. córdobas.

Banking and Finance

The Central Bank of Nicaragua came into operation on 1 Jan. 1961 as an autonomous bank of issue, absorbing the issue department of the National Bank. Its *Governor* is Noel Ramírez. There were 9 private commercial banks in 1994.

INDUSTRY

Production in 1993 (in 1,000 tonnes): vegetable oil, 27; wheat flour, 48; main chemical products, 13; cement, 258; metallic products, 2,483; rum, 9,868 litres; processed leather, 309 sq. yards.

Labour

The workforce in 1996 was 1,642,000 (64% males). In 1994, 37% of the economically active population were engaged in agriculture, fisheries and forestry, and 17% in trade, restaurants and hotels. There were 0·32m. unemployed in 1993.

INTERNATIONAL TRADE

Imports and Exports

Foreign trade in US$1m. (1997): exports, 678, consisting of cotton, coffee, chemical products, meat, sugar; imports, 1,335.

Main import suppliers, 1996: USA, 33·9%; Costa Rica, 8·4%; Guatemala, 8·4%; Japan, 7·7%. Main export markets, 1996: USA, 44·9%; Spain, 11·1%; Germany, 9·2%; El Salvador, 8·8%.

Nicaragua signed a letter of intent with the IMF for an enhanced structural adjustment facility up to 2000 and hoped to secure assistance of up to US$1·5bn. from a meeting in April 1998 of a consultative group of donor countries.

PANAMA

República de Panamá
Capital: Panama City
Population estimate, 2000: 2·86m.

KEY HISTORICAL EVENTS

A revolution, inspired by the USA, led to the separation of Panama from the United States of Colombia and the declaration of its independence on 3 Nov. 1903. This was followed by an agreement making it possible for the USA to build and operate a canal connecting the Atlantic and Pacific oceans through the Isthmus of Panama. The treaty granted the USA in perpetuity the use, occupation and control of a Canal Zone, in which the USA would possess full sovereign rights. In return the USA guaranteed the independence of the republic. The Canal was opened on 15 Aug. 1914.

The US domination of Panama has provoked frequent anti-American protests. In 1968 Col. Omar Torrijos Herrera took power in a *coup* and attempted to negotiate a more advantageous treaty with the USA. Two new treaties between Panama and the USA were agreed on 10 Aug. and signed on 7 Sept. 1977. One deals with the operation and defence of the Canal until the end of 1999 and the other guarantees permanent neutrality.

Torryas vacated the presidency in 1978 but maintained his power as head of the National Guard until his death in an air crash in 1981. Subsequently Gen. Manuel Noriega, Torryas' successor as head of the National Guard, became the strong man of the régime. His position was threatened by some internal political opposition and economic pressure applied by the USA but in Oct. 1989 a US-backed coup attempt failed. On 15 Dec. Gen. Noriega declared a 'state of war' with the USA. On 20 Dec. the USA invaded Panama to remove Gen. Noriega from power and he surrendered on 3 Jan. 1990. Accused as a drug dealer he was convicted by a court in Miami and is now serving a 40-year jail sentence.

On 31 Dec. 1999 the Panama Canal was legally handed over to Panama by the USA. All US military personnel left the country as part of the agreement reached in 1977.

TERRITORY AND POPULATION

Panama is bounded in the north by the Caribbean Sea, east by Colombia, south by the Pacific Ocean and west by Costa Rica. The area is 75,517 sq. km. Population at the census of 1990 was 2,329,329 (49% urban; 56·5% in 1997). July 1997 estimate, 2·7m.; density, 36 per sq. km.

The UN gives a projected population for 2000 of 2·86m.

The largest towns (1995) are Panama City, the capital, on the Pacific coast (658,102); its suburb San Miguelito (290,919); Colón, the port on the Atlantic coast (156,289); and David (113,527).

The areas and populations of the 9 provinces and the Special Territory were:

Province	Sq. km	Census 1980	1995 (est.)	Capital
Bocas del Toro	9,506	53,579	119,336	Bocas del Toro
Chiriquí	8,924	287,801	407,849	David
Veraguas	11,226	173,195	219,049	Santiago
Herrera	2,185	81,866	101,198	Chitré
Los Santos	4,587	70,200	79,935	Las Tablas
Coclé	4,981	140,320	189,579	Penonomé
Colón	7,205	166,439	226,139	Colón
San Blas (Special Territory)	3,206			El Porvenir

| Panama | 11,400 | 830,278 | 1,232,390 | Panama City |
| Darién | 15,458 | 26,497 | 55,538 | La Palma |

The population is a mix of African, American, Arab, Chinese, European and Indian immigrants. The official language is Spanish.

SOCIAL STATISTICS

1995 births, 62,000; deaths, 14,000; marriages (1994), 13,523. Birth rate, 1995 (per 1,000 population): 23·7; death rate: 5·2. Annual growth rate, 1990–95, 1·9%. Expectation of life at birth, 1997, was 71·8 years for males and 76·4 years for females. In 1994 the most popular age range for marrying was 25–29 for males and 20–24 for females. Infant mortality, 1997, 18 per 1,000 live births; fertility rate, 1997, 2·6 births per woman.

CONSTITUTION AND GOVERNMENT

The 1972 Constitution, as amended in 1978 and 1983, provides for a *President*, elected for 5 years, 2 *Vice-Presidents* and a 72-seat *Legislative Assembly* to be elected for 5-year terms by a direct vote. To remain registered, parties must have attained at least 50,000 votes at the last election. A referendum held on 15 Nov. 1992 rejected constitutional reforms by 64% of votes cast. Turn-out was 40%. In a referendum on 30 Aug. 1998 voters rejected proposed changes to the constitution which would allow for a President to serve a second consecutive term.

RECENT ELECTIONS

In the presidential election on 2 May 1999, Mireya Moscoso de Gruber of the conservative Arnulfist Party won, obtaining 44·9% of votes cast against 2 other candidates. She thus became Panama's first woman president. Turn-out was 75%, up from 74% in 1994 and 64% in 1989. In the Legislative Assembly elections, also held on 2 May 1999, the New Nation Alliance won 41 seats (Revolutionary Democratic Party, 34; Solidarity Party, 4; National Liberal Party, 3) with a combined 57·7% of the vote. The Union for Panama Alliance won 24 seats (Arnulfist Party, 18; Liberal Republican Nationalist Movement, 5; National Renewal Movement, 1) with a combined 33·8%. The remaining 6 seats went to Opposition Action (Christian Democrat Party, 5; Civil Renewal Party, 1) with 8·5%.

CURRENT ADMINISTRATION

President: Mireya Elisa Moscoso, b. 1946 (Arnulfist Party; sworn in 1 Sept. 1999).

First Vice-President: Arturo Ulises Vallarino. *Second Vice-President:* Dominador Kaiser Baldonero Bazan.

In Jan. 2000 the government comprised:

Minister of Government and Justice: Winston Spadafora. *Foreign Relations:* José Miguel Aleman. *Canal Affairs:* Ricardo Martinelli Berrocal. *Public Works:* Moises Castillo. *Economy and Finance:* Victor Juliao. *Agricultural Development:* Alejandro Posse Martínez. *Commerce and Industry:* Joaquin Jacome Diaz. *Health:* José Manuel Teran Sitton. *Labour and Labour Development:* Joaquin José Vallarino III. *Education:* Doris Rosas de Mata. *Housing:* Miguel Cardenas. *Women, Youth, Family and Childhood:* Alba Esther Tejada de Rolla. *Minister of the Presidency:* Ivonne Young Valdes.

DEFENCE

The armed forces were disbanded in 1990 and constitutionally abolished in 1994. Divided between both coasts, the National Maritime Service, a coast guard rather than a navy, numbered around 400 personnel in 1999. In addition there is a paramilitary police force of 11,000 and a paramilitary air force of 400 with no combat aircraft. In 1998 defence expenditure totalled US$118m. (US$42 per capita).

ECONOMY

Performance

Real GDP growth was 3·9% in 1998. For 1999 the growth rate was forecast to be 1·8% followed by a rise of 3·8% in 2000.

Budget

Revenues in 1996 were 2,140·3m. balboas (2,065·1m. balboas in 1995); expenditures were 2,255·3m. balboas in 1996 (1,953·3m. balboas in 1995).

Currency

The monetary unit is the *balboa* (PAB) of 100 *centésimos*, at parity with the US dollar. The only paper currency used is that of the USA. US coinage is also legal tender. Inflation in 1998 was 0·6%. In Feb. 1998 foreign exchange reserves were US$1,103m. In Dec. 1997 total money supply was 996m. balboas.

Banking and Finance

There is no statutory central bank. Banking is supervised and promoted by the National Banking Commission. Government accounts are handled through the state-owned *Banco Nacional de Panama*. There are 2 other state banks. The number of commercial banks was 108 in 1996. Total assets, June 1996, US$33,400m., total deposits, US$25,000m. (including offshore, US$15,900m.).

INDUSTRY

The main industry is agricultural produce processing. Other areas include oil refining, chemicals and paper-making.

Labour
In 1996 the workforce (persons 15 years and over) numbered 1,001,439, of whom 870,622 were employed.

INTERNATIONAL TRADE

Imports and Exports
Trade in 1996: exports, US$620m.; imports, US$2,780m. Main exports: bananas, shellfish, sugar. Chief export markets: USA, 37·5%; Germany, 12·2%; Sweden, 9%; Costa Rica, 7·1%; Belgium, 7%. Chief import suppliers: USA, 38%; Japan, 7·1%; Ecuador, 4%; Costa Rica, 3%.

PARAGUAY

República del Paraguay
Capital: Asunción
Population estimate, 2000: 5·5m.

KEY HISTORICAL EVENTS

Paraguay was occupied by the Spanish in 1537 and became a Spanish colony as part of the viceroyalty of Peru. The area gained its independence, as the Republic of Paraguay, on 14 May 1811. Paraguay was then ruled by a succession of dictators. During a devastating war fought from 1865 to 1870 between Paraguay and a coalition of Argentina, Brazil and Uruguay, Paraguay's population was reduced from about 600,000 to 233,000. Further severe losses were incurred during the war with Bolivia (1932–35) over territorial claims in the Chaco inspired by the unfounded belief that minerals existed in the territory. A peace treaty by which Paraguay obtained most of the area her troops had conquered was signed in July 1938.

A new constitution took effect in Feb. 1968 under which executive power is discharged by an executive president. Gen. Alfredo Stroessner Mattiauda was re-elected 7 times between 1958 and 1988. Since then, Paraguay has been under more or less democratic government. On 23 March 1999, Paraguay's vice-president Luis Maria Argaña was assassinated. The following day, Congress voted to impeach President Cubas who was said to be implicated in the murder. He then resigned.

TERRITORY AND POPULATION

Paraguay is bounded in the northwest by Bolivia, northeast and east
by Brazil and southeast, south and southwest by Argentina. The area
is 406,752 sq. km (157,042 sq. miles).

The population (census 1992) was 4·12m.; estimate (July 1998)
5·29m.; density, 13·0 per sq. km. In 1997, 53·9% lived in urban areas.

The UN gives a projected population for 2000 of 5·5m.

In 1995 the capital, Asunción (and metropolitan area), had an
estimated population of 1,081,000.

The population is mixed Spanish and Guaraní Indian. There are
some 46,700 unassimilated Indians of other tribal origin, in the Chaco
and the forests of eastern Paraguay. 40·1% of the population speak
only Guaraní; 48·2% are bilingual (Spanish/Guaraní); and 6·4%
speak only Spanish. Mennonites, who arrived in 3 groups (1927,
1930 and 1947), are settled in the Chaco and eastern Paraguay.
There are also Korean and Japanese settlers.

SOCIAL STATISTICS

1997 births, estimate, 172,000; deaths, 24,000. Rates, 1997
estimates (per 1,000 population): birth, 30·5; death, 4·2. 1997
growth, 2·62%. Expectation of life, 1997: 67·5 years for men and 72·0
for women. Infant mortality, 1997, 27 per 1,000 live births; fertility
rate, 1997, 4·2 births per woman.

CONSTITUTION AND GOVERNMENT

On 18 June 1992 a Constituent Assembly approved a new
constitution. The head of state is the *President,* elected for a

non-renewable 5-year term. Parliament consists of an 80-member *Chamber of Deputies,* elected from departmental constituencies, and a 45-member *Senate,* elected from a single national constituency.

RECENT ELECTIONS

Parliamentary and presidential elections were held on 10 May 1998. Raúl Cubas Grau of the authoritarian Republican National Alliance/ Colorado Party was elected President against 1 opponent with 55·4% of votes cast. At the parliamentary elections the Colorado Party gained 45 seats in the Chamber of Deputies with 53·8% of votes cast (and 24 in the Senate), the Authentic Radical Liberal Party 27 (and 13) and National Encounter 8 (and 7). The alliance of the liberal Authentic Radical Liberal Party and the centrist National Encounter received 42·7% of the votes.

CURRENT ADMINISTRATION

President: Luis González Macchi, b. 1947 (sworn in 28 March 1999).
   In Jan. 2000 the cabinet comprised:
   Minister of Agriculture and Livestock (interim), Finance and Economy: Frederico Zayas. *Education and Worship:* Nicanor Duarte Frutos. *Foreign Relations:* José Felix Fernandez Estigarribia. *Industry and Commerce:* Euclides Acevedo. *Interior:* Walter Bower Montalto. *Justice and Labour:* Silvio Ferreira. *National Defence:* Nelson Argana. *Public Health and Social Welfare:* Martin Chiola. *Public Works and Communications:* José Alberto Planas. *Secretary General for the Presidency:* Juan Ernesto Villamayor.

DEFENCE

The army, navy and air forces are separate services under a single command. The President of the Republic is the active C.-in-C. Conscription is for 12 months (2 years in the navy).

Defence expenditure totalled US$128m. in 1998 (US$24 per capita).

ECONOMY

Performance

Paraguay's economy has been experiencing a severe recession. In 1998 GDP growth was negative, at –0·2%, with a forecast for 1999 of a rate of –3·0%. It is anticipated that there will then be a recovery, with a growth rate of 1·3% in 2000.

Budget

In 1995 (in 1m. guaranís) revenue was 2,078,993 and expenditure 2,971,354; in 1994 revenue was 2,253,138 and expenditure 2,038,193.

Currency

The unit of currency is the *guaraní* (PYG), notionally divided into 100 *céntimos*. In Nov. 1997 total money supply was 1,607m. guaranís. In Feb. 1998 foreign exchange reserves were US$486m. and gold reserves were 30,000 troy oz. Inflation was 11·5% in 1998.

Banking and Finance

The Central Bank is a state-owned autonomous agency with the sole right of note issue, control over foreign exchange and the supervision of commercial banks (*Governor*, Hermes Gómez). In 1994 there were

28 commercial banks (mostly foreign), 2 other banking institutions, 1 investment bank, 1 development bank and 6 building societies. There is a stock exchange in Asunción.

INDUSTRY

Production, 1994 (1,000 tons): frozen meat, 45·8; cotton fibre, 136·8; sugar, 110·8; rice, 81·9; wheat flour, 47·8; edible oil, 78·9; industrial oil, 10·0; tung oil, 6·8; cement, 528·8; soybean, peanut and coconut flour, 468; cigarettes (1988) (1m. packets), 46,598; matches (1,000 boxes), 8,979.

Labour
The labour force in 1996 totalled 1,831,000 (71% males). Over 40% of the economically active population in 1993 were engaged in agriculture, fisheries and forestry. In 1993 there was a monthly minimum wage of 269,445 guaranís.

INTERNATIONAL TRADE

Imports and Exports
Imports in 1995 totalled US$3,144m. and exports US$919m.

Main exports in 1994 (in US$1m.): cotton fibre, 170·9; soya, 222·3; timber, 78·6; hides, 63; meat, 55·4. Main imports: machinery, 476·2; vehicles, 276·8; fuel and lubricants, 159·4; beverages and tobacco, 179; chemicals, 145; foodstuffs, 99·1.

Main export markets in 1994 (in US$1m.): Brazil, 323·7; Netherlands, 160; Argentina, 90·7; USA, 56·9; Italy, 24·2; Germany, 13·2. Main import suppliers: Brazil, 555; Argentina, 308·1; USA, 243·3; Japan, 193·3; UK, 58·2.

PERU

República del Perú
Capital: Lima
Population estimate, 2000: 25·66m.

KEY HISTORICAL EVENTS

The Incas of Peru were conquered by the Spanish in the 16th century
and subsequent Spanish colonial settlement made Peru the most
important of the Spanish viceroyalties in South America. On 28 July
1821 Peru declared its independence, but it was not until after a war
which ended in 1824 that the country gained its freedom. In a war
with Chile (1879–83) Peru's capital, Lima, was captured and she lost
some of her southern territory. Tacna, in the far south of the country,
remained in Chilean control from 1880 until 1929. In 1924 Dr Victor
Raúl Haya de la Torre founded the *Alianza Popular Revolucionaria
Americana* to oppose the dictatorial government then in power. The
party was banned between 1931 and 1945 and between 1948 and
1956 its leader failed regularly in the presidential elections but it was
at times the largest party in Congress. The closeness of the 1962
elections led Gen. Ricardo Pérez Godoy, Chairman of the Joint
Chiefs-of-Staff, to seize power. A *coup* led by Gen. Nicolás Lindley
López deposed him in 1963. There followed, after elections, a period
of civilian rule but the military staged yet another *coup* in 1968. In
1978–79 a constituent assembly drew up a new constitution, after
which a civilian government was installed. On 6 April 1992 the
President suspended the constitution and dissolved the parliament.
A new constitution was promulgated on 29 Dec. 1993.

TERRITORY AND POPULATION

Peru is bounded in the north by Ecuador and Colombia, east by
Brazil and Bolivia, south by Chile and west by the Pacific Ocean.
Area, 1,285,216 sq. km.

For an account of the border dispute with Ecuador *see*
ECUADOR: Territory and Population.

Census population, 1993, 22,639,443. 1998 estimate, 24,800,768.
Urban 17,732,549 (71·5%; 71·6% in 1997); rural 7,068,219. Density,
19 per sq. km.

The UN gives a projected population for 2000 of 25·66m.

Area and 1998 population estimate of the 24 departments and the
constitutional province of Callao, together with their capitals:

Department	Area (in sq. km)	Population	Capital	Population
Amazonas	39,249	391,078	Chachapoyas	17,527
Ancash	35,826	1,045,921	Huaraz	79,012
Apurímac	15,666	418,775	Abancay	49,513
Arequipa	63,345	1,035,773	Arequipa	710,103
Ayacucho	43,814	525,601	Ayacucho	118,960
Cajamarca	33,247	1,377,297	Cajamarca	108,009
Callao[1]	147	736,243	Callao	424,294
Cusco	71,892	1,131,061	Cusco	278,590
Huancavelica	22,131	423,041	Huancavelica	35,123
Huánuco	36,938	747,263	Huánuco	129,688
Ica	21,328	628,684	Ica	194,820
Junín	44,410	1,161,581	Huancayo	305,039
La Libertad	25,570	1,415,512	Trujillo	603,657
Lambayeque	14,231	1,050,280	Chiclayo	375,058
Lima	34,802	7,194,816	Lima	6,464,693
Loreto	368,852	839,748	Iquitos	334,013
Madre de Dios	85,183	79,172	Puerto Maldonado	27,407

Moquegua	15,734	142,475	Moquegua	44,824
Pasco	25,320	245,651	Cerro de Pasco	70,058
Piura	35,892	1,506,716	Piura	308,155
Puno	71,999	1,171,838	Puno	101,578
San Martín	51,253	692,408	Moyobamba	31,256
Tacna	16,076	261,336	Tacna	215,683
Tumbes	4,669	183,609	Tumbes	87,557
Ucayali	102,411	394,889	Pucallpa	220,866

[1]Constitutional province.

In 1991 there were some 100,000 Peruvians of Japanese origin. The official languages are Spanish (spoken by 80·3% of the population in 1993), Quechua (16·5%) and Aymara (3%).

SOCIAL STATISTICS

1996 births, 615,300; deaths, 156,800; infant deaths (under 1 year), 58,300. Rates per 1,000 population (1998 estimate): birth, 25·7; death, 6·5. Annual growth rate, 1990–95, 2%; infant mortality, 1997, 44 per 1,000 live births. Life expectancy, 1997: males, 65·9 years; females, 70·9. Fertility rate, 1997, 3·0 births per woman.

CONSTITUTION AND GOVERNMENT

The 1980 Constitution provided for a legislative *Congress* consisting of a *Senate* (60 members) and a *Chamber of Deputies* (180 members) and an Executive formed of the President and a Council of

Ministers appointed by him. Elections were to be every 5 years with the President and Congress elected, at the same time, by separate ballots.

On 5 April 1992 President Fujimori suspended the 1980 constitution and dissolved Congress.

A referendum was held on 31 Oct. 1993 to approve the twelfth constitution, including a provision for the president to serve a consecutive second term. 52·24% of votes cast were in favour. The constitution was promulgated on 29 Dec. 1993. In Aug. 1996 Congress voted for the eligibility of the President to serve a third consecutive term of office. All citizens over the age of 18 are eligible to vote. Voting is compulsory.

President Fujimori estimates that El Niño caused US$12m. worth of infrastructure damage, killed over 100 people and resulted in tens of thousands becoming homeless. The government declared a state of emergency in 9 out of the country's 24 regions. A programme to rebuild the infrastructure, namely communication lines (bridges, roads, railway lines and canals) and healthcare facilities, to prevent the spread of epidemics, has been initiated. President Fujimori regained popularity owing to his efforts to combat the effects of El Niño.

RECENT ELECTIONS

Elections were held on 9 April 1995 for President and a new 120-member, single-chamber Congress, to replace the former 80-member Constituent Assembly. The electorate was 12m. President Fujimori was re-elected by 64·42% of votes cast. In the Congressional elections, Change 90-New Majority won 67 seats with 52·1% of votes cast, Pérez de Cuellar's Union for Peru movement gained 17 seats, American Revolutionary People's Alliance 8, Moralising Independent Front 6, the Democratic Coordination-Possible Country 5, and 8 other parties got 4 seats or less.

The next presidential and parliamentary elections were scheduled to take place on 9 April 2000.

CURRENT ADMINISTRATION

President: Alberto Kenyo Fujimori Fujimori, b. 1938 (Change 90 Movement; sworn in 28 July 1990).

In Jan. 2000 the government comprised:

President of the Council of Ministers (Prime Minister) and Minister of Justice: Alberto Bustamante.

Minister of Economy and Finance: Efrain Goldenberg. *Fisheries:* Cesar Luna-Victoria Leon. *Foreign Affairs:* Fernando De Trazegnies Granda. *Interior:* Cesar Saucedo. *Defence:* Gen. Carlos Bergamino Cruz. *Public Health:* Alejandro Aguinaga. *Labour and Social Promotion:* Pedro Flores Polo. *Agriculture:* Belisario De Las Casas Piedras. *Energy and Mines:* Jorge Chamot. *Industry, Tourism, Commerce, Integration and International Trade Affairs:* Juan Carlos Hurtado Miller. *Transport, Communications, Housing and Construction:* Alberto Pandolfi Arbulu. *Education:* Felipe Ignaçio Garçia Escudero. *Of the Presidency:* Edgardo Mosqueira. *Promotion of Women and Human Development:* Luisa Maria Cuculiza Torres.

DEFENCE

There is selective conscription for 2 years. Defence expenditure totalled US$970m. in 1998 (US$39 per capita).

ECONOMY

Performance

GDP growth in 1998 was 0·7%, with forecasts for 1999 and 2000 of 2·2% and 5·3% respectively.

Budget

At US$10·2bn., the 1998 budget is 10% higher in real terms than in 1997. There was a trade deficit of US$1·7bn. in 1997. In 1997 the World Bank approved a US$150m. loan to help Peru overcome expected problems associated with El Niño.

Currency

The monetary unit is the *nuevo sol* (PES), of 100 *céntimos*, which replaced the inti in 1990 at a rate of 1m. intis = 1 nuevo sol. Inflation was 7·3% in 1998. Foreign exchange reserves were US$10,954m. in Jan. 1998 and gold reserves 1·11m. troy oz in Feb. 1998. In Dec. 1997 total money supply was 14,825m. sols.

Banking and Finance

The bank of issue is the Banco Central de Reserva (*Governor*, Germán Suárez Chávez), which was established in 1922. The government's fiscal agent is the Banco de la Nación. In 1995 there were additionally 17 domestic commercial, 1 foreign and 4 multinational banks. Legislation of April 1991 permitted financial institutions to fix their own interest rates and reopened the country to foreign banks. The Central Reserve Banks sets the upper limit.

There are stock exchanges in Lima and Arequipa.

INDUSTRY

About 70% of industries are located in the Lima/Callao metropolitan area. Products include pig-iron, blooms, billets, largets, round and round-deformed bars, wire rod, black and galvanized sheets and galvanized roofing sheets.

Labour

The labour force in 1996 totalled 8,652,000 (71% males). In 1993, 1,852,800 people worked in agriculture, 72,200 in mining, 783,900 in manufacturing, 255,000 in building, 1,167,000 in commerce, 347,500 in transport and 599,700 in services. In Dec. 1994 the minimum monthly wage was 132 sols. In 1999 an estimated 7·9% of the workforce was unemployed, up from 5·9% in 1991.

INTERNATIONAL TRADE

Imports and Exports

The value of trade has been as follows (in US$1m.):

	1990	1991	1992	1993	1994	1995	1996
Imports	2,930	3,630	4,090	4,123	5,596	7,761	7,897
Exports	3,323	3,391	3,594	3,536	4,598	5,591	5,897

In 1996 the main export markets (in US$1m.) were: USA, 1,154·4; UK, 424·2; Japan, 388; China, 419·4; Germany, 300·7. Main import suppliers: USA, 1,858·4; Japan, 317·8; Brazil, 328·6; Colombia, 633·2, Venezuela, 528·7. Main exports, 1996 (in US$1m.): fishmeal, 834·9; gold, 579·3; refined copper, 715·6, zinc, 273·3.

The central bank predicts that the combined effects of the Asian economic crisis of 1997 and El Niño will result in lower export earnings and increased food imports to compensate for lost agricultural production.

SURINAME

Republic of Suriname
Capital: Paramaribo
Population estimate, 2000: 452,000

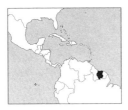

KEY HISTORICAL EVENTS

The first Europeans to reach the area were the Spanish in 1499 but it was the British who established a colony in 1650. At the peace of Breda (1667), Suriname was assigned to the Netherlands in exchange for the colony of New Netherland in North America. Suriname was twice in British possession during the Napoleonic Wars, in 1799–1802 and 1804–16, when it was returned to the Netherlands.

On 25 Nov. 1975 Suriname gained full independence. On 25 Feb. 1980 the government was ousted in a *coup* and a National Military Council (NMC) established. A further *coup* on 13 Aug. replaced several members of the NMC and the State President. Other attempted *coups* took place in 1981 and 1982, with the NMC retaining control. In Oct. 1987 a new constitution was approved by referendum. Following elections in Nov. Suriname returned to democracy in Jan. 1988 but on 24 Dec. 1990 a further military *coup* deposed the government. There was a peace agreement with rebel groups in Aug. 1992 and elections were held in May 1996.

TERRITORY AND POPULATION

Suriname is located on the northern coast of South America between 2–6° North latitude and 54–59° West longitude. It is bounded in the north by the Atlantic Ocean, east by French Guiana, west by Guyana, and south by Brazil. Area, 163,820 sq. km. Census population (1995), 407,000. Estimate, Jan. 1997, 417,000; density, 3 per sq. km. The UN gives a projected population for 2000 of 452,000.

In 1997, 50·3% lived in urban areas. The capital, Paramaribo, had (1997 estimate) 289,000 inhabitants.

Suriname is divided into 10 districts. They are (with 1992 population estimate and chief town): Brokopondo, population 7,554 (Brokopondo); Commewijne, 22,822 (Nieuw Amsterdam); Coronie, 3,151 (Totness); Marowijne, 18,339 (Albina); Nickerie, 37,200 (Nieuw Nickerie); Para, 13,693 (Onverwacht); Paramaribo, 240,000 – representing 66% of Suriname's total population (Paramaribo); Saramacca, 12,320 (Groningen); Sipaliwini, 26,458 (local authority in Paramaribo); Wanica, 69,114 (Lelydorp).

Major ethnic groups in percentages of the population in 1991: Creole, 35%; Indian, 33%; Javanese, 16%; Bushnegroes (Blacks),10%; Amerindian, 3%.

The official language is Dutch. English is widely spoken next to Hindi, Javanese and Chinese as inter-group communication. A vernacular, called 'Sranan' or 'Surinamese', is used as a lingua franca. In 1976 it was decided that Spanish was to become the nation's principal working language.

SOCIAL STATISTICS

Births, 1995, 10,100; deaths, 2,400. 1995 rates per 1,000 population: birth rate, 23·6; death rate, 5·6. Annual growth rate, 1990–95, 0·9%. Expectation of life, 1997, was 67·5 years for males and 72·7 for females. Infant mortality, 1997, 24 per 1,000 live births; fertility rate, 1997, 2·2 births per woman.

CONSTITUTION AND GOVERNMENT

Parliament is a 51-member *National Assembly*. The head of state is the *President*, elected for a 5-year term by a two-thirds majority by the National Assembly, or, failing that, by an electoral college, the United People's Conference (UPC) enlarged by the inclusion of regional and local councillors, by a simple majority.

RECENT ELECTIONS

Parliamentary elections were held on 23 May 1996. The National Democratic Party (NDP) won 16 of the available 51 seats (25·6% of the vote), followed by the National Party of Suriname with 9, the Progressive Reform Party with 9, the Party for National Unity and Solidarity (KTPI) with 5, Democratic Alternative '91 with 4, Pendawalima with 4, Democratic Party/Renewed Progressive Party Alliance with 3 and the Suriname Labour Party with 1. A coalition government was formed by the NDP, KTPI and the Basis Party for Renewal and Democracy.

The next parliamentary elections were scheduled to take place on 25 May 2000.

CURRENT ADMINISTRATION

President: Jules Wijdenbosch, b. 1941 (NDP; elected by the UPC on 5 Sept. 1996, sworn in 14 Sept. 1996).

Vice-President: Pretaapnarain Radhakisun.

In Jan. 2000 the government comprised:

Minister of Foreign Affairs and Defence: Errol Snijders. *Finance and Natural Resources:* Errol Alibux. *Justice and Police, Regional Development:* Yvonne Raveles-Resida. *Public Works, Education and Human Development:* Rudolf Vishnudath Mangal. *Transport, Communication and Tourism, Planning and Development Cooperation:* Dick De Bie. *Health, Social Affairs and Labour:* Soewarto Moestadja. *Agriculture and Fisheries:* Saimin Redjosentono. *Interior and Home Affairs, Trade and Industry:* Sonny Kertoidjojo.

DEFENCE

Defence expenditure totalled US$15m. in 1998 (US$35 per capita).

ECONOMY

Performance

Real GDP growth was 3·4% in 1998 (4·7% in 1997).

Budget

1996 revenue (in 1m. Sf) was 90,874·6 (68,918·0 in 1995), made up of direct taxes, 38,371·4; indirect taxes, 29,285·9; bauxite levy and other revenues, 22,697·4; aid, 519·9.

Total expenditure was 96,957·5 (94,900·7 in 1995), made up of wages and salaries, 27,598·4; transfers and subsidies, 13,235·3; interest, 1,659·5; social securities, 994·1; material cost, 595·1; other current expenditures, 52,463·2; development expenditure, 411·9.

Currency

The unit of currency is the *Suriname guilder* (SRG; written as Sf[lorin]) of 100 *cents*. Foreign exchange reserves totalled US$103m. and gold reserves were 210,000 troy oz in Feb. 1998. Total money supply in May 1997 was 61,792m. Sf. Inflation in 1998 was 21·1%.

Banking and Finance

The Central Bank of Suriname is a bankers' bank and also the bank of issue. There are 3 commercial banks; the Suriname People's Credit Bank operates under the auspices of the government. There is a post office savings bank, a mortgage bank, an investment bank, a long-term investments agency, a National Development Bank and an Agrarian Bank.

INDUSTRY

There are aluminium smelting, food-processing and wood-using industries. Production, 1994: cement, 24,665 tonnes (estimate); palm oil, 1,051,000 litres (estimate); beer 3,456,000 litres; alumina, 1,498,000 tonnes; aluminium, 26,700 tonnes; cigarettes, 443m.; shoes, 98,990 pairs (estimate); plywood, 6,864 cu. metres.

Labour

Out of 77,900 people in employment in 1994, 35,700 were in community, social and personal services, 13,400 in trade, restaurants and hotels and 6,300 in manufacturing. There were 11,300 unemployed persons, or 12·7% of the workforce.

INTERNATIONAL TRADE

Imports and Exports

In 1995 (provisional) imports totalled 258,916·7m. Sf and exports, 211,020·6m. Sf. Principal imports, 1995 (in 1m. Sf): raw materials and semi-manufactured goods, 94,254·3; investment goods, 65,128·7; fuels and lubricants, 28,629·4; foodstuffs, 24,987·6; cars and motor-cycles, 9,244·8; textiles, 3,986·0. Principal exports, 1994 (in 1m. Sf): alumina, 42,358·2; aluminium, 5,278·2; shrimps, 5,257·4; rice, 3,402·3; bananas and plantains, 1,274·3; wood and wood products, 261·4.

In 1995 (provisional) exports, including re-exports, (in 1m. Sf) were mainly to Netherlands (58,963·3), Norway (52,587·8), USA (47,126·1), Japan (12,835·7) and Brazil (10,889·0); imports were mainly from the USA (109,068·9), Netherlands (51,337·3), Trinidad and Tobago (19,071·5), Netherlands Antilles (6,582·5), Japan (5,513·7), UK (2,580·3).

URUGUAY

República Oriental
del Uruguay
Capital: Montevideo
Population estimate, 2000: 3·27m.

KEY HISTORICAL EVENTS

Uruguay was the last colony settled by Spain in the Americas. Part of
the Spanish viceroyalty of Rio de la Plata until revolutionaries
expelled the Spanish in 1811 and subsequently a province of Brazil,
Uruguay declared independence on 25 Aug. 1825. Conflict between
two political parties, the *blancos* (conservatives) and the *colorados*
(liberals), led, in 1865-70, to the War of the Triple Alliance. In 1903,
peace and prosperity were restored under President José Battle y
Ördónezo. Since 1904 Uruguay has been unique in her constitutional
innovations, all designed to protect her from dictatorship. A favoured
device was the collegiate system of government, in which the two
largest political parties were represented.

The early part of the 20th century saw the development of a
welfare state in Uruguay which encouraged extensive immigration. In
1919 a new constitution was adopted providing for a *colegiado* – a
plural executive based on the Swiss pattern. However, the system
was abolished in 1933 and replaced by presidential government,
with quadrennial elections. From 1951 to 1966 a collective form of
leadership again replaced the presidency. During the 1960s,
following a series of strikes and riots, the Army became increasingly
influential, repressive measures were adopted and presidential
government was restored in 1967. The Tupamaro, Marxist urban
guerrillas, sought violent revolution but were finally defeated by the
Army in 1972. The return to civilian rule came on 12 Feb. 1985.

TERRITORY AND POPULATION

Uruguay is bounded on the northeast by Brazil, on the southeast by the Atlantic, on the south by the Río de la Plata and on the west by Argentina. The area is 176,215 sq. km (68,037 sq. miles). The following table shows the area and the population of the 19 departments at census 1985:

Departments	Sq. km	Census 1985	Capital	Census 1985
Artigas	11,928	68,400	Artigas	34,551
Canelones	4,536	359,700	Canelones	17,316
Cerro-Largo	13,648	78,000	Melo	42,329
Colonia	6,106	112,100	Colonia	19,077
Durazno	11,643	54,700	Durazno	27,602
Flores	5,144	24,400	Trinidad	18,271
Florida	10,417	65,400	Florida	28,560
Lavalleja	10,016	61,700	Minas	34,634
Maldonado	4,793	93,000	Maldonado	33,498
Montevideo	530	1,309,100	Montevideo	1,247,920
Paysandú	13,922	104,500	Paysandú	75,081
Río Negro	9,282	47,500	Fray Bentos	20,431
Rivera	9,370	88,400	Rivera	56,335
Rocha	10,551	68,500	Rocha	23,910
Salto	14,163	107,300	Salto	80,787
San José	4,992	91,900	San José	31,732
Soriano	9,008	77,500	Mercedes	37,110
Tacuarembó	15,438	82,600	Tacuarembó	40,470
Treinta y Tres	9,529	45,500	Treinta y Tres	30,956

Total population, census (1996) 3,137,668 (89·3% urban). Population density, 17·8 per sq. km.

The UN gives a projected population for 2000 of 3·27m.

In 1996 Montevideo (the capital) accounted for 44·5% of the total population. Uruguay has the highest percentage of urban population in South America, with 90·7% living in urban areas in 1997.

13% of the population are over 65; 24% are under 15; 63% are between 15 and 64.

The official language is Spanish.

SOCIAL STATISTICS

1996 births, 55,000; deaths, 30,000. Rates (per 1,000 population), 1996: birth, 17·6; death, 9·7. Population growth rate, growth, 0·7%. Infant mortality, 1997 (per 1,000 live births), 18. Life expectancy in 1997 was 70·5 years among males and 78·0 years among females. Fertility rate, 1997, 2·4 births per woman.

CONSTITUTION AND GOVERNMENT

Congress consists of a *Senate* of 31 members and a *Chamber of Deputies* of 99 members, both elected by proportional representation for 5-year terms. The electoral system provides that the successful presidential candidate be a member of the party which gains a parliamentary majority. Electors vote for deputies on a first-past-the-post system, and simultaneously vote for a presidential candidate of the same party. The winners of the second vote are credited with the number of votes obtained by their party in the parliamentary elections. Referendums may be called at the instigation of 10,000 signatories. A referendum was held on 8 Dec. 1996 to prohibit parties from presenting more than 1 candidate in presidential elections, and to provide for 2 rounds of voting if no candidate gained an absolute majority in the first round. 50·2% of votes cast were in favour.

RECENT ELECTIONS

Elections for the General Assembly were held on 31 Oct. 1999. In elections to the Chamber of Deputies 40 seats were won by the Progressive Encounter (comprised of the Uruguay Assembly, Frenteamplio Confluence, Current 78, Movement of Popular Participation, Christian-Democratic Party, Communist Party of Uruguay, Party of the Communes, Socialist Party of Uruguay and the Social Democrats) with a combined 38·5% of the vote. The Colorado Party (PC) won 32 seats (31·3%), the National Party-Whites (PN) 22 (21·3%) and New Space 4 (4·4%). A coalition government was formed between PC and PN. In the Senate election, PC won 10 seats, PN 7, New Space 1 and Progressive Encounter 12.

In a runoff for the presidency on 28 Nov. 1999, Jorge Batlle won 54·1% of the vote and Tabaré Vázquez 45·9%. In the first round of voting, consisting of 4 candidates, Tabaré Vázquez had polled most votes.

CURRENT ADMINISTRATION

President: Jorge Batlle (PC; elected 28 Nov. 1999).
Vice-President: Hugo Fernandez Faingold.
    The government in Jan. 2000 comprised:
    Minister of the Interior: Guillermo Stirling. *Foreign Affairs:* Didier

Opertti. *Finance and Economy:* Luis Mosca Sobrero. *Transport and Public Works:* Lucio Cáceres Behrens. *Health:* Dr José Raúl Bustos Alonso. *Labour and Social Security:* Dr Ana Lia Piñeyrua. *Education and Culture:* Samuel Lichtensztejn. *Defence:* Juan Luis Storace. *Industry, Energy and Mining:* Dr Julio Herrera. *Tourism:* Benito Stern Prac. *Housing and Environment:* Juan A. Chiruchi Fuentes. *Agriculture and Fishing:* Luis Brezzo.

DEFENCE

Defence expenditure totalled US$309m. in 1998 (US$96 per capita).

ECONOMY

Performance

In 1997 the economy grew by almost 6% and in 1998 by 4·5%. In 1999, however, as a consequence of the devaluation of the Brazilian *real*, it was forecast to shrink by 2·7%. It is then forecast to recover in 2000 and grow by 3·5%.

Budget

Central government finance (millions of pesos):

	1992	1993	1994	1995	1996	1997
Revenue	6,695	10,030	15,095	21,141	28,845	38,180
Expenditure	4,661	9,039	13,968	15,657	19,628	25,535

Components of 1995 revenue: VAT, 44·9%; customs duties, 5·7%; fuel tax, 7·9%; income tax, 10%; capital gains tax, 5·7%. Expenditure included: social welfare and salaries, 60·8%; interest on public debt, 7%; capital expenditure, 10·9%.

Standard rate of VAT is 23%.

Currency

The unit of currency is the *Uruguayan peso* (UYP), of 100 *centésimos*, which replaced the nuevo peso in March 1993 at 1 Uruguayan peso = 1,000 nuevos pesos. Foreign exchange reserves were US$1,540m. and gold reserves 1·76m. troy oz in Jan. 1998. Inflation, which was over 100% in 1990, was 10·8% in 1998. Total money supply in Oct. 1997 was 9,436m. pesos.

Banking and Finance

The Central Bank was inaugurated on 16 May 1967. It is the bank of issue and supreme regulatory authority. In 1994 there were 22 commercial banks, 3 state-supported and 18 foreign-owned. Savings banks deposits were 1,993,029m. pesos in 1995.

The State Insurance Bank has a monopoly of new insurance business. There is a stock exchange in Montevideo.

INDUSTRY

Industries include meat packing, oil refining, cement manufacture, foodstuffs, beverages, leather and textile manufacture, chemicals, light engineering and transport equipment. 1991 output (in 1,000 tonnes): cement, 436; sugar, 86; motor cars, 11,794 units; lorries, 567 units; meat-packing, 1,132,000 head; petroleum, 1,587,000 cu. metres.

Labour

In 1996 the retirement age was raised from 55 to 60 for women; it remains 60 for men. The labour force in 1996 totalled 1,444,000 (59% males). In 1991, 40·2% of the workforce was engaged in services, 21·8% in manufacturing, 16·7% in trade, 6·9% in building and 5·6% in transport and communications.

INTERNATIONAL TRADE

Imports and Exports

The foreign trade (officially stated in US dollars, with the figure for imports based on the clearance permits granted and that for exports on export licences utilized) was as follows (in US$1m.):

	1991	1992	1993	1994	1995	1996
Imports	1,636·5	2,045	2,324	2,786	2,867	3,300
Exports	1,604·7	1,702	1,645	1,913	2,106	2,400

Principal exports in 1995 (in US$1,000): textiles, 421·3 (including washed wool, 25·8); meat, live animals and by-products, 561·8; agricultural produce, 304·1 (including rice, 163·0); leather, hides and manufactures, 250·7; footwear, 17·8.

The main import suppliers in 1996 were Brazil (22·4%), Argentina (20·8%), USA (12·0%) and Italy (5·2%). Leading export destinations in 1996 were Brazil (34·7%), Argentina (11·3%), USA (7·0%) and Germany (4·7%).

VENEZUELA

República de Venezuela
Capital: Caracas
Population estimate, 2000: 24·17m.

KEY HISTORICAL EVENTS

Columbus sighted Venezuela in 1498 and it was visited by Alonso de
Ojeda and Amerigo Vespucci in 1499 who named it Venezuela (Little
Venice). It was part of the Spanish colony of New Granada until 1821
when it became independent, at first in union with Colombia and then
as an independent republic from 1830. Up to 1945 the country was
governed mainly by dictators. In 1945 a three-day revolt against the
reactionary government of Gen. Isaias Medina led to constitutional
and economic reforms. In 1961 a new constitution provided for a
presidential election every five years, a national congress, and state
and municipal legislative assemblies. Twenty political parties
participated in the 1983 elections. By now the economy was in crisis
and corruption linked to drug trafficking was widespread. In Feb.
1992 there were two abortive *coups*. There was another abortive
coup in Nov. A state of emergency was declared. In Dec. 1993,
Dr Rafael Caldera Rodríguez was returned to the presidency with
30·5% of the vote. Dr Caldera's election reflected disenchantment
with the established political parties. He took office in the early
stages of a banking crisis which cost 15% of GDP to resolve.
Fiscal tightening backed by the IMF brought rapid recovery.

Hugo Chávez Frías, who took over as president in Feb. 1999,
instituted a wide range of reforms, notably the amending of the
constitution.

TERRITORY AND POPULATION

Venezuela is bounded to the north by the Caribbean with a 2,813 km coastline, east by the Atlantic and Guyana, south by Brazil, and southwest and west by Colombia. The area is 916,490 sq. km (353,857 sq. miles) including 72 islands in the Caribbean. Population (1990) census, 19,455,429 (84% urban; estimate, 86·5% in 1997). Estimate (1997) 21·8m.; density, 23·9 per sq. km.

The UN gives a projected population for 2000 of 24·17m.

The official language is Spanish. English is taught as a mandatory second language in high schools.

Area, population and capitals of the 23 states and 1 federally-controlled area:

State	Sq. km	Census 1990	Capital	Density; Inhabitants per sq. km
Federal District	1,930	2,265,874	Caracas	1,182·23
Amazonas	177,617	60,207	Puerto Ayacucho	0·55
Anzoátegui	43,300	924,074	Barcelona	24·88
Apure	76,500	305,132	San Fernando	5·43
Aragua	7,014	1,194,962	Maracay	202·30
Barinas	35,200	456,246	Barinas	15·48
Bolívar	240,528	968,695	Ciudad Bolívar	5·02
Carabobo	4,650	1,558,608	Valencia	443·00
Cojedes	14,800	196,526	San Carlos	16·31
Delta Amacuro	40,200	91,085	Tucupita	3·07
Falcón	24,800	632,513	Coro	29·01
Guárico	64,986	525,737	San Juan de los Morros	9·32
Lara	19,800	1,330,477	Barquisimeto	75·35
Mérida	11,300	639,846	Mérida	62·55
Miranda	7,950	2,026,229	Los Teques	305·01

Monagas	28,900	503,176	Maturín	19·86
Nueva Esparta	1,150	280,777	La Asunción	303·60
Portuguesa	15,200	625,576	Guanare	50·28
Sucre	11,800	772,707	Cumaná	67·79
Táchira	11,100	859,861	San Cristóbal	88·43
Trujillo	7,400	520,292	Trujillo	77·51
Yaracuy	7,100	411,980	San Felipe	68·65
Zulia	63,100	2,387,208	Maracaibo	50·21
Dependencias				
Federales	120	2,245		

37·3% of all Venezuelans are under 15 years of age, 58·7% are between the ages of 15 and 64, and 4% are over the age of 65.

Caracas, Venezuela's largest city, is the political, financial, commercial, communications and cultural centre of the country. Metropolitan Caracas had a 1995 population estimate of 3·01m. Maracaibo, the nation's second largest city (estimated 1995 population of 1·6m.), is located near Venezuela's most important petroleum fields and richest agricultural areas.

SOCIAL STATISTICS

1996 births, 595,816; deaths, 105,138; marriages, 73,064; divorces, 16,055. 1996 birth rate per 1,000 population, 26·2; death rate, 4·6; marriage rate, 3·2; divorce rate, 0·7. Annual growth rate, 1993–97, 2·1%. Life expectancy, 1997, was 70·0 years for males and 75·7 years for females. Infant mortality, 1997, 21 per 1,000 live births; fertility rate, 1997, 3·0 births per woman.

CONSTITUTION AND GOVERNMENT

Venezuela is a federal republic, comprising 34 federal dependencies, 23 states and 1 federal district. Executive power is vested in
the President. Re-elections can take place 10 years after the end of
the first term. The ministers, who together constitute the Council of
Ministers, are appointed by the President and head various
executive departments. There are 17 ministries and 7 officials who
also have the rank of Minister of State.

The Senate and Chamber of Deputies have similar legislative
powers. For a bill to become law, it must be approved by a majority in
both bodies. Differences between the 2 chambers are resolved
through majority vote of the Congress, meeting in joint session. The
constitution provides for procedures by which the President may
reject bills passed by Congress, as well as provisions by which
Congress may override such Presidential veto acts.

90% of votes cast in a referendum on 25 April 1999 were in favour
of the plan to rewrite the constitution proposed by President Chávez.
As a result, on 25 July the public was to elect a constitutional
assembly to write a new constitution, which was subsequently to be
voted on in a national referendum. In Aug. 1999 the constitutional
assembly declared a national state of emergency. It subsequently
suspended the Supreme Court, turned the elected Congress into
little more than a sub-committee, stripping it of all its powers, and
assumed many of the responsibilities of government. President
Chávez has also announced that he wants presidents to be able to
serve 2 consecutive 6-year-terms instead of terms of five years which
cannot be consecutive.

President Chávez has effectively taken over both the executive
and the judiciary.

Main political organizations: the president's party, Movimiento
Quinta República (MVR), which has 21 seats in the Chamber of

Deputies and 12 in the Senate; Acción Democrático (AD); Comité de Organización Politica Electoral Independiente (Copei); Proyecto Venezuela (PVVZL); Movimiento al Socialismo (MAS); Patria Para Todos (PPT); La Causa R (LCR); Convergencia; Apertura.

RECENT ELECTIONS

Congressional elections were held on 8 Nov. 1998. Acción Democrático won 55 of the 189 seats in the Chamber of Deputies and 17 in the Senate, ahead of Movimiento Quinta República with 49 in the Chamber of Deputies and 14 in the Senate. Presidential elections were held on 6 Dec. 1998. Hugo Chávez Frías (MVR) was elected President against 2 other candidates with 56·5% of the vote. In the election on 25 July 1999 for a new constitutional assembly, created specifically to produce a new constitution, the president's leftist Patriotic Pole (PP) alliance won 123 of the 131 seats. Not one candidate of the two traditional Venezuelan parties won a seat. This assembly was due to be dissolved on 30 Jan. 2000 when legislative power would fall to a Comisíon Legislativa appointed by the ANC, until a new National Assembly was elected.

CURRENT ADMINISTRATION

President: Hugo Chávez Frías, b. 1953 (MVR; sworn in 2 Feb. 1999).
Executive Vice President: Isaías Rodríguez.
In Jan. 2000 the government comprised:
Minister of the Interior and Justice: Ignacio Arcaya. *Foreign Affairs:* José Vicente Rangel. *Finance:* José Rojas. *Defence:* Gen. Raúl Salazar Rodríguez. *Infrastructure:* Alberto Esqueda. *Industry*

and Commerce: Gustavo Márquez Marin. *Environment and Natural Resources:* Jesus Pérez. *Health and Social Security:* Gilberto Rodríguez Ochoa. *Education, Culture and Sports:* Héctor Navarro. *Labour:* Lino Martínez. *Social Development:* Leopoldo Puchi. *Presidential Secretariat:* Gen. Lucas Rincon. *Co-ordination and Planning:* Jorge Giordani. *Production and Trade:* José De Jesus Montilla. *Science and Technology:* Carlos Genatios. *Planning and Development:* Jore Giordani.

DEFENCE

There is selective conscription for 30 months. Defence expenditure totalled US$962m. in 1997 (US$42 per capita).

ECONOMY

Performance
GDP contracted by 1% in 1996 but grew by 5·1% in 1997. In 1998 it contracted by 8·2%, and was forecast to contract again in 1999, by 6·0%.

Budget
The fiscal year is the calendar year. Revenues and expenditures in Bs 1m. for the period 1994 to 1997 were:

	1994	1995	1996	1997
Revenue	1,481,533	2,144,214	5,661,252	9,985,506
Expenditure	1,566,229	2,413,543	4,775,871	8,473,305

The expected revenue and expenditure for 1999 is Bs 13,969,059.

Currency

The unit of currency is the *bolívar* (VEB) of 100 *céntimos*. Foreign. exchange reserves were US$14,849m. in Dec. 1998 and gold reserves 11·11m. troy oz in Feb. 1998. Exchange controls were abolished in April 1996. The bolívar was devalued by 12·6% in 1998. The inflation rate in 1997 was 42·0%, in 1998, 29·9%, and forecast for 1999 to be 25·0%. Total money supply in Feb. 1998 was Bs 5,487m.

Banking and Finance

A law of Dec. 1992 provided for greater autonomy for the Central Bank. Its *Governor*, currently Antonio Casas González, is appointed by the President for 5-year terms. Since 1993 foreign banks have been allowed a controlling interest in domestic banks.

There is a stock exchange in Caracas.

INDUSTRY

Production (1994, tonnes): steel, 3·14m.; aluminium, 617,000; cement, 4·56m.

Labour

Out of 7,670,000 people in employment in 1995, 2,186,000 were in community, social and personal services, 1,739,000 in trade, restaurants and hotels, 1,047,000 in manufacturing and 1,012,000 in agriculture, fishing and forestry. In 1999 an estimated 11·7% of the workforce was unemployed, up from 8·6% in 1991.

INTERNATIONAL TRADE

Imports and Exports

In 1997 imports were valued at US$12·7bn. and exports at US$21·4bn. Crude petroleum and petroleum products account for approximately 75% of Venezuela's exports. The main import sources in 1995 were USA (42·6%), Colombia (7·6%), Germany (4·8%) and Japan (4·4%). The main markets for exports in 1995 were USA (51·3%), Brazil (9·0%), Colombia (7·6%) and Netherlands Antilles (4·9%).